ELIZABETH

*The Scandalous Life of
the Duchess of Kingston*

ELIZABETH

*The Scandalous Life of
the Duchess of Kingston*

Claire Gervat

CENTURY · LONDON

First published by Century in 2003

First published in the United Kingdom in 2003 by
Century, 20 Vauxhall Bridge Road, London, SW1V 2SA

Random House Australia (Pty) Limited
20 Alfred Street, Milsons Point, Sydney, New South Wales 2061, Australia

Random House New Zealand Limited
18 Poland Road, Glenfield
Auckland 10, New Zealand

Random House South Africa (Pty) Limited
Endulini, 5a Jubilee Road, Parktown, 2193, South Africa

The Random House Group Limited Reg. No. 954009

www.randomhouse.co.uk

A CIP catalogue record for this book is available from the British Library

Papers used by Random House are natural, recyclable products made from wood
grown in sustainable forests. The manufacturing processes conform to the environ-
mental regulations of the country of origin

Typeset in Janson Text by Palimpsest Book Production Limited,
Polmont, Stirlingshire
Printed and bound in the United Kingdom by
Mackays of Chatham PLC

ISBN 0 7126 1451 6

To Alexander and Perkins

CONTENTS

CONTENTS

Acknowledgements

Writing may be a lonely business but research never is, and I owe grateful thanks to the staff of the following national and university libraries and archives for their kind donations of time, advice and practical help: the British Library, particularly in the Rare Books and Music reading room; the Historical Manuscripts Commission; the National Archives of Scotland; the National Library of Scotland, especially the principal curator of manuscripts Dr Iain Brown; the National Library of Wales; the National Register of Archives for Scotland; the Public Record Office, Kew; the University of Durham Library; and the Department of Manuscripts and Special Collections, University of Nottingham.

I would also like to thank the staff at the following local record offices for their patient assistance: Bedfordshire and Luton Archives and Record Service; Derbyshire Record Office; Devon Record Office; Plymouth and North Devon Record Office; Hampshire Record Office; Centre for Kentish Studies; London Metropolitan Archives; Norfolk Record Office; Shakespeare Birthplace Trust Record Office; Staffordshire and Stoke-on-Trent Archive Service; Suffolk Record Office (Bury St Edmunds); Surrey History Centre; City of Westminster Archives Centre; and Wiltshire and Swindon Record Office.

Further help, for which many thanks, was given unstintingly by staff at other archives in this country: Brother Hodkinson at the Society of Jesus; staff at the House of Lords Record Office; Mark Pomeroy at the Royal Academy of Arts; Philip Winterbottom at the Royal Bank of Scotland; Henry Gillett at the Bank of England; Barbara Sands at C. Hoare & Co; Pamela Clark at the Royal Archives, Windsor; the Hon. Georgina Stonor and Victoria Crake at Stratfield Saye; Kate Gatacre at Christie's; staff at the Lambeth Palace Library; and, last but not least, Major Tatham and Martin Ford at the Royal Hospital Chelsea.

As Elizabeth Chudleigh travelled widely, information about her is scattered throughout Europe, as are those archives and people who provided much-appreciated aid. I would like to thank staff at the Archives Nationales de France; the Bibliothèque Municipale de Versailles; the National Historical Archive of Belarus; the Sächsische Haupstaatarchiv in Dresden; Snel Harmen at the Gemeentearchief (Municipal Archives) Amsterdam; Dottore Tino Gipponi at the Fondazione Maria Cosway in Lodi, Italy; Denison Beach at the Houghton Library, University of Harvard; Christopher Glover and staff at the University of Yale's Beinecke Rare Book and Manuscript Library; and Sirje Annist at the Estonian History Museum, Tallinn.

I am further most grateful to the Marquis of Bute and Gerald Barnett for permission to quote from items of the Duchess of Kingston's correspondence in their possession, and to all those who have been kind enough to allow me to reproduce paintings and drawings from their collections.

I must also thank all those 'miscellaneous others' who have, in one way or another, generously and enthusiastically helped in the creation of this book: Valerie Barnes at Lainston House, Robin Brackenbury, Anthony Cox, Professor Anthony Cross, Sue Hanson, Hugh and Ranji Matheson, Felix Pryor, Simon Sebag Montefiore, Clive and Gilly Venables and Helmut Watzlawick; plus Nijolè Bagdziute, Professor Berbec, Ben Chatterley, Professor Anthony Dexter, Miroslav Kutilek and Athol Stephen for essential translations.

My grateful thanks, as well, to Joanna Innes at Somerville, my former tutor, who gave up her precious time during term to read the manuscript and make wise suggestions; to my editor Anna Cherrett, and to Kate Elton, at Random House; and, of course, to my agent Jane Conway-Gordon.

Lastly, I would like to thank my mother, Elizabeth Gervat, who not only provided inspiration when my French failed me, but was always ready with encouragement and praise when it was most needed; Serena Mackesy for unselfish trail-blazing and writerly support; Mark Bottomley for being such a good friend and photographer; Lucy, Neel, Barbara, Cam and Lochie for all the cups of tea; and Alexander Martin, just for existing.

Illustrations

Miniature of Elizabeth Chudleigh, by Samuel Finney, on a snuffbox lid.
Courtesy of the Stratfield Saye Preservation Trust. Photograph: Photographic Survey, Courtauld Institute of Art

Conversation Piece: Augustus Hervey, 3rd Earl of Bristol with his mother, two sisters and their husbands (detail), by Gravelot, Liotard and others.
Courtesy of National Trust Photographic Library/Angelo Hornak

The Hon. Miss Chudleigh, engraved by S Bull, after an original portrait by Joshua Reynolds.
Private collection

Portrait of Elizabeth Chudleigh, by Francis Cotes.
Courtesy of Christie's (1928)

A Perspective View of the Grand Walk in Vauxhall Gardens and the Orchestra, published in 1765.
Courtesy of London Borough of Lambeth Archives Department

The Duchess of Kingston as she appeared at the Venetian Ambassador's Ball in Somerset House, engraving by F Chesham after Gainsborough.
Courtesy of the National Portrait Gallery, London

Evelyn, 2nd Duke of Kingston, circle of J B Van Loo, 1741.
Courtesy of Earl Manvers Will Trust. Photograph © Mark Bottomley

Kingston House, Kensington Gore, by T H Shepherd, 1854.
© Copyright The British Museum

Elizabeth Chudleigh, pastel by Francis Cotes, dated 1763.
Courtesy of Lainston House Hotel, Sparsholt, Hampshire (01962 863588).
Photograph © Mark Bottomley

The Duchess of Kingston, full length, in a White and Pink Dress,
circle of Sir Joshua Reynolds.
Courtesy of Bonhams Picture Library

A Prospect of Thoresby Hall with the Duke and Duchess of Kingston
on Horses in the Foreground, attributed to Nicholas Thomas Dall.
Courtesy of Nathalie Pierrepont Comfort

The Trial of the Duchess of Kingston, contemporary engraving.
Courtesy of Mary Evans Picture Library

The Duchess of Kingston, tinted drawing by Richard Cosway.
Courtesy of Gerald Barnett/Westcountry Books

Author's Note

In quoting from manuscripts, I have kept to the original spellings, use of capital letters, underlining and punctuation (or lack of it). Where the letters have been printed they have been quoted as they appear. Many of Elizabeth Chudleigh's later letters were written in French. In translating them into English I have followed the original punctuation and capitalisation as closely as possible, but used standardised spellings. The Georgians employed many abbreviations, which have been expanded, in square brackets, only where the meaning would otherwise be unclear.

The bibliography contains the details of most of the primary and secondary sources cited in the text. To avoid repetition, these are given in abbreviated form in the notes section.

Introduction

'This seems to be the Age of Women,'[1] exclaimed the anonymous correspondent to the pages of the *London Chronicle* that December 1775, signing himself only 'A profound Admirer of the Fair Sex'. History would, of course, beg to differ with the assessment, seeing it instead as the era in which Britain gradually lost control of its American colonies, the struggles over which had dominated the news since April. All the same, it was true that the papers had also been filled for months with the reports of two criminal cases where the main defendants were genteel, well-spoken and female: that of a Miss Butterfield for poisoning her lover and a Mrs Rudd for forgery.[2] A third was imminent, and promised to be the most enthralling, colourful and wonderfully shocking of them all, for it concerned a peeress of the highest rank, whose former beauty, connections and youthful indiscretions had long made her an object of gossip and curiosity, and who now stood charged with the shameful crime of bigamy.

The fifty-four-year-old Duchess of Kingston, born plain Miss Elizabeth Chudleigh, represented to the fascinated reading public everything that was simultaneously wicked and enthralling about the remote world of London high society. With apparently scant regard for decency or honesty, she had married one man and then, finding one whose wealth and title suited her better, she had denied *on oath* the first connection and wed again. Now her beloved Duke was dead, and his sister and brother-in-law were fighting to snatch, by any means possible, the immense fortune – land, paintings, silver and more – that he had left his supposed widow in his will.

The case seemed to confirm what many people had always known: that the world of the fashionable elite was rotten to the core. Some of its members certainly trod a narrow line between sin and salvation, if they ever even considered the two concepts: there was George Selwyn, for instance, who had an unhealthy appetite for young girls and public executions. More normal vices, however, were simply taken for granted in this select society.

The men's less obscure sexual needs, for instance, were admirably catered for by London's bagnios, which were upmarket bathhouses-come-brothels. There was even a printed annual guide to the best courtesans, called *Harris's List of Covent Garden Ladies: or, Man of Pleasure's Kalendar, containing the Histories and some curious Anecdotes of the most Celebrated Ladies now on the Town, or in keeping, and also many of their Keepers.* Having a mistress was so common it would hardly raise an eyebrow in one's own circle, unless you were the third Duke of Grafton, who was silly enough to squire *his* to the theatre in the presence of the Queen, which was felt to be a bit much given that he was the prime minister.[3]

The women of the *ton* also enjoyed a certain licence, particularly once they had dutifully borne a couple of healthy baby boys, an heir and a spare, to inherit their husband's titles and estates. It was not unheard of for at least some of the younger children to look nothing like their purported fathers. Dainty and fastidious Horace Walpole, for instance, the eighteenth-century's most famous letter-writer, was famously unlike the hearty Sir Robert, first minister and Norfolk squire.

What mattered most to this ruling elite was not so much what you did, but whether you were caught doing it. Discretion was everything, and the members of this tiny group were prepared to tolerate a surprising level of immorality in their own circle, provided that everyone concerned did their utmost to keep it from both the servants and the world beyond. By the 1770s, though, this task was becoming increasingly difficult. Of course, the mere mortals lower down the social scale had long been curious to know more about the rarefied world of those at its pinnacle, and for years had eagerly devoured every scrap of detail about it: the lavish entertainments, the expensive clothes, the almost unimaginably costly jewellery, the grand houses and fast carriages. However, they had only rarely been gifted an insight into the more private – and more disreputable – aspects of the world of the ruling class. Recently, that had begun to change. New publications such as *Town and Country Magazine* – with its monthly 'History of the Tête-à-Tête', profiling a different man of fashion and his mistress in each – had begun to make public what its subjects would rather have kept hidden. Readers who had formerly thrilled to reports of curiosities such as mermaids, Indian chiefs and dogs fluent in the Greek alphabet, could now lap up outrageous tales of the rich and famous which stirred up envy and disdain in equal measure.

In the midst of worrying rumblings against the excesses of the beau monde, it was clear that discretion was more important than ever. Unfortunately, this had never been Elizabeth Chudleigh's strong point. She had, as one reporter put it, 'paid too little regard to appearances and the public opinion; her propensity to pleasure having hurried her sometimes into scenes of levity and indiscretion, in which a young lady, more jealous of her reputation, would have blushed to make herself conspicuous'.[4] In her twenties she had appeared at a masquerade in a too-revealing costume, an episode that had been marked by a flurry of satirical verses and of prints of her in semi-undress. As her 'History of the Tête-à-Tête' put it, 'The tea tables pronounced this step as the test of her conduct',[5] and decided she was no better than a demi-rep – only half reputable in other words.

From the recent revelations in the press about her behaviour in the intervening years, of which most ordinary people at the time had known little beyond the seemingly innocent basic facts, this early judgement seemed to have been well founded. That Elizabeth, Duchess of Kingston was about to be tried, shamefully publicly, on a charge of bigamy was, though, no surprise at all to her own social circle. *They* had known of the 'secret' first marriage for years, but had discreetly said and done nothing to draw attention to a lapse of one of their own. To be sure, many of them had privately balked at her second marriage, but it was only a disputed will that had finally brought the felony to public notice.

The scandal threatened to damage not just Elizabeth's reputation, but that of the ruling class as a whole, including the royal family – and events in France would soon show how costly that could be. The result was the curious, and not exclusively eighteenth-century spectacle of those whose lives, in retrospect, would be revealed as less than pure, berating another for her lack of virtue. As *The Times* commented, with heavy sarcasm, 'Bigamy, it seems, is a greater crime than simple fornication or fashionable adultery.'[6] But what was she really like, this middle-aged woman with the gaze of the world upon her? And how had she found herself in the eye of this whirlwind of scandal?

Chapter 1

A Worthy Tribe

... the dignous family of Chudlegh [*sic*], which is very
ancient and worshipful in this country, and have
flourished successively many descents
Thomas Westcote, *A View of Devonshire in 1630*

There had been Chudleighs in Devon for longer than anyone could remember.[1] They were so embedded in the landscape that even its features – from rocks to caverns – bore their name. Since the reign of Edward III, generations of older sons had apparently lived out lives of unimpeachable respectability in the family seat of Place Barton in the tranquil village of Ashton, whose thatched, limewashed stone cottages and farmhouses were scattered down the steep side of a narrow valley, through which tumbled a small, lively tributary of the River Teign. They had served the local community as lords of the manor and sheriffs, toiled along the narrow lane up the hill every Sunday to worship in the ancient parish church where their ancestors were buried and commemorated, and married their children to equally worthy West Country families through whom they acquired other lands and manors. They had been rewarded for their service by knighthoods and, by James I in 1622, a baronetcy. At first glance it seemed an unlikely background for a woman who was to become one of the most notorious personalities of her times.

True, there were sometimes hints that the dusty official records might not tell the whole story, that Elizabeth Chudleigh's ancestors might have a spark of something more ambitious, more restless, more daring: there was the Elizabethan explorer Captain John Chudleigh, 'of a right martial, bold and adventurous spirit',[2] who sailed off to circumnavigate the world and died in the Straits of Magellan; and the seventeenth-century James Chudleigh, who fought valiantly on *both* sides of the Civil War in 1643, dying a few days after the siege of Dartmouth of gunshot wounds, 'a gallant young gentleman . . . a wonderful loss to the king's service'.[3]

James's father George, the first baronet, had also begun on the side of Parliament, of which he was a member. He, too, became disillusioned and changed sides, and soon after his son's death declared: 'I believe it hath gone too far; the destruction of a Kingdome cannot be the way to save it',[4] a change of heart for which 'that Grand Ambo-Dexter', as one pamphleteer called him, was soundly punished by Sir Thomas Fairfax and his New Model Army on their rampage through Devon a few years later. It was a blow; Place Barton's medieval mock fortifications were no protection against the Parliamentarian forces, who broke through the outer walls and laid waste to the imposing main house, trampled the formal gardens and plundered the fish-ponds and the deer park. However, it was not a death sentence, and by the Restoration, the Chudleighs were back serving crown and country and their secure way of life seemed as unchanging as ever.

All this time, the female Chudleighs had hovered in the shadows, almost invisible to posterity. Like so many other women, only the barest facts of their lives – birth, marriage, children, death – were recorded. The detail of how they passed their days, let alone what they thought of their life, are a mystery. Not until the beginning of the eighteenth century, when the Stuart kings were long gone and memories of England's Glorious Revolution were beginning to fade, did one of them slip quietly out of obscurity and into print. Lady Mary Chudleigh, Elizabeth's grandmother, had been writing for many years by the time her first work came to public notice. *The Ladies Defense* was published in 1701 as a spirited satire on a far-from-progressive marriage sermon that had come out a couple of years before. *Poems on Several Occasions*, with its dedication to the new Queen, Anne, followed two years later, and contains her most famous verse, 'To the Ladies', with its startling opening couplet: 'Wife and Servant are the same,/But only differ in the Name'.[5]

With little in the way of other evidence, biographers have tended to view Lady Mary Chudleigh's verses as autobiographical, suggesting that her own married life was a misery and her husband a tyrant. It is certainly true that the wit and intelligence of the poetry is shot through with a strong note of sadness and of stoical endurance. To her readers at the time, this would have been hardly worthy of comment. An ability to bear with Christian fortitude everything that life could throw at you was considered vital in an age when medicine could do little to cure disease and postpone death. Lady Mary celebrated this virtue in herself: 'I thank God, I cannot only patiently, but chearfully, bear a great many Things which others would call Afflictions; Life and Death are Things very indifferent to me.'[6]

Lady Mary had plenty to be stoical about. Her health was appalling, and she battled for years against the pain of what seems to have been rheumatism. In 1703, she wrote to a friend:

I am grieved to hear, you enjoy so little Health, 'tis a Blessing I heartily wish you, and all my other Friends, as being one of the greatest Pleasures of Life; while I had the happiness of possessing it, I could chearfully struggle with my Misfortunes, be pleasant in the midst of Storms, and easy without any other Company but my *Thoughts* and *Books*; but now my Body sinks under the Pressure, and will not keep pace with my *Mind*: Life is what I have for many Years had no Reason to be fond of.[7]

Nor was family life a source of unalloyed joy. Four of her six children died in early childhood, including her seven-year-old daughter Eliza Maria in 1701: 'She's fled, she's fled from my deserted Arms',[8] as Lady Mary later wrote. Between the perils of pregnancy and childbirth, the misery of her children's early deaths and the sheer time-consuming demands of running a household and raising her more robust offspring, it is a miracle she managed to find any time at all for her beloved books and writings. No wonder she resented the limitations that marriage placed on a woman's life. Whether she had cause to hate the man as well as the institution is impossible to determine, although if Sir George really were the model for the tyrannical Sir John Brute in *The Ladies Defense*, he must have been remarkably stupid not to have seen the resemblance and forbidden such a public mockery.

In the end, though, it was her own bad health that brought a premature end to Lady Mary's studies. She published just one more book, *Essays upon Several Subjects*, in 1710, before dying after 'the continuance of a long Sickness'[9] in Exeter – where she had gone to escape the damp winter air of Ashton – on 15 December 1710 at the age of fifty-five. She left behind the enigmatic Sir George and two grown-up sons: George, the elder, who was destined for the baronetcy and marriage to an heiress; and Thomas, who, with only a younger son's small inheritance to look forward to and his way to make in the world, headed for the army. This was then a very different, far more commercial organisation than it is now; commissions could be bought and sold, and rising through the ranks depended as much on money and recommendation as on talent. Thomas, luckily, though far from rich, had enough powerful patrons and skill as a soldier to compensate, and the war with Bourbon Spain and France from 1701 gave him an opportunity to prove himself. He rose steadily from infantry captain in March 1705 at the age of seventeen to colonel of the 34th Regiment of Foot by 1712, seeing active service on the Spanish mainland and along the French coast.[10]

With his financial future now looking more secure, Colonel Thomas Chudleigh was in a position to get married. His search for a wife did not take him far; only as far as the house of his uncle Hugh Chudleigh, in fact. On 8 December 1712, Thomas and his first cousin, Henrietta, Hugh's fourth daughter, were married by special licence* at the church of St Martin-in-the-Fields in London. Ten months later, their first child, George, was born, baptised – and buried.[11] He was followed almost exactly a year later by Susanna, who survived for four months before succumbing to what the parish burial book described as a 'convulson'.

By now, there was a new king, George I, who arrived in England from Hanover in 1714 unable to speak a word of the language of his subjects, and the War of the Spanish Succession had come to an end. Early the following year, Colonel Thomas was appointed Lieutenant-Governor of the Royal Hospital, Chelsea – Wren's vast architectural masterpiece on the banks of the Thames – with a salary of £200 a year,[12] an important boost to the family finances. A portrait of the time† shows

---

* From the sixteenth century, those who could afford it were usually married by special licence, avoiding the need for the publication of banns. It had the advantage of being quicker – banns had to be called three Sundays in a row – and less open to the vulgar public gaze.

† Current location of original not known; there is a black-and-white photograph in the Witt Library of the Courtauld Institute in London. Unfortunately, there are no known surviving portraits of his wife.

a satisfied-looking Colonel Thomas gazing out confidently from the canvas, his long hair curling over his armour-clad shoulder, a rather feminine pout to his full lips, and a double chin and protruding stomach testifying to a tendency to run to fat. It is the face of a man whose career was going well, and who had every reason to believe his success would continue.

It was all very gratifying; small comfort, perhaps, for the private disappointment of the death of two babies in a row, but there would, after all, be more children. There were, and in a heartrending, almost uninterrupted line, their births and rapid deaths were all recorded in the registers of the Royal Hospital chapel[13] and St Martin-in-the-Fields: another George, baptised 17 February 1716 and buried eight days later; Harriot [*sic*], who was laid to rest a fortnight after her christening on 23 January 1717; and Henrietta, born 1 August 1719 and buried at the end of the following May. Only Thomas, born 9 June 1718, interrupted the dismal pattern. With a record even worse than that of her late mother-in-law, Henrietta Chudleigh had given birth six times in six years, and had only one child to show for it. She, too, would have needed all the fortitude and resignation she could muster to cope with the physical exhaustion and emotional toll.

Worse was to follow. When Sir George Chudleigh died in early 1719, Colonel Thomas's inheritance – though much less than that of his older brother George – was enough to enable him to buy a small estate near Harford in Devon, called Hall, on the fringes of Dartmoor,[14] and an army commission of the lowest rank for his eleven-month-old son.[15] Hoping to boost his finances further, Colonel Thomas decided to invest in a relatively new joint-stock company that was already making fortunes for its backers. At the start of 1720, stock in the South Sea Company – which had been founded in 1711 as a Tory rival to the Whiggish Bank of England – stood at £128. In a whirlwind of speculation, its price had spiralled to close to £1,000 by the end of May.

So in June Colonel Thomas plunged £1,000 into the company's third issue of stock that year.[16] If he hoped to make a killing, however, he was too late; prices had already peaked. As rumours began to circulate that the company's assets and prospects were not what they seemed (hardly, alas, a uniquely eighteenth-century phenomenon), the 3rd Subscription struggled to maintain its issue level, until the arrival of September sent prices of all the company's stock issues tumbling. By the end of the month, no one was quoting for the 3rd Subscription at all. The South Sea Bubble had burst. 'All corners of the Town are filled with the Groans of the Afflicted,'[17] the *Weekly Journal* lugubriously informed its readers, and among them were surely those of Colonel Thomas Chudleigh.

In the midst of all this financial turmoil, Henrietta Chudleigh discovered she was pregnant yet again, the seventh time in seven years. It was hardly an ideal time to have another child; Thomas's job at the Royal Hospital might come with a good salary and a gracious set of rooms, but there would be little left over to put by, whether for a daughter's marriage portion or a second son's career. That was supposing the child even lived, which, going by experience, was hardly likely. It must have been a miserable few months.

CHAPTER 2

Wednesday's Child

The Small-Pox continues to make great Breaches,
especially in the Families of our Nobility and
Gentry this Week.
Applebee's Original Weekly Journal, 11 March 1721

The child *did* live, and was baptised – in miserably cold weather and the middle of an outbreak of smallpox – at St Martin-in-the-Fields in London on 27 March 1721.[1] 'Elizabeth Chidley of Thomas and Henrietta. [Born] March 8', the clerk wrote, making the same spelling mistake that the one at Chelsea had done the first time he heard the unfamiliar West Country name.

Back in the Lieutenant-Governor's neat rooms at the Royal Hospital, the baby girl and her older brother Thomas continued to thrive. Chelsea was then a peaceful retreat just outside the capital, a 'town of palaces'[2] as Daniel Defoe called it, with a string of noble mansions stretched along the banks of the Thames. Even thirty years later, a Swedish traveller described it as somewhere that gentlefolk came in summer to escape the heat and smell of nearby London. The air was clean and healthy, and the hospital grounds were bursting with places for childish games: orchards and gardens, summerhouses and echoing stone-flagged corridors. Here, Thomas and Elizabeth had not only freedom but also playmates, such as the treasurer's son Horace Mann, who became Britain's representative in Florence, and a fey little boy also called Horace, son of the first minister Sir Robert Walpole, in whose famous letters Elizabeth Chudleigh was later to feature regularly in less-than-flattering terms.[3]

Of course, life at the hospital was not without its drawbacks. In those days, the King's road to Chelsea from London was barely more than a country lane, and sections of it were in extremely poor condition. It was also a favourite haunt of footpads, the downmarket version of highwaymen, as Mrs Chudleigh discovered for herself in the spring of 1723. On 2 May, as she was heading past Buckingham House* on her way home, her coach was set upon by a notorious gang of five. 'Tho' she had with her two Servants and two of the Patrole Guard armed,' the *British Journal* informed its readers, 'they had the Boldness to fire at the Coachman for not stopping soon enough.'[4] It was not a first offence for the thieves, but for one of them it was certainly the last. Mrs Chudleigh, showing a remarkable amount of sangfroid considering she had been woken by having a pistol thrust at her, leaned calmly out of the coach window and ordered her two Pensioner escorts to fire.[5] Presumably needing no encouragement they obeyed, and Joseph Rice was fatally shot. The others escaped into nearby fields, but were caught a few days later trying to rob someone else.

Footpads aside, life for the Lieutenant-Governor's young family would have been relatively easy and comfortable. Contemporary biographers made much of the terrible state of the Chudleighs' finances after the South Sea Bubble, which finally forced the Colonel to sell his commission in early 1723. It is true that he *did* resign his regiment; the news appeared in several of the newspapers of 11 May, although it seems from army records to have happened several months before.[6] Money cannot have been in such short supply, however; the year before, Colonel Chudleigh had more than doubled his property in Harford, and in 1723 and 1724 he added to his holdings again.[7] The South Sea Company may not have made him a rich man as he had hoped, but it did not make him a pauper, either. Perhaps it was the Colonel's health instead that was shaky – too shaky for active service – for he was not destined for a long life. Early in 1726 he sickened, dying on 14 April at the age of thirty-eight. He was buried in the Royal Hospital cemetery.

Now the family's affairs *were* in a precarious condition. The young widow was deprived at a stroke not only of her husband's salary of £200 a year, but also of the family's graceful quarters and many of

* Built 1702–1705 for the first Duke of Buckingham, it was bought by George III in 1762; the earliest parts of the current palace date from the early nineteenth century.

their contents. Barely a week after Colonel Thomas Chudleigh's death, the Hospital commissioners were already fussing about drawing up an inventory of the furniture that had been supplied to the Lieutenant-Governor's lodging, worrying that Mrs Chudleigh might take some scrap of it away with her.[8] From now on, Henrietta Chudleigh would have to rely on the income from the land on the edge of Dartmoor to support her young family, for even the wives of serving army officers were not guaranteed a pension, and those that *were* awarded did not generally exceed £50 a year. It is possible that the Royal Hospital granted Henrietta a small annual payment in recognition of her husband's long, loyal service, but by no means probable.

Henrietta Chudleigh was forced to summon all her considerable courage, somehow conquer her grief and find somewhere for herself and her two young children, eight-year-old Thomas and five-year-old Elizabeth, to live. She headed for the new district of London at the growing city's westernmost edge, called May-Fair.* Building had begun here, in a desultory way, at the end of the seventeenth century. However, with the accession of George I in 1714, there had been a surge in the pace of the development. To the amazement of Londoners, new squares and broad streets appeared to rise up daily 'to such a prodigy of buildings that nothing in the world does, or ever did, equal it'.[9] The patriotically named Hanover Square was the first to be laid out, from about 1714 onwards, and no sooner had work finished ten years later on the neighbourhood church of St George's, with its graceful and much-admired portico, than the fashionable world began to move in from the more crowded areas of Soho and Covent Garden to the east. Here, in 1726, Henrietta Chudleigh took a house 'fit, in that less refined period of time', as one anonymous late-eighteenth-century biographer sniffily put it, 'for a fashionable town residence',[10] which is as good a description of Maddox Street Stable Yard[11] as any. To boost her income in the only way possible – for she could hardly go out to work; no respectable woman did – she reputedly took in a lady lodger.

London, with its 600,000 or so inhabitants,[†] would have seemed

---

* Named, with admirable straightforwardness, in honour of a fair held there in May from the 1680s.

† Estimates vary from around 500,000 to 750,000; the first census was not until 1801.

a vast, noisy, dirty place after the genteel tranquillity of Chelsea and the spacious calm of the Royal Hospital. At least May-Fair was better than other parts of the city, which one disgusted commentator described as a 'confused Babel',[12] with a 'Hotch-Potch of half-moon and serpentine narrow Streets, close, dismal, long Lanes, stinking Allies, dark, gloomy Courts and suffocating Yards &c'. At this west end of London, the countryside still lapped at its fringes, and not until the second half of the century would the fields north of Piccadilly between Swallow Street* and Hyde Park be entirely covered over. Nevertheless, even May-Fair's airy thoroughfares echoed with sound: the rattle of coach wheels on small cobbles, not to mention the clatter of horses' hooves and the metallic clink of the pattens that people wore on their feet to lift them out of the mud on wet days; the shouts and handbells of street traders selling everything from lavender to newspapers; and even the noise of farm animals being driven through the streets, who also made their own important contribution to London's notable smell.

However, at least Henrietta had close family in London, which was not merely comforting but practical. Her nearest relatives were her brother Colonel George Chudleigh and his wife Isabella, only a short walk away in a house in Great George Street.† Here there were already two slightly younger cousins – three-year-old Isabella and another Elizabeth, just past her first birthday – to keep her children company; Isabella, especially, was to be a lifelong friend of Colonel Thomas's daughter. Moreover, there was another little cousin due any day, the couple's only son as it turned out, and George's wife Isabella would have been glad of her sister-in-law's help looking after the other children. If that meant there were often three extra mouths to feed at mealtimes, it would hardly have been worthy of notice.

As Isabella's brood continued to grow – she eventually had ten children, most of whom survived to adulthood – Henrietta's help would have been even more valued, especially when it came to teaching them to read, write and count. How far the young female Chudleighs' learning extended beyond these basics we do not know. Genteel girls usually received an informal education at home, and how much and what they learned depended on the quality of the

---

* Redeveloped as Regent Street in the early nineteenth century.

† Now St George Street, it was known as George Street from 1737 onwards.

teaching they received from family members or paid tutors. They might study a little history and geography; read the classics in translation and other 'improving' books; learn music, dancing, fine needlework and a foreign language. Elizabeth certainly picked up enough French to be able to write it in later years, though the spelling was often of her own invention, and she danced beautifully. However, in the only account of her life that purports to be from her own lips – though so full of mistakes it must be taken with a vast pinch of salt – she claims that she 'did not get much instruction in her youth, or rather she did not take that which was offered her, for although masters of all kinds were employed for her education, the vivacity of her disposition prevented her from being an attentive pupil'.[13]

Despite family help, however, bringing up her son and lively daughter was plainly a struggle for the widowed Henrietta. Although her poverty was relative, it would still have taken all her skill in elegant economy to maintain a genteel way of life. Elizabeth would have grown up well aware that every penny counted, and that there was nothing to spare for extravagances. In 1730 the local poor rate* assessor noted that 'Mrs Harriat [*sic*] Chudleigh', as she was sometimes called, was refusing to pay her poor rate, 'agrived' as the margin note pointed out, as she might well be by a sudden increase in the rateable value of her house and a proportionate increase in the tax she was expected to pay on it. The difference was nearly seventeen shillings a year, enough for two sets of children's clothes, though we do not know whether Henrietta disputed the payment out of necessity or on principle. She did win the battle, however, for the following year she paid her arrears, and the rate returned to its original level. But Maddox Street Stable Yard was not to be home for much longer. By spring 1733 a Mrs Hughes had moved in, and thought the former occupant might have moved to James Street, just off Golden Square. But no Mrs Chudleigh appears in the rate books for that street; perhaps she was renting, or lodging with her sister Susanna Merrill round the corner on the north side of the Square itself.

In fact, there is a vast hole in our knowledge of where the young family was living in the 1730s and Henrietta, reverting to the invisibility of earlier Chudleigh women, left no letters to fill the gaps.

---

* A property-based tax levied by the parish, to pay for the relief of the local poor.

Unfortunately, neither did her daughter. Elizabeth's eighteenth-century biographers were forced to extemporise with fanciful stories: that an attack of smallpox when the girl was fifteen – from which she recovered without a scar – prompted her mother to remove the family from London to their house on the edge of Dartmoor, where the girl roamed, fishing in the upland streams and following the hounds. Here, half-charmed, half-savage, the girl with the double dose of Chudleigh blood grew into a beauty, irresistible both to animals and to the local boys. The whole of west Devon, no less, resounded with the crack of breaking hearts.

Of course, it is not unreasonable to think the Chudleighs might have spent some time at Hall, 'this Fairy land'[14] as Elizabeth after-wards called it, their house in Harford, particularly in summer when London was so unpleasant – and certainly Elizabeth's love of fishing later in life was well known. There were other places they could expect a welcome, too, with plenty of younger cousins for Elizabeth to order around: Ashton, perhaps, or Haldon, Sir George's new brick house near Kenn, not far from Exeter, built in a more satisfyingly modern taste than Place Barton; Henrietta's brother George's country residence at Chalmington in Dorset; or her sister Susanna Merrill's at Lainston in Hampshire. In short, they could easily have spent several years constantly on the move from one pleasant family home to another, both in London and in the country.

Of other members of the Chudleigh clan we know more, but for all the wrong reasons. These years were not kind to the men of the family. Henrietta's oldest brother John had died in 1729. Then, in October 1738, her brother-in-law Sir George Chudleigh followed him to the grave, leaving a widow, four daughters – Mary, Frances, Margaret and yet another Elizabeth – without a father, and his title to his nephew Thomas, Elizabeth's brother, who became the fifth baronet. The following September, death claimed Henrietta's brother Colonel George Chudleigh of the 2nd Regiment of Foot-guards, clearly without any warning as the notice of it in the *Gentleman's Magazine* remarked that 'he had play'd at Cricket and at Bowls the same Morning'.[15] He left another eight children, seven of them girls, fatherless and his wife Isabella seven months pregnant with another girl.

Two years later, in June 1741, it was the turn of Elizabeth's brother Sir Thomas Chudleigh, playing not at bowls but at soldiers at Aix-la-Chapelle, for Britain was fighting the Spanish and French again, having been drawn into the War of the Austrian Succession by way of the curiously-named War of Jenkins' Ear. The baronetcy passed to John, the only son of Colonel George and Isabella, who was to enjoy his position for only four years before he too met an early end at the age of eighteen, this time at the siege of Ostend in 1745. Here, showing at least as much recklessness as courage, he 'gloriously preferred to die with his colours in his bosom rather than accept of quarter of a gallant French officer who, in compassion for his youth, three times offered him his life for that ensign, which was shot through his heart'.[16] The baronetcy expired with him.

One person, at least, felt sure he knew the reason for such a whole-sale sweeping away of the Chudleigh men. The final baronet's corpse was barely cold before Hugh Yarde, vicar of Ashton, turned up to play on the grief and religious sensibilities of the young man's aunt, Lady Frances,* and 'told her that it was my Opinion that the ruine of the Family was owing to their Sacrilege, which they had often been guilty of, by adjoyning the Mills &c to the Barton . . . and bringing all down to a Composition for twelve pound a year'.[17] In short, the Chudleighs were being punished for underpaying their tithes. By persistence, the wily and mercenary Hugh Yarde won his point; the church taxes were eventually paid in full. No more male Chudleighs died – but, then, there were none left in that branch of the family.

As death cut a swathe through the men, it altered the fortunes of the Chudleigh women for better or, more usually, for worse. The sisters of the last baronet, John, faced an uncertain future with neither a father nor a brother; the income from Chalmington, their prop-erty in Dorset, would not be enough to provide marriage portions for all of them, though their mother was able to keep her London house. John's death, however, actually improved the prospects of the late Sir George's four daughters, for with the extinction of the male line they finally inherited the estates in Devon that had once belonged to their father.

For Henrietta Chudleigh and her daughter Elizabeth, the death of the young Sir Thomas in 1741 at the age of just twenty-two was the worst possible news. Sir Thomas's burgeoning army income,

* Widow of Sir George Chudleigh of Ashton, the fourth baronet.

which would have been a vital contribution to the family fortunes in the years to come, was gone. Elizabeth was twenty years old when her brother was killed and, although the gentry generally frowned on finding husbands for their daughters at too young an age, the question would soon arise. Unfortunately, her prospects on this score had taken a turn for the worse for, in an age when marriage announcements in the newspapers matter-of-factly quoted the bride's portion, she would have barely any money at all to attract appropriate suitors.

The gloom was relieved by the knowledge that Henrietta still had influential friends who might take pity on a family that had run short of men. One of these was William Pulteney – a bitter opponent of George II's first minister Sir Robert Walpole – who in 1742 became Earl of Bath. The fanciful 'spirit of Dartmoor' school of thought believed the connection was the result of a chance encounter between Elizabeth Chudleigh and Pulteney while he was out shooting in Devon: for, according to them, this was where Elizabeth had grown to womanhood. 'Madame,' he reportedly said, 'he is a fortunate hunter who can come out of a wood and meet a divinity.'[18] The truth was more prosaic for he was, in fact, as Elizabeth herself put it, 'my fathers friend'.[19] Moreover, although it is unclear exactly where Elizabeth and her mother were living in this early part of the 1740s, they would have had a vested interest in spending as much time as possible in London. Devon was remote, a hard five days' journey from the capital, and Elizabeth's grandmother Lady Mary had warned one visitor that 'you will find very little agreeable Company here, most of the Persons you will converse with, will speak a Language you will hardly understand; you will find us as rough and unpolished as our Country.'[20] London, however, had a wider choice of both suitable marriage partners and potential patrons.

If William Pulteney had the power to help his old acquaintance Colonel Thomas, then the oldest of the gaggle of Chudleigh girls was a promising candidate. Elizabeth had grown into a beautiful young woman, if not quite a divinity; a little below the average height perhaps, but graceful and with, an anonymous contemporary opined, 'unquestionably, a fine complexion, good features, and penetrating eyes'[21] that sparkled with vitality. A likeness from around this time by a then unknown Joshua Reynolds,[22] of which only later prints survive, confirms this assessment, for even in three-quarter profile one can see that there was a warmth and strength to her gaze. Perhaps more importantly, she was also cheerful, lively and witty, with a sweet temper, [23] and though she was too easily bored to apply herself to one topic long enough to master it, she had a talent for picking up useful bits of knowledge with which, one Frenchwoman later noted, 'she afterwards adorns her conversation so skilfully, that, at least for a time, she would deceive one as to the extent of what she knew'.[24] She was courageous, too, and spirited, the word most often used in her praise throughout her life.

Quite how personal an interest the new Lord Bath took in this sparkling young woman was the subject of a great deal of speculation. Later eighteenth-century writers hinted slyly that they developed a relationship that was not altogether platonic, in short that the young woman became his mistress, an insinuation with no foundation although it was a classic example of how much of Elizabeth Chudleigh's past was rewritten unflatteringly in the light of later events. Again, the truth was a lot less racy. The young woman had long been fatherless, and Lord Bath, whose political career had been at a low ebb since he accepted a peerage, had recently lost his only daughter. With her talent for making people laugh, Elizabeth would certainly have been a welcome diversion for Pulteney at a difficult and dull time. According to Elizabeth, he adopted her 'as his daughter'[25] and gave her 'a Real Estate', though where and what is unknown.

Not content with such a practical gift as property, Lord Bath used what influence he still possessed in certain quarters to obtain a post for Elizabeth in the royal household or, rather, that of Frederick, Prince of Wales. A recommendation was made, and in the last gasp of 1743[26] the beautiful Miss Chudleigh was appointed Maid of Honour to Augusta, Princess of Wales. It was a marvellous stroke of good fortune, a chance to make potentially valuable contacts, for at twenty-two she was still of marriageable age. Moreover, the position paid £200 a year and those Maids unfortunate enough to lack a title of their own were allowed to call themselves 'Honourable'.

Such a wonderful piece of good fortune called for new clothes to show Elizabeth's beauty to its best advantage, something suitably grand but not too expensive.[27] The most characteristic eighteenth-century dress was the 'sacque' or 'sack', a loose open gown with sleeves to the elbow, which instead of being fitted at the back fell in soft folds straight from the shoulders to the floor. This was worn over a tight square-necked bodice and full underskirt. Below the underskirt was a contraption called a hoop, which had started life as a circular frame but had, by the 1740s, metamorphosed into a shape that stuck out sideways from the hips. This style of hoop was massively inconvenient to wear. Apart from the alarming tendency it shared with all hoops to swing up on one side revealing more of the woman than was at all decent in the days before knickers, it made it very difficult for modish women to squeeze into their sedan chairs. Some hoops were so wide the wearer had to go through doors sideways, so that their skirt arrived in the room several seconds before the rest of them. Fashion-conscious house owners had their doors widened specially, which was not a bad idea as hoops, despite their obvious drawbacks, would remain the general fashion until the 1760s.

The royal family, however, clung to a style of dress that dated from the late seventeenth century, appropriately called the court mantua. This had a fitted bodice with a stylised train looped up over a decorative petticoat, and remained the accepted court dress into the nineteenth century, long after fashion had moved on. This, too, from the 1740s to the 1820s or so, was worn over wide, flat-fronted hoops; perfect for showing off expensive silks and rich embroidery in silver or gold. At least it required less fabric than the sacque, whose elegant drape of fabric consumed up to twenty-two yards of silk. A dressmaker might charge only a guinea to make up a sacque and petticoat (plus £1. 8s. for a hoop), but the fabric could cost anything from £10 to £70. As for silver embroidery, it is unlikely that the new Maid of Honour was in a position to buy such a lavish, or heavy, court mantua. She would have to begin her career in the household of the Princess of Wales less extravagantly dressed.

CHAPTER 3

Court and Courtship

. . . a comical circumstance at Leicester House:
one of the prince's coachmen . . . has left his son
three hundred pounds, upon condition that he
never *marries* a maid of honour!
Horace Walpole to Horace Mann, 12 May 1743

The Honourable Miss Chudleigh's new royal mistress had arrived in England from Saxe-Gotha in 1736 at the age of seventeen without even her governess for company.[1] The only relic of her former life was a large doll, to which she clung like a drowning woman to a life raft. To Lord Hervey, that acerbic chronicler of George II's court, it was a clear sign of her imbecility. One of her Ladies of the Bedchamber, less biased, thought her 'a very agreeable woman, very affable in her behaviour, a good deal of address, and her person what may be called a pretty woman; she speaks not one word of English, French tolerably, and though I speak it intolerable, with her good humour and civility I have made myself understood by her'.[2] Within a year, this supposed imbecile spoke English better than the rest of the royal family – though, to be fair, that was not such a great challenge.

Her royal husband, the Prince of Wales, had endured a lonely childhood that would nowadays provide work for an army of therapists and social workers. When the Elector of Hanover, his grandfather, became George I in 1714, seven-year-old Frederick was left behind as all the other members of the family – his father, mother and siblings – decamped to London. He did not see his mother again for fourteen years, when George II reluctantly allowed his son to come to England. Contemporaries found him agreeable and obliging, with lively eyes. For some unfathomable reason, however, his parents loathed him, his mother vehemently so, once calling him 'the greatest ass, the greatest liar, the greatest canaille, and the greatest beast in the whole world and I heartily wish he was out of it'.[3] There had even been a plan to cut him out of the succession in favour of his younger brother William, Duke of Cumberland.

Money and popularity were the two main areas of conflict. The King, partly out of parsimony and partly to prevent Frederick forming a serious opposition – though initially he showed no signs of wanting to – kept his son short of funds, pocketing a large part of his allowance for himself. For years after the Prince's arrival, he was not permitted a separate establishment either, and had to put up with being snubbed by his family on a daily basis. Matters had come to a head in 1737, when the Prince of Wales tried once again to settle the matter of his income through a debate in Parliament, and had followed this by whisking Augusta away from his parents' presence at Hampton Court to St James's when she went into labour with their first child. The King's reaction was to throw the couple out of St James's – a classic example of history stupidly repeating itself, for George I had done the same to him in 1717 – without the furniture from their apartments or even chests to carry their clothes in. Society was told in no uncertain terms that if they visited the Prince's court, they would be turned away from the King's.

By the time Elizabeth Chudleigh took up her post, she joined a court that was still in opposition to the King's, though its political influence was at a low ebb. The Prince's harshest critic, his mother, was dead, as was her confidant Lord Hervey. There were occasional thaws in the frost between father and son, but they rarely lasted long because of the King's determination to keep his heir sidelined. The good-natured Prince remained popular, however, largely thanks to his father's ill treatment of him, and Leicester House – a large, architecturally unremarkable seventeenth-century house at the north-east corner of Leicester Square – was an enjoyable place to be. The Prince and Princess of Wales were on easy, affectionate terms with their children, and took an interest in subjects such as painting, music, the theatre and gardening. Lord Egmont thought Frederick's main passion, if he had one, was 'to pass the evening with six or seven others over a glass of wine and hear them talk of a variety of things, but he does not drink. He loves to play, and plays to win, that he may satisfy his pleasures and generosity.'⁴

Elizabeth fitted easily into this agreeable environment and soon proved popular. Charlotte Dives, another Maid of Honour, who became Lady Masham, was to be a lifelong friend, and she remained on cordial terms with others such as Lucy Boscowen, later Lady Frederick. Another enduring friendship was with the eccentric and strong-willed Duchess of Queensbury, whose husband was one of the Prince of Wales's Gentlemen of the Bedchamber. Part of Elizabeth's appeal was her gift for story-telling and witty repartee – no doubt helped by her supposed unfailing maxim that one should always be 'short, clear and surprising'⁵ – which enabled her to turn even disasters into amusing anecdotes. In one example some years later, for instance, after someone had thrown a firework into her coach, burning a new lace ruffle, Elizabeth turned the episode into a long story '& diverted all the Company'.⁶ Aided and abetted by her 'penetrating eyes' and her 'fine complexion', the beautiful and lively Maid made an encouraging debut, although she was as yet only on the fringes of fashionable society. She was not yet its toast: that honour was reserved for acknowledged aristocratic beauties such as Lady Caroline Fitzroy, the high-spirited daughter of the Duke of Grafton; Miss Lepel Hervey, by now Mrs Phipps, the granddaughter of the Earl of Bristol; and Miss Jenny Conway, daughter of Lord Conway and the handsomest of the lot, who was destined to die in 1749 after drinking tainted lemonade at a masquerade, the rhyming possibilities of which did not elude the jingle writers.

However, even for those who were not yet the talk of the town, London was full of elegant diversions, particularly in the warmer months. The newest of these were the new pleasure gardens in the grounds of Ranelagh House adjoining Elizabeth's childhood home, the Royal Hospital, Chelsea. From its opening night in May 1742, which was attended by the Prince and Princess of Wales, and a large and glittering crowd of London's smartest, most glamorous people, Ranelagh became a fashionable meeting place. At its heart was a large rococo rotunda, beautifully painted and gilded inside, with an ornate central fireplace in the middle, and tiers of boxes where the company could sup or drink tea, and listen to music. The main activity, however, was simply promenading in endless circles, talking and looking at the other promenaders. Outside were the gardens themselves, small but well laid out. The overall effect was impressive, especially when it was crowded with 'the great, the rich, the gay, the happy, and the fair'[7] in their finest clothes. It became a compulsory stop for foreign visitors, who generally agreed with the German count who wrote in his diary: 'The numbers of people who are generally assembled here, and who are walking round and round, present a curious sight, which, together with the quantity of lights and music, astonishes people who see it for the first time.'[8]

On the other side of the Thames was Vauxhall, a much larger and older pleasure garden which had been improved to great acclaim in 1732. Until 1750, when Westminster Bridge opened, the only way to reach it was by boat or by making a huge detour and crossing the river over London Bridge, aptly named as it had been the city's only one for many years. Once inside, which cost one shilling, visitors amused themselves by strolling down the long avenues, lined with lamp-festooned trees and spanned by ornate arches, admiring the classical ruins, statues and cascades, before pausing for refreshment in one of the elegantly painted supper boxes where they might catch a glimpse of the Prince of Wales and his party. Most people brought their own food, for Vauxhall's prices were exorbitant and the ham was notorious for being so thin you could read through it. An orchestra played every evening from the comfort of a pretty raised bandstand. Off the main walks were narrower and darker paths, a terrible temptation to indecent behaviour in the eyes of the more prudish members of society, which doubtless made them irresistible to others.

Aside from these summer frolics, there were plenty of fashionable year-round amusements at which seeing and being seen was at least part of the pleasure. At the Theatre Royal, Drury Lane, David Garrick had recently begun his triumphant reign as actor-manager, with a different play staged every night. There was also the Royal Opera House in Covent Garden, for which Handel wrote many of his operas and oratorios, and plenty of private and public concerts. Fancy-dress parties called masquerades – again, public or private – were relatively new and very popular. Otherwise, there was the Tower of London with its menagerie, which included several lions and other big cats; freak shows of the weird and wonderful, such as satyrs and mermaids; Mrs Salmon's Waxworks in Fleet Street; and trials to attend, the more sensational the better. London's much-praised shops, with their bow-fronted windows and lavish displays, were another diversion for those who could afford them.

But when summer came, everyone who possibly could abandoned London for some rural retreat, escaping the dust and, more particularly, the smell, which even in England's indifferent summers could become stomach-turningly pungent. As the Prince and Princess of Wales generally removed with their children and a much-reduced household to Cliveden, their house on the banks of the Thames in Buckinghamshire, Elizabeth was released from her duties. She, too, headed away from the city to reflect on her first months in her new employment. In general, it had not been the most sparkling of seasons; fears at the start of the year of a Jacobite uprising in Scotland with French help, continuing conflict in Europe, and France's eventual official declaration of war against Britain in March had not unnaturally had a dampening effect on everyone's spirits. For one of Elizabeth's sister Maids of Honour, however, who had been appointed at the same time as her, it had been a great success. Having begun the year as pretty Miss Drax, daughter of a mere Esquire, in May she had become the wife of the fourth Earl Berkeley. According to many of her biographers, however, Elizabeth had made an even more exalted conquest, no less than James, sixth Duke of Hamilton, though clearly no one else had noticed for there was no recorded gossip about it. At this time the Duke was only nineteen, not yet legally an adult, and the reputed romance was, it was said, interrupted by his departure for a tour of the Continent, with which no young gentleman's education was complete, forcing the supposed lovers to part with many promises on both sides.

Elizabeth was to spend part of the summer at her cousin John Merrill's seat at Lainston in Hampshire, where her aunt Ann Hanmer was already ensconced. It was, and still is, a beautiful stretch of countryside, and Lainston was a harmonious addition to the landscape. The elegant E-shaped brick house was typical of the kind put up after the Restoration with due regard for proportion and form, not lavish but comfortable, and entirely appropriate for a gentleman's dwelling. It was conveniently close to the Salisbury to Winchester road, near enough for the post boy to not object to a detour through the grounds, especially if he was rewarded with 'money and strong beer'9 for his trouble, but set back from it in a small park with a fine avenue of lime trees pointing towards the racecourse on Worthy Downs.

Winchester Races had been the highlight of the local social calendar for years, providing an excuse for a lively procession of dinners and dances in the neighbourhood mansions. There were three days of racing on Worthy Downs at the end of June, as well as 'the Subscription Cock-Match every Morning during the Races; the Thursday Morning and Afternoon, and a Ball as usual Thursday Evening',[10] as the newspaper advertisements promised. Visitors descended on the area, old friendships were renewed and new introductions made. Among the latter was one that was to have consequences no one could have foreseen. At some point during the first three days of the race meeting, during which Mr Martindale's grey horse Starling beat Mr Aislabie's chestnut gelding Bucephalus to win 'His Majesty's Plate of 100gns, for six yrs old',[11] Elizabeth Chudleigh was introduced to a young naval lieutenant on leave from his ship the *Cornwall*, then lying at Portsmouth.

The Honourable Augustus John Hervey had two things to recommend him. Firstly, despite being too fleshy to be truly handsome, he was evidently charming. His diary reveals that, although he was only twenty when he met Elizabeth, he already had a not-inconsiderable experience of being pleasing to women,[12] though it would pale into insignificance compared with the number and variety of the future conquests he recounts. Secondly, he was the grandson of the Earl of Bristol, and only a frail older brother stood between him and the title. On both counts he was a perfectly acceptable escort, and it would have been no dishonour for the pretty Maid of Honour to lead off the dancing at the race ball[13] with the 'gallant and gay Lothario',[14] as she called him.

After the races, Hervey invited the Lainston party on an outing to Portsmouth to show them over the *Victory*, the pride of the British fleet with its hundred and ten gleaming brass guns, which was then riding at anchor there.* That invitation was reciprocated with one to Lainston for Hervey, which obviously went well for it turned into two or three further visits. Then, apparently out of the blue, there was a startling development. As Mrs Hanmer's maid Ann remembered years later: 'She . . . was informed by her Mistress . . . that Mr Hervey . . . was going abroad but that before he went he was to be married to her niece Miss Chudleigh.'[15]

The great mystery is how the young woman who was supposedly

---

* It sank off Alderney in October 1744, with the loss of 900 men.

in love with James Hamilton had become, in a matter of weeks, betrothed to someone else. Sadly, Hervey's surviving diaries break in 1743 and do not resume until 1746, and if the other principals in the drama ever committed anything to paper it has not survived. Only Mrs Hanmer's maid ever spoke of the events of that summer, and her knowledge was limited to what she was allowed to see or hear. With nothing in the way of evidence, contemporary biographers tried to fill in the gaps with various theories, the most popular being that Mrs Hanmer, to further a match with the charming Hervey, had intercepted and destroyed a series of passionate letters from Hamilton to her niece, so the girl believed she had been jilted and accepted Hervey out of pique. Others suggested that it was Elizabeth who had jilted the Duke, after hearing rumours that he was sowing wild oats on his European travels or had fallen in love with someone else. All agreed on one thing, though: that something of the kind *must* have happened, for only in the absence of any solid proof of Hamilton's enduring affection could Elizabeth have been persuaded to give up on her suitor. A clever young duke with large estates was, after all, a good match, and not to be turned down lightly, particularly by a girl who, in an age when the bride's portion was an important part of the marriage negotiations, had no money at all.

There is another possible explanation, however: that perhaps there was, as yet, no love affair at all between Elizabeth and Hamilton. When the Duke had inherited his title at the age of eighteen the previous March, he discovered that his father had bequeathed him not only his dukedom but also substantial debts[16] and several guardians to watch over him until he came of age at twenty-one. He graduated a month later from St Mary Hall, Oxford, and spent a little time in London – it is not clear how long – but by February 1744 he was on his way not to Europe but to Scotland[17] for a prolonged visit to sort out his estates and flirt with Jacobitism. It was not impossible for him to have encountered Elizabeth in those opening months of 1744, especially as his great-aunt Lady Archibald Hamilton was the Prince of Wales's mistress. Guardians and debts, however, were a considerable hindrance to anyone wanting to woo young women in London.

If that was the case, then Hervey might well have been Elizabeth's most promising, or even only prospective suitor so far. He had a good chance of becoming the Earl of Bristol one day, and probably sooner rather than later. Even if his older brother defied the odds and lived a long and unhealthy life, Hervey's prospects in the Navy were promising and by a mixture of natural ability and patronage he seemed certain to flourish in his career. Against these potential benefits of the match were some all-too-real and present drawbacks. Hervey might be rich one day, but for now he had only an allowance of £50 a year left to him by his father, and whatever he could make in prizes from plundered enemy ships. The couple would not even have Elizabeth's £200 a year, for only single women could be Maids of Honour. Even the future was not that secure; if the Earl of Bristol disapproved of his grandson's choice of bride – and it certainly was not a prudent one for a penniless younger son – he might cut him out of both his will and the succession. In short, it was, as Elizabeth later said, 'the extent of human folly, for I had little & he had nothing'.[18] Worse, Hervey would shortly be sailing for the West Indies and would be away for two years, which was hardly the ideal foundation for lifelong wedded happiness, for what was his wife to do in his absence?

These considerations ought to have given all those involved an extended pause for thought. Marriage was not something to be entered into lightly or in haste, not least because for all but the richest, it was a bond 'which nothing, nothing can divide'.[19] Divorce was possible, but as it required a private Act of Parliament it was rare. Only 325 were obtained between 1670 and 1857, all but four of them by men,[20] and most of these were in the later part of the period. Queen Anne's reign saw only six divorces, George I's just two, and even George II's thirty-three years on the throne produced a mere twenty-nine.[21] With no second chances, families tried to make sure that their children – especially their daughters – made a prudent choice of life partner. Matchmaking was often a long-drawn-out negotiation involving both sets of relatives. Romance was not entirely left out of the equation, but the older generations certainly regarded it as their duty to consider the more practical matters and prevent the young from allowing their feelings to run away with them.

In this Mrs Hanmer failed her niece. If, as her maid reported, it was indeed Mrs Hanmer's wish 'that they should not be married till Mr Hervey returned',[22] she did both parties a disservice by not being firmer and making her wish prevail. After all, there was no need for such haste, even if her spirited niece had been conquered by Hervey's 'soft perswasion, and soothing eloquence'.[23] Elizabeth, at a time when the average age for marriage among the better-off was around twenty-five, was several years away from being an old maid. As for Hervey, in the eyes of the law he was a minor, yet he was about to take one of the most important steps in life without the advice and support of his own family. Folly was allowed to win the day; the wedding would go ahead – but, so that Elizabeth could retain her job, in secret.

Accordingly, late on the evening of 4 August, the principal members of the house party began to drift discreetly in the direction of the small medieval private chapel, nowadays a roofless ruin, a short distance from the house.[24] This was hardly used, except as a mausoleum; the family usually worshipped at nearby Sparsholt. For a secret wedding, however, it was perfect. In its musty interior, standing at the old reading desk, the Reverend Thomas Amis, rector of the one-house parish of Lainston, was waiting for them: Hervey and Elizabeth, Mrs Hanmer and her maid Ann, John Merrill and Mr Mountenay, a close friend of his and almost permanent resident at Lainston. In the interests of discretion, the only light was a candle held by Mr Mountenay, which he shaded with his hat so that the Reverend Amis could only just see to read. In the gloom, surrounded by shadows, everyone – except Mrs Hanmer, who sat on a bench in the aisle – stood huddled together to hear the Reverend murmur and stumble his way through a marriage ceremony that Elizabeth was later to describe as 'such a scrambling shabby business . . . and so much incomplete that she should have been full as unwilling to have taken a positive oath that she was married as that she was not married'.[25]

Hervey, though, was quite sure of his new status and of its pleasurable benefits. After the maid had been sent ahead to make sure none of the other servants were awake, the wedding guests walked back through the garden to the house where the new husband lost no time in taking his bride upstairs to bed. Aunt Hanmer was furious, though she can hardly have been surprised, for this was the carrot that had been dangling before the besotted young man all along. Undaunted, she made them both get up, determined the servants should have no cause for damaging gossip. Eventually, however, tiredness defeated her; she fell asleep and the newlyweds spent the rest of the night together. For the next two or three days the couple remained at Lainston, strolling in the grounds and eating greengages, until it was time for Hervey to return to his ship at Portsmouth and sail away.

The maid Ann later remembered how she had woken Hervey at five on the morning of his departure, and how reluctantly he took his leave, 'and as he . . . went away from the House he desired the dep[onen]t to go up stairs and give her (meaning his wife . . .) all the comfort she could which the dep[onen]t accordingly did and found her in a flood of tears'.[26] This the maid took to be a sign that Elizabeth was sorry to see Hervey go. But perhaps, in the cool, clear light of dawn, she was already regretting bitterly having wed him. To be sure, hers was not the only irregular marriage of the time. There was a brisk trade in suspect weddings at and around the Fleet prison for debtors, for there were often needy parsons among the inmates happy to undercut Church rates; in fact, in the 1740s, at least half of all London marriages took place here.[27] Smarter couples, around seven hundred a year, were married without licences or banns at Mr Keith's notorious establishment in May-Fair, a faintly church-like house in Curzon Street. A decade later the concern about these irregular ceremonies had reached such a pitch that Hardwicke's new Marriage Act was brought in to tighten the rules in England.

All this did not alter the fact, though, that Elizabeth had put herself in an unenviable position. At the end of the summer, she would have to return to court, ostensibly still the desirable 'Honourable Miss Chudleigh', flirtatious and available, yet keeping admirers at arm's length. If one of them should offer her his hand, Elizabeth would have to turn him down, and the world would begin to wonder why. If her secret became known, her only source of income would be taken from her, and she would have to rely on the feeble earning power of a husband who was several thousand miles away. It would be a difficult act to carry off. Perhaps not surprisingly, Elizabeth made little noise in society in the following months as she tried to come to terms with the consequences of that August night when she had tied herself for life to a man she hardly knew. Nor could she console herself with happy memories of the ceremony itself for, even in a pragmatic age where weddings were relatively simple affairs, hers had been particularly wretched.

The world at large, however, had more pressing concerns as 1744 drew to a close and 1745 began. The French under Marshal de Saxe were making important gains in the Austrian Netherlands, and in May they inflicted a heavy defeat at Fontenay on the allied forces led by the Duke of Cumberland. For Elizabeth, the campaign brought personal sadness, for it caused that 'glorious' death, already mentioned, of her cousin John Chudleigh, the last baronet, at Ostend. To add to the gloom, in July Charles Edward Stuart – Bonnie Prince Charlie, the Young Pretender – landed in Scotland to seize the throne, causing George II and his son the Duke of Cumberland to hurry back to England from Hanover, which was, not unnaturally, one of Britain's allies in the War of the Austrian Succession. The Jacobites, an army of some 2,000, marched steadily south with surprising success. On 8 November they finally crossed into England, and a week later took Carlisle, before marching on to Manchester and Derby. Their rapid advance caused widespread panic among the English, who believed a French invasion fleet would appear off the south coast at any moment to take advantage of the situation.

While his favoured younger brother marched north to confront the rebel army, the Prince of Wales languished in London at his father's command. With his heavily pregnant wife resting in bed, he took to giving dinners for selected Ladies of the Bedchamber and Maids of Honour, whom he harangued about politics from the head of the table.[28] The nearest he came to battle was when, for the supper to celebrate the christening of his newborn son, he had a model of Carlisle Castle made in sugar so that everyone could besiege it with sugar plums. Walpole could not resist mentioning another piece of frivolity: that when it was reported that William Pitt had been made secretary of war, Frederick 'said, Miss Chudleigh, one of the maids, was fitter for the employment, and dictated a letter, which he made her to write to Lord Harrington, to desire he would draw the warrant for her'.[29] The joke was that Miss Chudleigh was not in the least interested in politics, except in so far as it affected her friends, whom she chose with no regard to 'party' allegiances. At least the frustrated Prince turned out to be right in not taking the uprising too seriously. In early December at Derby, the Jacobites – tired, their shoes worn out, and with no sign of the French – decided to retreat. The Jacobite Rebellion was effectively over, and was finally brought to a bloody full stop at the Battle of Culloden the following April, which earned the King's son the epithet 'Butcher' Cumberland among the Scots, and later among the English, too.

Notwithstanding a smallpox epidemic, the feeling of relief in London that spring of 1746 was palpable; 'all was joy and hilarity among loyal subjects',[30] wrote one observer. 'The season at Vauxhall was very prosperous, and songs of triumph were sung every night.' On the evening that the news of the final defeat of the rebels arrived, the whole town was brilliantly illuminated. Everyone put lights outside their houses; the smart folk put flaming torches on their railings and candles round their windows and roofs, so that the whole effect was of a Chinese festival. The delighted mob, no doubt after a surfeit of loyal toasts, took to smashing the windows of any houses foolishly left dark. As for the fireworks, Londoners could barely hear themselves think over the noise of explosions. At last, it was acceptable to be frivolous again. At a crowded benefit concert, the composer Mr Gluck played a concerto on twenty-six glasses filled with spring water;[31] the Prince and Princess of Wales, presumably with Elizabeth in attendance, graced Epsom Races with their presence; and, in June, the Prince of Hesse, who had been in Scotland, was fêted with dinners and a performance of *The Beggar's Opera* by command of the Prince of Wales.

In all this gaiety Elizabeth sparkled, and people began to notice the vivacious Maid of Honour. She was even honoured in print that June, in a poem written as a rebuff to 'Mr Eckardt the Painter' who had taken the love of classicism too far and been dismissive of British womanhood. The author turned out to be the ubiquitous Horace Walpole:

> Desponding Artist talk no more
> Of Beauty of the Days of yore,
> Of Goddesses renown'd in Greece
> And Zeuxis' Composition Piece, . . .
> In Britain's Isle observe the Fair,
> And curious chuse your Models there.[32]

There, among the established beauties, such as Hervey's sister Mrs Phipps, and Lady Caroline Fitzroy, was Elizabeth:

> Whose Eyes shall try your Pencil's Art,
> And in my Numbers claim a Part?
> Our Sister Muses must describe
> CHUDLEIGH, or name her with the Tribe.

No doubt well pleased with the mention, Elizabeth left London for the summer. It was delightful being the toast of the court, of course, but a strain having to conceal her marriage from everyone for so long. It would soon be harder still, for in the middle of August Hervey came back to England to discover that his liaison with Elizabeth was not as secret as he thought. In his diary, he wrote, 'My B^r told me, both Ld Bristol & himself had been told I was engaged to Miss—— (still Maid of Honor to the Pss of Wales) & desir'd to know if it was so, for that if I own'd her he had got Ld Bristol to consent to the receiving her – however, I evaded the question by saying the world always advanced more than they knew of – Yet my B^r told me she herself did not deny it'.[33] Hervey, though, resolved to tread carefully until he had a better idea of his family's true feelings on the matter, for he was still dependent on them financially; his total fortune was, by his own admission, only about £300, plus an annuity of £50 a year, which would rise to £200 on the death of his grandfather Lord Bristol.

He was also eager to find out how matters stood with his wife after a two-year absence. The news was not encouraging. Lady Townshend made 'some inuendo's that were sufficient to ground some sort of suspicions in me, that Miss—— Conduct was not altogether as Vestal-like as I might have wished from her Connections'.[34] Still, Hervey resolved not to panic, and to wait until he had seen Elizabeth before he formed an opinion, 'knowing how ready people in gen^l are to Censure others, or to endeavour to Levell them with themselves, whenever they are fall'n rather beneath the Standard of Proof'. To his growing concern, however, Elizabeth remained stubbornly out of town in the West Country. Moreover, though he stayed in London for several weeks while his new ship, the sloop *Porcupine*, was being fitted up at Deptford, he heard nothing from her, 'tho' I did of her'.[35] Undaunted, Hervey consoled himself as best he could, with two women; 'the Galli & the Campioni both famous in their way on the stage admitted my attentions, the latter was beautiful, & as she wd accept of nothing from me being kept by the Count Hasslang, I found it most suitable as well as most agreeable to stick to her'.

Eventually, Elizabeth must have realised she could put off the meeting with her husband no longer. Dragging her heels, she finally arrived back in London in the middle of October, a full two months after Hervey's return. It was a clear sign of how reluctant she was to see him again. She summoned him to meet her at her aunt Mrs

Hanmer's house, where they argued at once. 'She thought I sd have gone down to Devonshire to see her,' Hervey remembered, '& I, that she might have come up to attend her Duty on the Princess, if she had any Inclination to see me'.[36] It was not a good start; however, they *were* married and it was important to at least try to make a go of it – Hervey was eager to, Elizabeth seemingly more resigned. The quarrel blew over, and while Hervey remained in London they met several times in secret 'at Mrs. Hanmer's (who was not in Town) about midnight & passed together quite uninterrupted 'till 4 or 5 in the morning'.

It would take more than these brief encounters to rescue their doomed marriage, however. In the two years since Hervey's departure, Elizabeth had had to make a life for herself, one in which her absent and unacknowledged husband naturally had no part. Naively, Hervey complained that he 'found her much more taken up with her pleasures, with the Court & with Particular Connections, than she was with our attachment'. He had not altogether given up hope, though, despite the disquieting stories that he heard about his wife and her mysterious 'Particular Connections', and was resolved 'to gratifye my own Inclinations which were still to please her if I cd'. What Elizabeth felt about the situation is not recorded. Whatever her feelings for Hervey in the past, however, her behaviour towards him now was not that of a woman madly in love. On the other hand, she could not afford to quarrel with him during what would be, after all, only a short stay in England, for in anger he might make their marriage known. If she was to grant Hervey his conjugal rights, therefore, she made sure he had the conjugal responsibilities that went with them. Playing on his sense of honour, she persuaded him to pay her debts, though he had to borrow money himself to do so. Hervey even 'gave her an Onyx Watch set with diamonds, & in short, whatever People wd trust me with, trusting to the Chance of War & Success of Prizes to be able to repay it all'.

By the end of October, only two weeks after his first meeting with Elizabeth, Hervey was already making plans to leave again. London was boring, and Elizabeth was being difficult and elusive. Two weeks later he sailed, only to discover that his sloop was as disappointing as his stay in the capital, for the *Porcupine*'s green timbers made the crew ill. As if that was not discouraging enough, he soon had the dubious pleasure of learning from Mrs Hanmer's letters to him one of the reasons for his wife's elusiveness: Elizabeth was being courted by someone else, the very person who had supposedly jilted her two years earlier. Now, however, there was definitely a connection, for in early December Hervey wrote to Elizabeth to complain about her aunt's news that she 'wd receive the <u>Duke of Hamilton</u> & . . . they were very often together'.[37]

Exactly when the connection could have begun is unclear. The Duke had definitely been in London at the beginning of August, however, for he was reported to be planning his first visit to court, with the intention of pleading for the life of one of the Scottish rebels, Lord Kilmarnock, whose trial had taken place in Westminster Hall the previous month. In this he had no success. Kilmarnock, with Lord Balmerino, was eventually hanged, and their awful severed heads made a gruesome display at Temple Bar for many years to come. In wooing Elizabeth, however, the Duke – tall and elegant, with strong but refined features and an air of confidence – seemed to be doing better, and was obviously sufficiently encouraged to offer her his hand in marriage at around this time.[38] Naturally, Elizabeth had no option but to turn him down.

By early December, the Duke was in poor health,[39] and a few days before Christmas left London for his estate in Hampshire.[40] Illness seemed to be the fashion that season, for Elizabeth was also laid low with a bad cold, one that nearly proved fatal. On 12 January, several of the newspapers reported: 'A few Days ago a melancholly Accident happened to Miss Chudleigh, one of the Maids of Honour to her Royal Highness the Princess of Wales; which was, as we are inform'd, in the following Manner: The young Lady having caught a Cold, which had occasioned her to be thick of Hearing, she was advised to drop a small Quantity of Laudanum in her Ear; and sending for a Bottle, she did as prescribed. A Medicine being sent some Time after for her to take inwardly, she ordered her Servant, a young Country Girl, to pour it out, and give it her, but she mistaking the Bottle, gave her the Laudanum instead of the Medicine, The Lady's Mother coming soon after into the Room discovered the Mistake, and sent directly for a Physician, who advised them by all means to keep her awake, for if she went to sleep she would certainly die; which by Shaking and other Methods they have hitherto effected, and there are great Hopes of her Recovery.'[41]

While Elizabeth battled for her life in London, the Duke of Hamilton was faring little better and towards the end of the month was reported to be dangerously ill at Portsmouth 'having been twice taken with very severe Vomitting of Blood'.[42] Hervey, who was there to supervise preparation for his new ship, added: 'they say he can't (poor Man) live many days longer; No Wonder! for the Instant he recovers a little, he drinks 'till four, five, & six in the Morning'. The unhappy announcement of the Duke's death duly appeared in the newspapers near the end of January. Not until several days later was the report contradicted and the Duke found to be well on his way to recovery. With the help of his doctors, over the next two months he regained enough of his health to be able to carry out his plan of sailing to Lisbon, where he arrived in April.

At least Hervey had something to celebrate, for in mid December he had been asked to be a captain under Admiral Byng, with a fine ship, the *Princessa*, which would sail shortly for the Mediterranean for a lengthy stay. He returned to London on 9 January to accept his new command and went at once to see Elizabeth, where he discovered that she was 'very much alive' and recovering from her accident – though Horace Walpole cannot have been the only person to voice doubts over whether it really was such an accident.[43] If Hervey's career was flourishing, the same could not be said for his marriage. While he remained in town, Elizabeth saw him grudgingly and only when she could not avoid it, which Hervey hated for he was not the type to find pleasure in forcing his company on any woman. There were, he complained, 'great mysteries, great falseness, & every mark of what I wholly disapproved – However I determined to shut my Eyes & Ears as much as I cd to it all, as I was so very shortly to go abroad.'[44]

That they did meet privately is certain, however, for despite the sly hints of one anonymous late-eighteenth-century biographer that 'the connubial rites were attended with consequences, injurious to health, as well as unproductive of fecundity',[45] it soon became clear to Elizabeth that she was pregnant. Some time that spring, while London fizzed with celebrations for the end of the Scottish Rebellion and Hervey battled to overcome a painful and dangerous attack of what he called rheumatic pleurisy, which laid him low for most of April and May, Elizabeth retreated discreetly to Chelsea, where she had spent the first years of her childhood. The spot was well chosen: comfortable lodgings were easy to come by in Chelsea, which was still a popular summer resort for gentlemen; the air was clean and healthy; and her mother – who was either still in ignorance of her daughter's

marriage or so angry about it that her daughter was avoiding her –
never went there, 'by reason her husband and son were buried there'[46]
in the Royal Hospital cemetery. Quite *how* Elizabeth explained her
removal there is a mystery, though a popular option for young women
obliged to vanish to the country for three or four months was to say,
gravely, that it was for the sake of their health.

Hervey finally sailed for the Mediterranean in June, and Elizabeth
stayed closeted in Chelsea until her baby was born sometime in the
autumn. Present at the birth was, of all people, Caesar Hawkins, surgeon
to the Prince of Wales; Elizabeth must, then, have told her royal
mistress about her pregnancy, and probably about her marriage as well.
On 2 November 'Augustus-Henry Hervey son of ye Honble Augustus
Hervey'[47] was baptised by his father's uncle, the Honourable Reverend
Henry Aston.* The child was left in Chelsea to be nursed, while
Elizabeth returned to court and the gossip about her unexplained
absence. In a story that had also been told of other women, and whose
accuracy is consequently in doubt, she apparently said to Lord
Chesterfield,† 'Do you know, my Lord, that the world says I have had
twins?' To this Chesterfield replied dryly, 'Does it? For my own part,
I make it a point of believing only half of what it says.'[48]

Hervey, who had been lucky enough to capture two richly laden
enemy ships, was able to send Elizabeth £200 by way of his uncle
Aston,[49] but Elizabeth still had to borrow another £100 from Aunt
Hanmer to buy baby things. Sadly, they were not needed for long.
On the very day that Ann, Mrs Hanmer's maid, was to be taken to
see the boy who looked very like Hervey, Elizabeth 'came in great
grief'[50] and told her it had sickened and died. Little Augustus-Henry
was buried in Chelsea on 21 January 1748. Elizabeth was heartbroken,
but possibly also a little relieved. It was one less secret to keep, one
less complication, one thing less to bind her to Hervey. Life could
now return to relative normality.

---

* Born Henry Hervey, but changed his name to Aston after marrying an
  heiress of that name.
† Philip Stanhope, fourth Earl of Chesterfield (1694–1773), politician, wit
  and famous letter writer.

CHAPTER 4

Peace

To crown the triumphs o'er subjected France,
See all the gay, in jubilee, advance;
See Heroes, Statesmen, flaunt it in disguise,
See maids, and matrons, all illustrious rise;
See Belles, Coquettes, and each gay straying wife,
Behold the soft varieties of life.

'A Poetical Epistle to Miss C—h—y'

The general mood that spring of 1748 was one of relief and celebration. The War of the Austrian Succession, which had been rumbling on since 1740, had finally come to an end, and a preliminary peace treaty was signed at the end of April. It had been an unpopular conflict in England, for in its early stages it seemed the country was being dragged into it only to protect George II's beloved Electorate of Hanover. Even the King's heroics at Dettingen in 1743 – where he was the last British monarch to lead troops into battle – had done little to soften public anger at an apparently pointless and definitely expensive war in which many fine young men, including Elizabeth's brother Thomas and her cousin John, had died. Now, at last, it was over.

For Elizabeth, the peace brought welcome news about Hervey. His ship was safely at anchor at Lisbon and, as he told one correspondent, 'if 'tis Peace, I hope not to see England [for] some time, as I'm in a Ship that I flatter myself will be station'd here'.[1] Elizabeth no doubt shared his hope. Better yet, he had written to her to let her know he would pay all her debts 'if she wd let me know what they were',[2] and had given her £500 in the meantime. With her more pressing bills paid off and Hervey away, Elizabeth could forget her problems and throw herself into the social whirl with renewed enthusiasm. She was by now an established member of the '*élite de la jeunnesse*'[3] – along with the likes of Lords Eglinton, Bute and Barrington, William Pitt, Lady Charlotte Johnston and Miss Neville – who made the most of that lively season and were seen frolicking at all the early summer balls at Ranelagh.

From London, Elizabeth and her set moved on to the fashionable spa town of Tunbridge Wells. Its popularity as a resort had grown rapidly since the beginning of the century, particularly since 1732 when Beau Nash, who had revolutionised the winter season at Bath, was also appointed Master of Ceremonies here for the summer season. Under his aegis, the routines that governed every waking hour at Bath were now applied to the picturesque Sussex town. New arrivals paid a fee, a subscription, which covered two balls a week at the Assembly Rooms, four card assemblies and on Sunday evenings the Upper Rooms were laid out for public tea-drinking. Aside from this, the daily routine was unchanging. It began, for a very few people, with an early-morning visit to the spa itself to drink the waters. Afterwards everyone promenaded on the Upper Walk before breakfast – tea, coffee or chocolate and toast or buns – at ten. At noon they returned to the shady Walk, this time in their formal day clothes, to listen to a band of flutes, hautboys and violins, do a little shopping or pause at the circulating library to look at novels or read the latest verses by visitors. Dinner, the fashionable hour for which was around four, occupied the rest of the afternoon. This was followed by another couple of hours of promenading in the early evening or, for a welcome change, an excursion to High Rocks for tea, or a syllabub at the Fish Ponds on Mount Ephraim. The evening concluded with either a concert, ball or cards, which closed punctually at eleven.

At Tunbridge Wells that summer, Elizabeth continued to turn heads and attract comment: 'a lively, sweet-tempered, gay, self-admired, and, not altogether without reason, generally admired lady',[4] the novelist Samuel Richardson called her. 'She moved not without crowds after her. She smiled at every one. Every one smiled before they saw her, when they heard she was on the Walk. She played, she won, she lost— all with equal good-humour.' A contemporary drawing shows her, modishly wide-hooped, a picture of elegance, strolling past Evans Coffee House with Beau Nash and Mr Pitt.[5] Her behaviour did not always attract favourable comment, however. One particularly riotous evening ended on a farcical note when one of the young men, Thomas Scrope, went too far with his horseplay, for

> after drinking four bottles, which had made me mad, and the rest of the company drunk, I strapped and carried Baron Newman, alias Crook-fingered Jack, in a chair, quite up to the end of Joy's long room, at nine o'clock, where all the company then in Tunbridge were assembled. I tore open the door and top of the chair, and down dropped, to all appearance, a dead man. Miss Chudleigh, who is very subject to fits, struck with the odd appearance, fainted, and was carried off. This, in less than quarter of an hour, spread among the ladies like a contagion; I am informed of eight at least, who fell into fits.[6]

On the face of it, it seems implausible that the spirited, bold Miss Chudleigh should be the swooning type. However, she was also not particularly tall, so that every surplus pound in weight would show all too clearly. To keep her unruly flesh in order, she perhaps needed rather tighter stays than her contemporaries, restricting her rib cage and making her more prone to breathing problems and fainting.

Among her many admirers at Tunbridge was the dramatist and actor Colley Cibber, for it was not only the young men who were captivated. The seventy-seven-year-old Mr Cibber

> was over head and heels with Miss Chudleigh. Her admirers (such was his happiness) were not jealous of him: but, pleased with that wit in him which they had not, were always for calling him to her. She said pretty things – for she was Miss Chudleigh. He said pretty things – for he was Mr. Cibber; and all the company, men and women, seemed to think they had an interest in what was said, and were half as well pleased as if they had said the sprightly things themselves; and mighty well contented were they to be second-hand repeaters of the pretty things. But once I faced the laureat squatted upon one of the benches, with a face more wrinkled than ordinary with disappointment. 'I thought,' said I, 'you were of the party at the tea-treats – Miss Chudleigh is gone into the tea-room.' – 'Pshaw!' said he, 'there is no coming at her, she is so surrounded by the toupets' – And I left him upon the fret – But he was called to her soon after; and in flew, and his face shone again, and he looked smooth.'[7]

To the disappointment of many, Elizabeth had moved on from Tunbridge by the beginning of August, and it is not unreasonable to assume she may have gone for a quiet visit to her family in the West Country. It had been a busy year, after all, and the demands of being one of the fashionable set would have depleted both her energy and her finances. Moreover, there was every sign that the new season would be even more glittering, more joyful and more expensive than the last. The Peace of Aix-la-Chapelle was formally signed on 18 October and for months the papers could talk of little else but the celebrations that would follow George II's return to England in late November. In the meantime, the King's birthday and the anniversary of his coronation were marked by great receptions at Leicester House, for Frederick still tried to please his father if he could, and with bonfires and illuminations in the evening. The end of the war also brought Hervey – who had not been granted the Lisbon command – back to England at the beginning of December. Elizabeth, for once, almost welcomed his arrival for she had more than a few pressing bills to pay. Hervey obliged with £500 'to pay her debts a list of which she gave me, & in a few days afterwards gave her £200 more . . . The 30th, I gave Miss—— £100 more – This was a very idle time now – & I was very much displeased with many things I heard of Miss Ch——'s Conduct, especially from her own Relations too which put me out of humour.'[8]

The marriage, a mistake from the outset, was on its last legs. Elizabeth had long ago given up on it, but Hervey – who had always been the more keen – hung on a little longer. Now even he had had enough. On his return to town in the early days of 1749, he 'carried it very cool'[9] with Elizabeth whenever he met her. On 25 January, there was an argument, some 'éclaircissements as to Miss Ch—— Conduct with her which she did not approve . . . In short I took a Resolution from this afternoon of going abroad & never having any more to do in that affair.' The incompatible couple had finally separated for good, but in law they were bound as tightly as ever. Moreover, they seemed likely to remain that way for although divorce was possible, it was hugely expensive and well beyond Hervey's means. Both were trapped in a way that would affect their whole life. Hervey, if he ever became Earl of Bristol, would never have a legitimate heir to whom to pass his title; but at least he could have a career. For Elizabeth, the situation was far graver. The only income she had was

£200 a year as Maid of Honour, a post she would be forced to give up if her marriage became public knowledge, which was only a matter of time; her 'single' state at the age of twenty-seven, rumours of her rejection of eligible suitors such as the Duke of Hamilton and the Duke of Ancaster,[10] and her sudden departure from town in 1747 would all have made people curious about her. Financially, women were usually dependent on their husbands, but Elizabeth could expect nothing more from Hervey. She urgently needed to find someone else to support her in the style to which she had become accustomed.

Accordingly, she flung herself into that spring's official celebrations for the end of the war with unusual enthusiasm and purpose. It was a busy season of concerts and balls, fireworks and masquerades; the newspapers were full of it. 'Yesterday,' the *Daily Advertiser* of 18 April informed its readers, 'the Musick compos'd by Mr Handel for the Fireworks in the Green Park, was rehears'd at his House in Brook-Street, Grosvenor-Square. The Band consists of upwards of a hundred Trumpets, Bassoons, Hautboys, French Horns, Kettle Drums, and other Instruments.'[11] There was a public rehearsal in Spring Gardens in Vauxhall a few days later, with tickets at half a crown each, before twelve thousand of 'the most numerous, and brightest Assembly of Ladies and Gentlemen, that ever met together on such an Occasion'.[12] Such were the crowds that the traffic on London Bridge came to a standstill and 'no carriage could pass for 3 hours'.[13] Music poured from every corner of London, with a new anthem and Te Deum being tried out at St James's Chapel and concerts of 'Musick and Breakfasting' at Ranelagh.

More thrilling still to the majority of the population were the preparations for the great firework display in Green Park. Crowds of people visited the park just to see the magnificent structure decorated with statues of Greek and Roman gods that was being built there 'for the pompous* displaying the Fireworks, in honour of the late concluded Peace',[14] as the *London Evening-Post* put it. Celebrations began in earnest on 25 April, the day appointed for a General Thanksgiving. The King and the rest of the royal family went to the Chapel Royal at St James's, where they were regaled with sermons based on Psalm 29, and Handel's new Te Deum and anthem, which

---

* At the time, 'pompous' merely meant 'characterised by pomp or splendour'.

must have been much more enjoyable. In the evening, the whole of London was illuminated, which made for a pretty sight.

The next day was the Royal Jubilee Masquerade at Ranelagh 'in the Venetian manner', as the organisers called it, if only because, according to the advertisements, it contained 'a Representation of Le Boteghe* della Piazzo di San Marco at Venice'.[15] Its advent was far from universally welcomed; the grumpy Middlesex magistrates declared 'that such meeting, as it tends to the encouragement of gaming, lewdness and all manner of debauchery and the corruption of the morals of both sexes is unlawful and a public nuisance',[16] and vowed to suppress it. Masquerades were constantly under attack as sinful entertainments, for it was supposed – often with reason – that anonymity would lead people to behave in ways they would not otherwise. However, on this occasion the magistrates were disappointed and more than six thousand people crammed into Ranelagh to enjoy a spectacle that even the demanding Horace Walpole thought was the prettiest he ever saw: 'nothing in a fairy tale ever surpassed it'.[17]

Everywhere you looked there were people in fancy dress, charming little tents to sit in, and bands of masked musicians – in fact, everyone had their face covered. In one corner was the rustic scene of a maypole with dancers moving to the sound of a pipe and tabor, and there was 'a troop of harlequins and scaramouches, in the little open temple on the mount'. To add to the noise, there was a 'Royal Salute of Cannon'[18] on the hour every hour until the ball ended. One of the few Venetian touches was the gondola on the canal, festooned with flags and streamers, and with another group of musicians on board; another was the collection of booths round the amphitheatre, to mimic those of St Mark's Square, selling all sorts of exotic goods. The amphitheatre itself was illuminated, and the central area filled with tall firs and orange trees to make a scented bower, 'and below them all sorts of the finest auriculas in pots; and festoons of natural flowers hanging from tree to tree'.[19] Round the edge were booths where people could take refreshments such as wine and tea, and there were card tables and a space for dancing. In short, it was magnificent.

The next day came the eagerly awaited firework display, preparations for which had been going on since November. That evening, an immense crowd gathered in Green Park; the roads were blocked

* Shops.

with carriages, and every window and balcony with a view was crammed with people, except at St George's Hospital where the governors had been forced to keep spectators out because of the danger to them from its disturbed women patients. As if to emphasise that peace in Europe did not mean peace in the royal family, the King and the favoured Duke of Cumberland had gathered with their entourage in the library at St James's, while the Prince and Princess of Wales – in the absence of an invitation from his Majesty – were watching from Lady Middlesex's house in Arlington Street.

At half past eight, the deafening display began with the firing of two large rockets, and several cannons, 'after which a great Number of Rockets of different Sorts, Ballons, &c. were discharged, to surprizing Perfection'.[20] The 'Ballons' were hollow globes of paper filled with stars, which were fired from mortars and burst high in the air: some of these 'were remarkably fine'.[21] There was particular praise for the 'Grand Girandole', which was a collection of rockets fired simultaneously from a large chest. This particular one 'surpassed all imagination in the beauty and greatness of its appearance, for it covered the whole heavens, forming a canopy of diversified fires, which, together with the rapidity of the flight of these rockets, and the reports which attended their bursting, inspired the immense multitude of spectators with the utmost transport'. This was at least some consolation for the fireworks on the ground, which were a disappointment, partly because part of their pavilion burnt down, so most of them could not be set off. As for the illumination with its triumphant inscriptions, Walpole complained that it 'lighted so slowly that scarce anybody had patience to await the finishing'.[22] Almost inevitably given the fever of anticipation, the event was generally regarded as an anticlimax.

Four days later, there was a Subscription Masquerade at the King's Theatre in the Haymarket. This was a much more exclusive affair, where, as the *Daily Advertiser* put it, 'his Majesty supp'd in Publick with the Quality',[23] and was thrilled when someone failed to recognise him – 'well disguised in an old-fashioned English habit'[24] – and asked him to hold their tea cup. He was accompanied by the Duke of Cumberland, in a similar outfit, looking immensely fat. Other revellers came as figures from Elizabethan paintings, a Jacobean mayoress, Rubens' wife, characters from Don Quixote and a starry night. Glittering with diamonds in the candlelight, many of the women looked particularly beautiful, especially Mrs Pitt as a canoness whose face was concealed by a red veil. However, the costume that caused the most comment was that of Miss Chudleigh, who had come as Iphigenia, the daughter of Agamemnon, ready for the sacrifice. Her dress, 'or rather undress',[25] as one masquerader described it, left her 'so naked ye high Priest might easily inspect ye Entrails of ye Victim'. The other Maids of Honour – hardly models of modesty themselves, though they might wish to pretend so – were so shocked they refused to speak to her.

Precisely how revealing the outfit was is hard to say, since no one thought to leave a detailed description of it. Moreover, as the story grew, the costume shrank until, in several of the prints that followed, it became nothing more than a flimsy gauze with one strategically placed wreath round her hips. It is unlikely that Elizabeth would have left off her stays, however, for they were an essential tool to creating and showing off the fashionable figure. More likely is a combination of low-cut, flesh-coloured stays – which could be adjusted to reveal an impressive amount of bosom even in normal circumstances – and layers and layers of gauze that, in the candlelit interior of the theatre, hinted strongly at the shape beneath without actually revealing all.

Whatever the precise makeup of Elizabeth's masquerade outfit, it succeeded in making her the centre of attention. The Duke of Cumberland was all admiration, and his Majesty was delighted. It was even said he had asked, like a besotted youth, if he might touch Miss Chudleigh's breast, to which Elizabeth had apparently responded by taking his hand and, saying 'Your Majesty, I can put it to a far softer place',[26] had guided it to his own head. The King, charmed out of his usual parsimony, had immediately ordered another Jubilee Masquerade at Ranelagh for the following week, at which he amazed everyone still further by spending thirty-five guineas of his own money on a present for Elizabeth at one of the booths.[27] As for the newspapers, they were thrilled to report such scandalous goings-on in the fashionable world, and in the months that followed there were endless prints and verses about the scantily clad Maid of Honour. One typical example was 'A Poetical Epistle to Miss C—h—y', which appeared in June. This, in common with the prints, moved the event from the private subscription ball at the Haymarket to the public one at Ranelagh, which made it all the more wonderfully shocking, provided fuel to those who railed against the evils of the pleasure gardens and left an indelible, and none too flattering, impression of the immodesty of Elizabeth's character on the public consciousness.

> But you, O C—h—y! born mankind to please,
> To dress with freedom, and gallant with ease;
> O learn my fair, all censure to dispise,
> And trust alone the lightning of your eyes;
> Nay sometimes deign your snowy breast to show,
> For Beauty still does captivate the Beau: . . .
>
> Why should those parts, by nature meant to shine,
> Be veil'd? since beauty has a power divine.
> Why should the bosom of surpassing white,
> Be hid (thrice cruel!) from the wond'ring sight? . . .
>
> But tow'ring far, above each pigmy elf,
> Deign fairest creature, deign to view yourself;
> All eyes are gazing, as you move along,
> All hearts are fluttering, in the shining throng;
> Fond admiration scans the wond'rous show,
> Each rival envies, and adores each Beau;
> Beauty display'd, in native lustre charms,
> The rising bosom every heart alarms;
> Each feels a pang, which the severe call sin,
> And all admire an alabaster skin . . .[28]

May's entertainments were not yet finished, however. Using the excuse of a visit to England by the Duke of Modena, his Grace of Bedford gave a reception at his house in Bloomsbury Square; the following evening, the Duke of Newcastle did the same at Lincoln's Inn Fields; and two nights later the Duke of Richmond trumped them all with a firework display at Whitehall, on the banks of the Thames. It was a great success. After a concert of water music, huge numbers of rockets were fired from barges on the river, then more were set off from smaller boats on every side. The Catherine wheels, which had failed so dismally in Green Park, were displayed to great effect along the terrace railings. Even the illumination – a pavilion flanked by pyramids – was much admired. 'You can't conceive a prettier sight; the garden filled with everybody of fashion',[29] Walpole commented.

It had been a sparkling month, but also an expensive one for Elizabeth. Her debts must have been worrying enough for her to pay a visit at the beginning of June to Hervey – then making final preparations to go away to France – though she had not seen him for months. 'She suddenly came in upon me at Mrs. Aston's',[30] Hervey wrote in his diary, 'which I impute to their having sent to her & told her of my design—but I was deaf to all the Syrens Voice.'

It was now more important than ever for Elizabeth to find someone else to support her. Of course, it was flattering that the old King should believe himself in love with her, but – no matter what the gossips might claim – she had no intention of becoming the mistress of a man who would offer little in return. Being close to the throne might give her some modicum of political influence, and in the fashionable world in general it was a great advantage to have powerful supporters, but Elizabeth would not be able to pay her dressmakers, milliners and the rest that way. All the same, there was no harm in keeping the King interested but at arm's length; socially, it was pleasing to be one of the few people welcome at both George II's and Frederick's courts, and the connection with the King might prove useful some day. It was a connection she clearly maintained with great skill, for even the following February it was noted that George II had left a masquerade '*fort* cross'[31] because Elizabeth had pleaded gout and stayed away.

But, as 1749 fizzed to an end and a new decade began, it was the natural world, not the fashionable world, that was capturing everyone's imagination. First, parts of the country were treated to an aurora borealis, which had strayed as far south as Oxfordshire. The ripple of light in the sky made, said one correspondent to *The Gentleman's Magazine*, 'a most glorious appearance'.[32] At the end of January, there were terrible storms at Bristol and Norwich, worse than anyone could remember. Then, on 8 February, 'the Shock of an Earthquake was felt all over the Cities of London and Westminster, and Parts adjacent'.[33] The tremors sent the lawyers scurrying in fear from Westminster Hall, and 'in most Parts of the Town People ran out of their Houses, the Chairs shaking, and the Pewter rattling on the shelves'. However, it caused little damage – a few chimneys, the odd hayloft – and its main effect was to trigger a steady trickle of letters and poems to the papers about the causes of earthquakes, whether scientific or divine.

In March, the trickle turned into a flood as London was hit by a second and worse earthquake, exactly four weeks after the first. This time, the city's inhabitants were shaken awake at half past five in the morning, and in the worst-affected parts 'the people ran from their houses and beds almost naked'.[34] Even the dogs 'howl'd in an uncommon manner, and fish jump'd half a yard above water'. In the great scheme of things, it was still only a tiny tremor, but it produced an immediate effect on many Londoners' minds. The now rather smug poet who, in the pages of February's *Gentleman's Magazine*, had warned 'Britain! attend the warning voice,/ And dare be deaf no more!/ The God that makes *still sounds* his choice,/ Can bid his thunders roar'[35] was joined by a host of other doomsayers. Clergymen rushed at the chance to swell their congregations and funds by producing what Walpole called 'a shower of sermons and exhortations'.[36] Following swiftly on the heels of the Bishop of Oxford, the Bishop of London published a 'Letter of Admonition to mend our Lives to loock on this as a Warning',[37] in which – to the scorn of many, it must be said – he blamed everything from heretical books, infidelity and blasphemy, to depraved writings and pictures, bawdy houses, popery and 'unnatural lewdness'* for these recent shakings of the earth.

While reasonable minds bought learned volumes on past earthquakes and scientific treatises on their causes, the more superstitious were filling their heads with books such as *God's Revenge against the Breakers of the Ten Commandments* and taking note of the ravings of a 'crazy Lifeguard-man'[38] who prophesied that a third earthquake four weeks after the second would swallow up London entirely. As *The London Evening-Post* wrote with scorn, it 'is almost impossible to conceive the Degree of Consternation which many credulous People were seiz'd upon such a silly Prognostication.' As 5 April drew nearer, more and more people began to leave town, with the excuse that it was the unseasonably mild weather that called them to the country. Such was the panic that in the first days of April more than seven hundred coaches passed Hyde Park Corner on their way out of London,[39] and presumably still more left the capital in other directions. In the columns of *The Daily Advertiser*, there was even a notice

---

* Given the accompanying reference to the destruction of Sodom by fire from heaven, this can only mean homosexuality.

that 'On Monday next will be publish'd, (Price 6d.) A True and exact List of all the Nobility and Gentry, who have left, or shall leave, this Place through fear of another Earthquake',[40] which, had it ever appeared, would have contained some surprising names.

On the eve of 5 April, 'incredible numbers of people',[41] dressed in their warmest clothes, 'left their houses, and walk'd in the fields, or lay in boats all night; many people of fashion in the neighbouring villages sat in their coaches till daybreak; others went to a greater distance, so that the roads were never more throng'd, and lodgings were hardly to be procur'd at Windsor: so far, and even to their wit's end, had their superstitious fears, or their guilty conscience, driven them'. The moment, of course, passed without the foreseen cataclysm, and although some nervous types delayed their return to town until after 8 April – the previous two quakes having happened on that day – it was not long before the whole bizarre episode was forgotten. Life returned to normal, and soon another ball at Ranelagh 'after the Venetian manner' was being advertised for the middle of the month.

On 11 April, the King announced he would be leaving in five days for another visit to Hanover. In his absence, the Princess of Wales gave birth to another son, before setting off with her Prince on a summer tour of the West Country. All the conversation, however, was of a dashing gentleman highwayman called James Maclaine, who in late July was arrested for robbing the Salisbury stagecoach. At his smart lodgings in St James's Street, the officers also found twenty purses, and a rich coat and blunderbuss belonging to Lord Eglinton, who had been held up less than an hour after the Salisbury coach. A few days later, Maclaine was brought in front of Justice Lediard where 'before a large company of lords, ladies, &c.' he admitted that he 'with one *Plunket*, committed these robberies, also the robbing Mr *Walpole* in *Hyde Park*, when a pistol went off undesignedly'.[42] He appeared so contrite, this 'very genteel, tall Fellow . . . very gay in his Dress', that several of the women were moved to tears. It became quite the thing to visit Maclaine at Newgate, and many fashionable ladies in particular went to weep at his fate and admire his person. A torrent of prints and pamphlets fed the public appetite for information about him. None of it could save him, however. He was duly tried, convicted and sentenced to hang, spending his last ten days of life in prison almost suffocated by the great weight of adoring visitors.

In early November, George II returned from Hanover, and

London's social life fell back into the familiar royal patterns. There was a glittering court to celebrate the King's birthday halfway through the month, to which all the nobility and even the Prince and Princess of Wales with their own attendants – including, presumably, his Majesty's favourite Miss Chudleigh – duly went to pay their compliments. This renewed acquaintance of monarch and Maid of Honour was soon to bear valuable fruit, for one of the parties at least. It so happened that the housekeeper at Windsor died in early December,[43] and the newspapers confidently appointed several women as her successor. George II, however, chose Mrs Henrietta Chudleigh for this sought-after post,[44] which, although not as lucrative as gossip suggested – there were reports it paid £800 a year, though the *Court and City Register* gives it as £320[45] – still provided a tidy income. At the next Drawing Room* the King, well pleased with his actions, marched up to Elizabeth and said 'he was glad to have an opportunity of obeying her commands . . . and hoped she would not think a kiss too great a reward'.[46] Plainly, it was not, and to everyone's amazement he promptly kissed her in front of everyone. It was now surely only a matter of time, it was whispered, before she became the King's mistress and was rewarded by George II with a title.

---

* The name both of the magnificent room in St James's Palace, lined with tapestries, and of the receptions regularly held there by senior members of the royal family; it was on these occasions, for example, that new peeresses would be presented to the King.

CHAPTER 5

New Admirers

To Licentiousness I then gave way,
Miss Chidley I was called,
At balls and plays I bore the sway,
Which many ladies galled.

Ballad

Speculation about where the King's obvious admiration for Miss Chudleigh might lead continued during the early months of 1751, through the eternal round of balls, masquerades, dinners and concerts. Life went on as usual, and no one paid too much attention when in early March the Prince of Wales developed a cold 'consequent of his Highness's attending his Gardeners forming a new Plantation at Kew this piercing damp Season'.[1] He was well enough to attend an unusual performance of *Othello* on 7 March at the Theatre Royal, Drury Lane, acted by an amateur company of ladies and gentlemen before a select audience. 'The Company was the most brilliant ever seen in a Playhouse in this Kingdom,' *The Penny London Post* enthused. The audience must have been rather less gorgeous from the knee down, however, for 'the Streets and Avenues were so filled with Coaches and Chairs, that the greatest Part of the Gentlemen and Ladies were obliged to wade through Dirt and Filth to get to the House, which afforded good Diversion and Benefit for the Pickpockets'.

Unfortunately, the Prince's cold soon took a turn for the worse. He developed pleurisy, brought on, the newspapers said, by travelling back from the House of Peers with the windows of his coach down. Doctors were summoned, and under their care Frederick seemed to rally, seemed certain to recover in time. On the evening of Wednesday 20 March, Frederick felt well enough to send his doctor home, but not long afterwards he was gripped by a terrible pain in his chest and stomach, accompanied by an unpleasant smell in his nostrils. Almost at once, he 'flung himself back and expired'[2] while his aghast wife looked on helplessly.

The shock of Frederick's death was enormous, for even those close to him had believed his condition was improving. However, an autopsy revealed a large abscess on the Prince of Wales's lungs which had burst, and the talk was that it had been caused by a blow from a cricket ball some years before. Not surprisingly, the Princess of Wales – several months pregnant – was said to be devastated by the loss of a husband 'whose Virtues',[3] *The Penny London Post* declared, 'were too many to be as yet describ'd by any English Pen, and whose Loss to this Nation, we have only to hope, may not be felt in the future Records of Time'. An announcement was made that a general mourning period would begin at the end of March. Meanwhile an awful silence fell over the whole country, as playhouses and other places of entertainment closed. As the court went into deep mourning, which would last until the end of June, even their footsteps were muffled by the black chamois leather shoes they had to wear. The only sound was Spitalfield's silk weavers groaning at the prospect of losing an entire season of sales of colourful silks, which by November had resulted in an estimated 15,000 or more of them being out of work.[4]

Preparations for Frederick's funeral – a private one, as Queen Anne's had been – took several weeks as builders erected extra seating in Westminster Abbey for the mourners, giving the country's amateur versifiers plenty of time to publish their thoughts on the man who 'To all Opprest his Goodness did extend:/A general Benefactor, Master, Friend.'[5] But by 13 April, everything was ready, and at half past eight that evening Frederick's coffin draped in black velvet was carried from the Prince's Chamber to the Abbey. As the long procession of peers and members of the Prince's household began their slow walk to the Abbey doors, two rockets were set off in Old Palace Yard, as a signal for the guns of the Tower to begin firing every minute until midnight. To add to the noise, the bells of St Peter's Church in Westminster, St Paul's Cathedral and many others began their dismal tolling. On the other hand, the newspapers noted, 'though the Populace were extremely noisy before the Procession began'[6] – for, despite the rain, huge crowds had turned up – 'there was during the whole, a Silence, that, if possible, added to the Solemnity of so awful a Sight'.

Even once the Prince was interred, there were many practical matters to be dealt with: creating Frederick's fourteen-year-old son and heir George Prince of Wales, making plans for a regency if it should prove necessary, providing an income for Augusta, choosing new members for her household and re-appointing others, including Elizabeth as Maid of Honour.[7] In all this flurry of activity, there was one small consolation for the widowed Princess, which others were not slow to notice. The Countess of Oxford, for instance, commented, 'I Hear ye King has on this meloncholy occasion Behaved to the Pss of Wales wth ye utmost Tenderness & Compassion & that she is sensible of it.'[8] Whatever his motives – guilt, perhaps, at not loving his son – he paid several visits to Augusta in the unhappy days before and after the funeral. Others noted his affectionate behaviour to his grandchildren, for he was not the first person to be more relaxed with a later generation than with his own offspring.

In the following months – as the rest of the world got on with the business of going to plays, operas and oratorios – this apparent rapprochement with the King and the tender care of servants and friends such as her lively Miss Chudleigh were a valuable support to the pregnant Augusta. Princess Caroline was eventually born in July, entering a grey world by then in the second stage of mourning for her father. Barely had this drab period ended, however, when the black crape had to be pulled out again for the death of the King's son-in-law the Prince of Orange. Socially, it would not be remembered as a sparkling year.

The new one, though, seemed from the start to be much more promising. In the middle of January, 'there was a very great Company at the Masquerade at the Opera-House in the Hay-Market',[9] among them Elizabeth's former admirer the Duke of Hamilton who, over the past few years, had become noted more for his passion for gaming, whoring and drinking than for his better qualities.[10] There, too, were the Gunnings, that pair of impoverished Irish beauties who had been much admired since their arrival in London eighteen months before. Hamilton promptly fell in love with the younger, another Elizabeth; so much so that at another entertainment three weeks later, he lost more than a thousand pounds at cards because his attention was entirely taken up with wooing her. Two nights after that, he made up his mind to marry her and, the parson that he summoned refusing to oblige without a licence, the ceremony was performed at half past midnight at Mr Keith's 'chapel' in Curzon Street, with – so Walpole averred – the bride having to make do with the ring from a curtain. The *Daily Advertiser* merely noted the date of the nuptials as 14 February, made no mention of the haste, and added that 'their Graces soon after set out for his Seat in Wiltshire'.[11] His former sweetheart's reaction was not recorded, but it must have been a bitter moment for Elizabeth.

To add to the gossip, Maria Gunning soon followed her sibling into the ranks of the aristocracy. Two days after the new Duchess of Hamilton was presented to the King at an impossibly crowded court, her older sister married the Earl of Coventry. In the circumstances, it was only natural that the now thoroughly overexcited public should turn their thoughts to those peers who remained single. Among the names that were mentioned was that of Evelyn Pierrepont, the forty-one-year-old Duke of Kingston. He was a shy but good-natured man – a generous but exacting master 'endowed with many shining virtues',[12] according to his valet Thomas Whitehead – who was happiest when he could be on his country estates in Nottinghamshire and elsewhere. His great pleasures were his horses and dogs, fishing and shooting; indeed, he 'was reckoned the best noble-man-shot in England, except Lord Ravensworth'.

He took pains with his appearance: Whitehead called him

> very whimsical in dressing in the country. I have known him change his shooting-dress four times in a morning before he went out, returning often to change something or other. I shall give you a list of articles taken to [Holme] Pierrepoint only for one week's shooting, viz. Six frocks or jackets; twelve waistcoats, different sorts; thirty pairs of breeches; twenty pair of different sorts of stockings; sixteen shirts; six pair of boots; six pair of half boots; six pair of spatterdashes; six pair of shoes; six pair of gloves; three hats, with other things in proportion; add to these his guns, &c. so that his carriage was loaded inside and out, like a stage coach.

Given the entries for 'a pint of violet perfum'd Water'[13] and 'finest juniper water' in the Duke's household accounts, he appears to have taken trouble with the impression he left on people's noses as well.

The Duke of Kingston was not a complete stranger to the world of gossip. Although in recent years his name was more likely to appear in the horse-racing reports than in another part of the newspaper, it had not always been that way. In 1736, he had caused plenty of raised eyebrows when he had returned from the continent in a great hurry, swiftly followed by a beautiful – and married – Frenchwoman. As Lord Hervey, Augustus's father put it, 'The Duke of Kingston is not to go back to France. France is come to him, and lodges in St James's Street.'[14] The episode caused such an outcry in Paris 'one should have imagined the Duke . . . had seduced a Vestal from her sacred Fire, rather than only suffered a forsaken mistress of the Duc de la Trémouille's to follow him to England',[15] Hervey added. Madame, as she was called, continued to be an object of fascination for some years, though her situation was far from enviable; one 1739 visitor to Thoresby, the Duke's main estate in Nottinghamshire, pointed out that 'no ladies in the country will take notice of her'[16] and added, 'Most people here think he is tired of her, and if so, the poor soul, must lead a miserable life, for she never sees the face of a woman.'

In 1745, the Duke had again been in the public eye. First, his house at Thoresby had burnt down, although 'he saved all his Paper's most of ye best furniture & all his Plate'[17] and the offices and stables had been spared the flames. Then, during the Jacobite Rebellion later that year, he was one of the first nobles to raise their own Regiment of Horse, with the expenses – everything from saddles to iron skull caps – paid partly by patriotic local supporters and partly by his Grace.[18] He had then returned to decent obscurity in the country, turning the surviving buildings at Thoresby into a makeshift residence.

In recent years, however, the retiring Duke had been more in town than usual. Perhaps this was not unconnected with his sister Lady Frances's decision in 1749 to move herself from London to Thoresby, along with her husband Philip Meadows and their children. Maybe it was a way of saving money – Meadows had an income of less than £900 a year, completely inadequate for the lifestyle of a peer's sister – but there was another motive, for she brought with her Madame, whose connection with the Duke was clearly faltering at best, though he supported her financially. If that relationship could be rekindled, it would prevent the Duke from marrying and the Meadowses would eventually inherit his considerable worldly goods. As the Duke's aunt Lady Wortley Montagu put it, 'I think Lady F. Meadows pays very dear for whatever advantages she may gain. But Interest is so commonly preferr'd to Honor, I do not doubt her conduct will be applauded by many people.'[19]

Whatever the reasons, London society was more and more aware of the presence of the Duke of Kingston in the early 1750s: in the upper gallery at Drury Lane for the famous performance of *Othello*;[20] at Vauxhall Gardens in a party with Horace Walpole; vying for the post of Master of the Horse, though he admitted to Lady Oxford he 'ws indiferent whether He had it, or not, & I hear his inducemt to chuse it, ws to provide for his Flaterers'.[21] A wealthy bachelor – generous to a fault, kind and still handsome, though Walpole thought his good looks were 'at the fall of the leaf'[22] – could hardly expect to go unnoticed by parents with daughters to marry off. So it was no great surprise when, at the start of 1752, the newspapers were suggesting that the Duke was about to marry the Earl of Portmore's second daughter. There was, however, no truth in the rumour; 'the town says he is rather engaged in a flirtation than a matrimonial affair'.[23]

Still, during his long stay in London that spring the Duke continued to be the subject of enough speculation for Madame, languishing in Nottinghamshire, to talk 'of retireing to Dr Wells at Cotness fr: Thoresby in May by her own choice & sent many Goods ye Duke has given Her'.[24] By June that year, there were hints that his Grace had formed a new connection. The occasion was the installation of several new Knights of the Garter at Windsor, at which the exhausted-looking Duke stayed for the briefest time possible: 'Miss Chudleigh was not here',[25] one Windsor resident explained, 'she has been very ill, and was not enough recovered to venture; I am really sorry for Madame.' By August, the suspicion that Elizabeth and the Duke were more than mere acquaintances was confirmed by their being seen together constantly at Tunbridge Wells: 'that is a surprising affair, we are so used at Windsor to their coming together here to her mother, who is housekeeper, that now 'tis scarce mentioned,'[26] Lady Jane Coke informed her correspondent.

Exactly when Elizabeth had caught the attention of the shy Duke is impossible to tell for certain. Clearly, however, by the time the first whispers about it were broadcast in June 1752, their attachment was already strong. After all, they could hardly have met while Elizabeth was so ill, and she evidently had been seriously indisposed, for at Tunbridge she was 'so altered' that people were surprised to see her by daylight. Whenever it was formed, however, it was not long before Elizabeth was deriving practical benefit from the connection. By April 1753, she was able to afford to build a house in Hill Street, part of the recent development around Berkeley Square, with a coach house and stables behind in Farm Street.[27] Reassuringly, Madame had also been persuaded to leave England in return for £800 a year for life, so that when Elizabeth quipped at the time that there was 'some sense in belonging to a king who turns off an old mistress when he has got a new one',[28] it was perhaps this – rather than her supposed link with George II – that she was thinking of.

For the first time in many years, Elizabeth could begin to feel reasonably secure. Financially, her position was promising, for the Duke was a generous man – though a very discreet one, for Elizabeth's name is not mentioned in his bank records at Hoare & Co. While it may later have suited others to portray Elizabeth's interest in the Duke as purely mercenary, though, there was much more to it than that. Of course it was important for Elizabeth to find money from somewhere, for society offered no way for gentlewomen to support themselves by work. However, if all she had wanted was money, there were almost certainly other men – the parsimonious King aside – whose indulged mistress she could have become far sooner. But between her and the Duke there seems to have been real feeling. When she was again 'taken very ill'[29] at Windsor in October that year the Duke sat up all night with her, and Elizabeth was far too bright and sensible a woman not to appreciate that evidence of more than casual concern.

As 1753 became 1754, society had less and less to say about Elizabeth. There were occasional stories: on 27 April 'there was a very crowded audience at the King's Theatre in the Haymarket, and the weather being warm, one of the ladies of honour to her Royal Highness the Princess of Wales fainted away, as did one of the soldiers on the stage'.[30] That the 'lady of honour' was Elizabeth we know from Walpole's highly embellished account of the evening which mentions the 'tragi-comedy'.[31] Miss Chudleigh's 'theatric fit of kicking and shrieking' was, apparently, so impressive that several other women who had been planning their own fits gave up the idea, and for half an hour there was complete uproar in the theatre. Otherwise, the world had nothing more to notice until November, when there was more finery than usual on the King's birthday 'and Miss Chudleigh danced minuets',[32] something she did well; even in old age, she was described as moving with 'all the grace and majesty of a goddess'.[33] That winter's bathers at Bath, their days as regimented and pleasantly dull as those at Tunbridge Wells, might chuckle over the latest verse which revealed quite how widely known Elizabeth's supposedly secret marriage and pregnancy had become:

> A wife, who to her husband ne'er laid claim,
> A mother, who her children ne'er dare name,
> Is this a wonder, more may yet be said,
> This wife, this mother still remains a Maid.[34]

However, they had nothing new to say about Elizabeth – although they certainly smiled at the idea of a 'virginal' Maid of Honour being kept by a Duke – and all the gossip was about younger beauties and their escorts, the new *elite de la jeunesse*. Away from the public notice, Elizabeth and her Duke lived a life that followed conventional patterns: London for the season, the fashionable spas in summer and country retreats when the pleasures and perils of town became too much. At some point, Elizabeth had rented a villa in leafy Finchley, a pretty village outside London. But in summer 1755, that house was given up, and the Duke decided to take Percy Lodge, a small house near Iver in Buckinghamshire,[35] which his valet later called 'a delightful spot'.[36] There Elizabeth and the Duke had both privacy and an opportunity to indulge their mutual love of one particular country sport: fishing. After a few days at the Lodge

> cold provisions were got ready, to take the next morning to a little farm-house, near Rickmansworth, close to the water, where was the best trout-fishing, and the largest and finest-coloured fish. Hither they repaired in his Grace's coach, passing away the time till evening, when they returned to Percy-lodge, frequently without catching a single fish. This was the usual jaunt every other day, until Miss C—— was obliged to attend in waiting.[37]

On 18 January 1756, however, the leisurely rhythm of Elizabeth's life was interrupted by the death of her mother.[38] Three days later, Henrietta Chudleigh was buried in the cemetery of the Royal Hospital, Chelsea, next to her husband and son.[39] Elizabeth was devastated by the loss of this last member of her immediate family. Even at court, in public, she could not restrain her tears, which earned her a cruel epigram from the reputed wit George Selwyn, beginning: 'What filial piety! what mournful grace,/ For a lost parent, sits on Chudleigh's face!'[40] To add to Elizabeth's misery, there were rumours that her Duke – under pressure to have an heir – was on the verge of agreeing to wed the Duke of Marlborough's eldest daughter. It was only at the end of May that the gossip about the Duke stopped and, according to one letter writer, 'his mistress is said once more to have resumed her ascendant'.[41] Guessing that the Duke's feelings for Elizabeth might be stronger than his need for an heir, the writer perceptively added, 'I fancy one may say – 'Here end the *Pierpoints.*'

Elizabeth celebrated in her preferred way: with property. At the beginning of February 1757, she acquired a three-acre plot of land in Knightsbridge, 'abutting on the Kings Highway leading from Hyde Park Corner towards Kensington towards the North'.[42] She next employed an architect, Henry Flitcroft, who had built the Duke's London residence in Arlington Street nearly twenty years before, to design a house for her. Unfortunately, the plans and building accounts have not survived, though Flitcroft later said the cost 'amounted to many thousand pounds'.[43] While the work progressed, Elizabeth continued in her habitual round of activities with the Duke; this included a tour of the south and west, for the couple were spotted in Newport, in the Isle of Wight, early that September.

By the late spring of 1758, the work at Knightsbridge was finished. Elizabeth immediately sold her Hill Street house to 'Hugo Meynell Esq'[44] and moved into her fine new Knightsbridge home. Built in the style that Flitcroft admired most, the austere neo-classicism of Palladianism, the two-storey villa with basement and attics floors was flanked by service wings joined to the main house by one-storey corridors.[45] The only decoration to the façade was a Venetian window on the first floor. It was an elegant, if conventional and slightly old-fashioned building; what made it special was the beautiful setting, with views over Hyde Park's deer herds and the Serpentine River to the front and towards Chelsea at the rear.

As for the interior decoration, opinion was divided. One German visitor thought it could 'justly be called a gem; it contains a quantity of handsome and costly furniture and other curiosities and objects of value, chosen and arranged with the greatest taste, so that you cannot fail to admire it greatly. There is hardly a place in the whole house left bare or without decoration, like a doll's house.'[46] Those with more classical tastes such as Walpole thought it 'not fine nor in good taste'[47] for exactly the same reason – that it was crammed to the rafters with finery. Everywhere you looked there were pieces of Dresden china, varnished boxes, toothpick cases, filigree, cameos, amber and lapis lazuli: all the glorious, glittering trinkets that Elizabeth had accumulated over the years from indulgent admirers and on enjoyable shopping trips.

As far as society in general was concerned, however, the most note-worthy thing about the house was that its cost far exceeded Elizabeth's income as Maid of Honour. Her new calling cards might give her address as Chudleigh House, 'but the vulgar beings say she lives in Concubine Row'.*[48] The Duke's bank account, however, was discretion itself; though it might be reasonable to assume it was his money that paid for the house, any payments have been well hidden as 'To recipient'. The *Times*, though, would one day suggest that Elizabeth had indeed paid for the house herself – by playing cards with the Duke, who scrupulously settled his losses but never took his winnings.[49]

With the Knightsbridge house finished, Percy Lodge was also given up; 'the piece of water near Rickmansworth was then taken by the Duke, at a yearly rent of £.10 of one farmer Budd'.[50] Thomas Whitehead, who had been the Duke's valet for a year, later recalled:

A new route now took place: the party to Budd's farm set out from London of an afternoon, lying at the White-horse at Uxbridge, where they met Miss Chudleigh and companion, with a man and maid servant. I took care to provide plenty of cold victuals and beer, that poor Budd's family might have a belly-full . . . sending the provisions to the little farm, with plenty of rum for Miss C—— to *put in her shoes*. I have known her use two quarts in a day; being obliged to change her clothes twice or thrice during that time;

* Sophia von Walmoden, Countess of Yarmouth and mistress of George II, lived next door but one.

standing from morning till evening in the wet; sometimes too without catching a single fish. When they began angling, I set about preparing a stew of chickens . . . which was done in a silver pan, fixed in a box about twice the size of a large tea-chest; keeping it hot, till wanted, by an iron heater put in the box. After dinner, by the time the empty things were packed up, and sent away, coffee and tea succeeded; which soon brought on night, when we returned to our inn. This continued sometimes for three or four days successively, if they met with sport. I believe every pound of fish they caught, on an average, cost the Duke five guineas; as he never grudged any expence attending these parties.[51]

That summer was not entirely devoted to fishing, however. In early August, Elizabeth was spotted with friends at the seaside resort of Scarborough, popular since the 1720s for its healthy air and its sea bathing. The occasion was a review of some of the soldiers then stationed there: 'the uniform is very pretty, and I never saw anywhere such goodlooking men, and so exactly of a size', said one genteel onlooker. 'It was by Miss Chudleigh's desire, they exercised at this hour; all her party was there.'[52] His Grace of Kingston was there, too, for towards the end of the month a neighbour was writing about the Duke's return from Scarborough.[53] Perhaps it was even for his benefit that Elizabeth had ordered the special troop review, to give him pleasure, for as the events of 1745 show he had a keen interest in military matters. With a fine new house in Knightsbridge, after all, she had every reason to show her gratitude to the man who had paid for its construction.

CHAPTER 6

A Fatal Mistake

There is now in the Tower, among the other wild
Beasts, &c. an Animal found upon the Snows in
Greenland; it is much about the size of an Otter.
Daily Advertiser, 2 January 1759

Early in 1759, Elizabeth made a curious decision, one that would
later come back to haunt her. The Reverend Mr Amis, who
had conducted her marriage service, was seriously ill and
seemed certain to die at last. However, Lainston had never had a
parish register, so there was no written record of that foolish ceremony fifteen years earlier. In mid February, Elizabeth suddenly
resolved to have one made, for although Hervey's older brother was
then in good health thanks to the climate of Madrid where he had
been posted as ambassador, that might easily change. If he died,
Augustus would become the next Earl of Bristol and Elizabeth would
be his Countess, as long as she could prove that their marriage had
taken place.

Elizabeth made her way to Winchester to see the Reverend Mr
Amis. His wife afterwards recalled that on 12 February, at about six
o'clock in the morning, she had received a message informing her
that there was a gentlewoman at the Blue Boar inn who wanted to
speak to her immediately. Mrs Amis hurried at once to the inn, which
was almost opposite her house, where to her great surprise she found
Miss Chudleigh. 'When I went to her,' Mrs Amis remembered, 'she
asked me if I thought Mr. Amis would give her a register of her
marriage. I told her I thought he would.'[1]

The two then bustled over in the darkness to the Reverend's house,
where Mrs Amis went upstairs to her husband 'who was then confined

to his Bed with Illness'[2] to put Miss Chudleigh's request to him, to which he agreed. This brought Elizabeth upstairs as well, and soon afterwards her cousin John Merrill arrived and climbed up to Mr Amis's room. Here, the two cousins consulted on which attorney to send for, finally settling on James Spearing who was a local 'Master Extraordinary in Chancery'.[3] 'In about half an hour the sd Mr Spearing came and just before he came into the Bed Chamber the sd Elizabeth . . . sayd she did not care that Mr Spearing should know she was there and therefore she would conceal herself in the Closet which she accordingly did in a light Closet near the Bed Chamber that opened on the Stair Case.'[4]

On Spearing's arrival, Mr Merrill gave him a sheet of stamped paper with which to make a register, but the attorney proved less compliant than they had hoped, for he 'said it would not do, it must be a book, and that the lady must be at the making of it'.[5] Elizabeth had no choice but to come out of hiding, whereupon she sent Spearing to buy the appropriate volume in which – 'seated up in his Bed'[6] and in the presence of his wife, Elizabeth, Mr Merrill and the lawyer – Amis duly entered the details of the marriage along with the record of the burial of Susannah Merrill in 1742, to give it more authenticity. 'Then Mr. Amis delivered it to the lady; the lady thanked him, and said it might be a hundred thousand pounds in her way.'[7] Elizabeth 'cut out two long strips of paper and put the same on the outside of the sd Book and sealed the papers together to prevent the Book being opened',[8] before returning it to Mrs Amis, with the request that she should deliver it to Mr Merrill after her husband's death, which was duly done six weeks later.

When the events of this chilly February morning became public knowledge more than fifteen years later, they were not unreasonably seen as utterly mercenary and snobbish on Elizabeth's part. If she were as devoted to her dear Duke as she always claimed, why did she go to such lengths to create evidence of a marriage ceremony with a man she cared nothing for? Did the thought of being Countess of Bristol override all other considerations? Most people assumed it did, but in truth her actions proved nothing about whether or not she loved the Duke. No matter what her feelings for his Grace of Kingston, it did not alter the fact that her future was no more secure than that of any other mistress and sooner or later she might easily share the fate of Madame in being pensioned off. Moreover, even if the Duke *never* tired of her, he might still decide to put practicality first and marry for the sake of an heir to his titles. This way, she at least had proof of her status safely – so she thought – under her control, to use or not as she saw fit.

Quite how she planned to use it and why it might be worth a hundred thousand pounds to her, however, is much less clear. If Hervey inherited the Bristol money, he would at last be able to afford all the expense of a divorce. Perhaps this was the sum she expected to receive in return for making the process easy for him. Whatever her reasoning, Elizabeth was now in a position to prove her marriage if it suited her.

Elizabeth returned to London as 'Miss Chudleigh', although privately most of the beau monde had been convinced for some time that she had long been Mrs Hervey. Indeed, in a legal document that year, connected with the acquisition of more land in Knightsbridge, she was referred to as 'otherwise Elizabeth Hervey but commonly called Elizabeth Chudleigh'.[9] Moreover, it was also well known that it was not the income from her estates in Devon, as she sometimes claimed, that paid for her to be a lady of fashion. The fine Knightsbridge house, the clothes and jewellery, even the little black page boy 'that she dressed . . . in an elegant style, taking him with her to most public places she frequented; especially to the play, where he sat in the boxes with her'[10] – the Duke of Kingston, everyone assumed, discreetly paid for it all. Despite this, Elizabeth remained a Maid of Honour, a valued royal servant, and in this role was part of the procession for the funeral of Augusta's eighteen-year-old daughter Princess Elizabeth that September, walking with her three fellow Maids immediately behind 'The Countess of Tankerville as Chief Mourner'.[11]

As well as her normal duties Elizabeth had also, it seems, taken it upon herself to become an unofficial party giver for the royal family. The following March, 1760 – after a winter so mild that pear trees and primroses flowered in December – she gave a breakfast and concert at Chudleigh House for Prince Edward's birthday, 'and at three a vast cold collation'[12] to which the whole town came, according to Walpole. On a sultry night in June, she followed this with a magnificent ball in honour of the young Prince of Wales's twenty-second birthday. It was a great success: as the guests arrived the house and courtyard looked delightful lit up as they were with small lanterns, and inside there was not too large a crowd. There was a little dancing, which the Duke of York in pale blue watered silk led off with his hostess; a fine supper in two rooms where every flat surface seemed to be covered in overflowing dishes of cherries and strawberries; and card tables for gambling set up in the unusually well-appointed garret. The Duke of Kingston was there, too, 'and seemed neither ashamed nor vain of the expense of his pleasures'.[13]

Away from London and its costly diversions, Elizabeth and the Duke continued to enjoy their shared hobbies. In May, Elizabeth had 'bid 5000 Guineas for the late Mr. Dicker's House at Walton Bridge. Fishing being one of her favourite amusements',[14] the Duchess of Northumberland noted in her diary. The bid was unsuccessful, but in September the Duke bought a small estate near Farnham in Surrey,[15] with a river 'flowing in full view of the House',[16] which he promptly renamed Pierrepont Lodge. The Duke's valet later recalled how his master 'was so delighted with this place, its situation, distance from London, and other circumstances, that he began making many improvements'.[17]

Work could hardly have progressed far, however, before the news came from Kensington that on 25 October Elizabeth's old admirer King George II had been 'suddenly seized . . . by a Violent disorder, and fell down speechless, and soon expired'.[18] He was not a young man, but nevertheless his death was unexpected for, as the *Annual Register* and other journals pointed out, 'His late majesty rose in the morning at his usual hour, without any apparent signs of indisposition.'[19] After drinking the chocolate his page brought, he had opened his window and, seeing what a fine day it was, had announced he would walk after breakfast in the gardens. But, when the page left the room, 'he heard a deep sigh, immediately followed by a noise like the falling of a billet of wood from the fire, and, returning hastily, found the king dropt down from his seat, as if in attempting to ring the bell'. His Majesty's last, faint words were 'Call Amelia.' Mr Pitt, whose carriage happened to be waiting to take him to his country seat, was ordered to go instead to Kew at once to tell the twenty-two-year-old Prince of Wales of his grandfather's death. The following day, George III was officially proclaimed King.

Once again, London ground to a halt. A mourning period of six months was proclaimed, and the playhouses were closed until after the old King's funeral, which was to be on 11 November. The day before, the royal corpse – minus the bowels, which according to custom had already been privately interred in King Henry VII's Chapel in Westminster Abbey – was removed with great formality from Kensington to the Prince's Chamber, near the House of Lords. The royal hearse, covered with purple velvet and drawn by eight cream-coloured horses, was preceded by a line of carriages, led by the Earl of Rochford's, and followed by the royal trumpeters 'in their rich habits, sounding the dead march',[20] a large number of Life Guards and a final coach. 'On each side of all the royal carriages, except the last', the *Annual Register* went on to inform its readers, 'a train of men walked in black cloaks, with lighted torches in their hands.' This was as nothing, however, to the majestic ceremonial of the funeral itself the following evening – for which the lighting alone was reported to have cost more than a thousand pounds[21] – with its seemingly endless line of peers, privy counsellors, archbishops and heralds accompanying the King's coffin on its last journey to the royal vault. Vast crowds turned out hoping for a glimpse of the magnificence; many were disappointed, but at least they could hear the church bells tolling and the minute guns firing at the Tower and in the Park.

The playhouses soon opened again and, to set the tone for the rest of the season, the King and the royal family were among the first to attend. On 21 November, their presence at Drury Lane for a performance of *Richard III* drew such crowds that many hopeful theatre-goers had to be turned away. Three days before, even more people – 'unanimous in testifying their applause'[22] – had cheered George III's visit to the House of Lords to open parliament, for not only was the new ruler young and charming, he was also a true Briton, the first of his dynasty actually born here. Society fizzed with the optimism of a new reign, but there were some favourite old topics of conversation they were not prepared to consign to the past, and one of these was Elizabeth Chudleigh.

That winter, the story – or, rather, stories, for there were several variations – spread that there was a print in which Lord Bute's admirer the Dowager Princess of Wales was rebuking Elizabeth for something. The Maid of Honour's reply was a play on the French word for 'goal' or 'aim': *'Madame, chacun a son But.'*[*][23] In another version, she had made the answer as a result of 'being pressed to resign her Post as Maid of Honour soon after the Accession . . . in favour of a

* 'Madam, everyone has their aim' – or Bute.

Scotch Lady related to Lord Bute with whom as 'tis well known the Princess was supposed to be too intimate'.[24] In this variation, Elizabeth was more voluble, too; for her full reply was, '*Votre Altesse Royale doit sçavoir, que chacun a son But; le mien est de servir votre Altesse Royale jusqu'à la fin de ma Vie.*'* The tales were almost certainly apocryphal, and aimed as much as anything against the unpopular Lord Bute, who was felt with good reason to have too much influence on George III. The resentment was fed by the fact that his wife had just inherited an astonishing amount of money, more than a million pounds, from her father.[25]

This fascination with Elizabeth reflected the fact that in recent years, in spite of her unusual position, she had become not only an established society hostess but a patroness as well. At some point in the previous two years, she had come into contact with a woman called Mrs Cornelys, an Italian singer and former mistress of Casanova† by whom she had a daughter. With Elizabeth's help, Mrs Cornelys rented and later bought Carlisle House, on the east side of Soho Square, and began holding a series of evening assemblies with cards, music and dancing for select subscribers in 1760. Thanks to patrons such as Elizabeth, who persuaded members of the royal family to attend, these evenings were a huge success from the beginning, and were to remain popular with the smart set for more than a decade. Mrs Cornelys was evidently not insensible of the help Elizabeth had given her, for in the late nineteenth century a small copper plaque was found in the grounds of Carlisle House, on the site of a small eighteenth-century garden building, with the following inscription:

> Not vain but grateful
> In honour of the Society
> And my first protectress ye
> Honble Mrs Elizabeth Chudleigh
> Is laid the first stone
> Of this edifice

* 'Your Royal Highness must be aware that everyone has their aim in life; mine is to serve your Royal Highness to the end of my days.'

† Elizabeth was destined to meet Casanova in 1764 during his visit to London, for he came off his horse in front of Chudleigh House, spraining his leg, and was carried into her drawing room to be tended.

June 19, 1761
By me
Teresa Cornelys.[26]

However, royal events continued to dominate the social scene in 1761, for in early July the King finally announced his choice of a bride: the seventeen-year-old Princess Charlotte of Mecklenburg-Strelitz, who according to him was 'distinguished by every eminent virtue, and amiable endowment'.[27] As a flood of inaccurate prints and descriptions of the future Queen poured from the presses, the King made arrangements for bringing Princess Charlotte over to her new home, even down to such details as choosing new scarlet uniforms for the hand-picked boatmen who would bring her down the Elbe. The King's ambassador Lord Harcourt and his party reached Strelitz on 14 August where, despite the ravages of the recent war, the court mustered two days of splendid entertainments before sadly parting with its princess. After considerably more feasting on route to the coast, Princess Charlotte finally set sail for England on 28 August. Not until nine days later, 'after three different storms, and being often in sight of the English coast, and often in danger of being driven on that of Norway',[28] did the fleet finally reach Harwich. The future Queen was promptly whisked off to St James's Palace, and on 8 September, some time after eight in the evening, was married at St James's Chapel with all due pomp to George III. 'The evening concluded', the *Annual Register* reported, 'with the utmost demonstrations of joy.'[29]

Everyone was eager for a glimpse of the young Queen. At the levee the day after the wedding, a crush of nobility, gentry and foreign ministers in their finest clothes came to pay their respects. There was even more excitement for Queen Charlotte's first trip to the theatre five days later; the streets were packed from St James's to the playhouse, and in spite of the escort of guards 'it is said the crowd pressed so violently upon her majesty's chair, that she discovered some signs of fear'.[30] Inside the theatre, those lucky enough to gain entry glittered in their most costly clothing and jewels, while outside the unlucky ones in the great crowd round the entrance were forcibly reminded of the events of the Black Hole of Calcutta three years before. Only one person was killed and another seriously injured in this particular scrum, however.

By the day of the coronation itself on 22 September, London was bursting at the seams. The whole route of the procession from St James's to Westminster Abbey was lined with crowded tiers of seating full of people in their best outfits cheering and throwing their hats in the air, while faces craned from every window for a better view of the spectacular pageantry below. The seemingly endless line of royal servants – led by the 'King's herb woman, with her six maids, strewing the way with herbs'[31] – and peers and peeresses in their gorgeous robes, among them the Duke of Kingston carrying St Edward's Staff, eventually reached the Abbey at about half past one. The Dowager Princess of Wales was already there, having made a lower-key entrance with her children and 'those who had not a right to walk with their majesties', which would surely have included her notorious Maid of Honour. There followed an exhausting six hours[32] of sermons and oaths, investitures and anthems, before the procession reassembled for the walk to Westminster Hall. On the way back, the great diamond in his Majesty's crown fell out 'but was immediately found and restored', the *Gentleman's Magazine* reassured its readers.

A few days later, her crowned Majesty, dressed 'in Pink and Silver',[33] made her first trip to Covent Garden, to see *The Beggar's Opera*. The evening was a great success, and the Queen vowed to attend every week. Not everyone was happy about this news; Lady Mary Coke and Lord Strafford, for instance, were dismayed to find that the only box available for royal nights was one over Miss Chudleigh, which would not do.[34] If the Duke of Kingston's valet is to be believed, this was not mere snobbery, though higher boxes were preferred. At the time when 'the Beggar's Opera had such a run, and when Miss Brent was the chief vocal favourite with the public'[35] – which if Whitehead's memory is right would be the autumn of 1759, when the country was celebrating General Wolfe's defeat of the French in North America – Elizabeth had apparently made herself deeply unpopular at Covent Garden with her high spirits. 'Miss Chudleigh and her party attended almost every night, and drank tea in their box; making such a noise, and disturbing both the performers and the audience so repeatedly, that at last they were determined to rout her.' This, Whitehead claims, they did by putting a 'smart paragraph in the news-papers; after which, she was received at the theatre with hissings, groanings, and such strong marks of disapprobation, that she and her whole party were obliged to decamp before the opera was over'.

However, it was the young Queen who dominated the talk that autumn and soggy winter, though it was whispered that Augustus Hervey, in the West Indies, had 'full proof against another person'[36] and was planning to seek a divorce. For her Majesty's birthday in January 1762, 'there was the most brilliant appearance at court that ever was known, the nobility and gentry vying with each other in the grandeur of their equipage and dress'.[37] The vying was not restricted to personal appearance, however; particularly in these early years of the new reign, it was important to be seen to be giving the best, most admired parties, for a high social profile could translate into political influence. Elizabeth, though neither she nor the Duke had any interest in politics, nevertheless relished the role of fashionable hostess.

That spring, for instance, she gave a concert at Chudleigh House for the Queen's brother the Prince of Mecklenburg and 'a large and select company'.[38] Count Kielmansegge, a German who was one of the company, later recalled with pleasure: 'About half-past two, when the concert was over, we were invited to lunch in the dining-room downstairs, where music was going on with two good French horns; a so-called "ambigue" was served at a very long table, on which there was everything which could be brought together – cakes, sandwiches, cold and smoked meat, ham, jelly, fruit, etc. Small side-tables were arranged for coffee, tea, chocolate, etc., so that I must say it was the most perfect feast of its kind.'

That a 'large and select company' would flock to Chudleigh House was a sign of how flexible eighteenth-century morals could be, at least at its upper levels. By now, even foreign visitors such as Count Kielmansegge were well-versed in the facts of their hostess's unusual life: that she had married Hervey secretly and was separated from him, that 'although every one knows that she has a husband, she has kept on her appointment as Maid of Honour', and equally that she had been kept all this time by the Duke of Kingston, whose money funded the entertainments her guests so enjoyed. It was also known, however, that she enjoyed not only the protection of the Duke but also the support of the young King's mother and other members of the royal family, which gave her a claim to respectability that the Duke's former mistress had so conspicuously lacked.

Social success and wealth, however, brought with it problems as well as pleasures. One night that June there was an attempted robbery at Elizabeth's Knightsbridge house, 'as believed by a desperate Gang of House-breakers, who found Means to get over her Garden-Walls'.[39] Luckily for her, one of her servants saw the thieves trying to break in and disturbed them, though it was less fortunate for him as he was 'immediately fired at with a Blunderbuss, by one of the Villains, and shot through one of his Hands by a Ball'. Elizabeth was not the sort to allow this to scare her into moving somewhere less remote, however, and in July she added another six acres of garden to her holdings in Knightsbridge.[40]

In all the years since her rash marriage, Elizabeth had apparently remained on good terms with her aunt Ann Hanmer, and it was to her she wrote in August to pass on the news that the King and Queen had been blessed with a healthy son. Her aunt replied: 'Her Majesty has I think finishd the year compleatly,—I am sorry you are not well, am afraid you got cold a fishing & fear you sent me all yr sport, for wch I should have wrote a line or two of thanks but it being late I would not detain yr servant.'[41] Evidently, the boots filled with rum had been inadequate to stave off the effects of standing in cold water for hours, for in mid September Elizabeth was asking to be allocated particular accommodation at Windsor for the coming investiture of several new Knights of the Garter. She was, she wrote, 'solicitous to have them knowing them to have been well air'd for some years and I am a very great invalyd being just recover'd from a violent fit of the Rhumatis'.[42]

During all this time, the Duke had been adding to his estate in Surrey and making his planned alterations to Pierrepont Lodge, turning it into a villa that was later described as 'uniform and commodious'.[43] According to his valet, 'He built an excellent kitchen and many conveniencies, made a good coach-road over the heath to Farnham, and erected a ball-room capable of holding thirty couples to dance with ease.'[44] There was also a kitchen garden, kennels, an ice house, a pheasantry, a dairy and 'a Corn Mill with a Water Engine to supply the House'.[45] When the work was finished, the Duke invited Elizabeth and a party of their friends to spend the Christmas holidays. These included Elizabeth's companion Miss Bate and her half-brother Richard Shuckburgh, a great favourite of Elizabeth's; her cousin Bell Chudleigh; Miss Fielding, the daughter of the novelist Henry; and Sir James Laroche and his wife. It was a bitterly cold season. To the distress of the ferrymen, the Thames froze in several places, and a thick blanket of snow covered the ground for the whole of the first month of 1763. At Pierrepont Lodge, the housebound guests kept themselves amused with a dance every evening in the new ballroom, to the accompaniment of 'Warner the harper and Prosser the violin'. The first, on Christmas Eve, was opened by the Duke dancing a minuet with Miss Chudleigh before gallantly partnering the other ladies in turn. This was followed by country dances until about eleven, when there was supper and bed. Thanks to the weather, this continued every night for a month, except on Sundays.[46]

As the thaw set in at the end of January, and England was submerged by meltwater, Elizabeth took up her pen again. This time, she wrote to the Dowager Princess of Wales's trusted adviser Lord Bute, then the King's first minister* and as such in a position to appoint his favourites to rewarding sinecures. The position on which Elizabeth had apparently long ago set her heart was 'Gardener of Kensington', for 'as Ladies are not exempt from vanity she makes no Doubt that she shall do herself credit in that employ; it has been held by a Duke of Ormond in former Reigns, and therefore not unworthy the acceptance of an <u>Old Maid</u>; and as much in Charecter for a Lady as Ranger of a park is for Lady C Pelham'.[†47] There was only one problem, one she herself put forward: that she could not take the post if it meant forgoing the pleasure of remaining in service with the Dowager Princess, for whom she felt an 'affectionate respect'. Apart from that, 'if you will assist an old friend I may once more sing our old song, oh the merry merry hours of pleasure, the happy little hours of pleasure etc etc, and you will for ever oblige a person who has a gratefull heart, but nothing to boast she can serve you with, except with sincerity and truth doing justice to the goodness of your character'. Unfortunately, Elizabeth was out of luck with her request, and by April Lord Bute was out of power, having been forced to resign by the strength of opposition to him – vilification, even – from many different quarters, though the King continued to take his advice privately for several years.

Unlike Lord Bute, Elizabeth's own favoured status in the royal family brought her no problems apart from the occasional raised eyebrow. She continued to entertain lavishly on their behalf, and in May gave a firework display and dance to mark the Queen's real

---

* First Lord of the Treasury; the post of Prime Minister was not officially recognised until 1905.

† Lady Catherine Manners (1701–1780), married Henry Pelham in 1726.

birthday, which was otherwise not celebrated, and for which the Queen's family paid her the compliment of putting aside their mourning for the Margrave of Brandenburg-Bayreuth. The evening began with the fireworks, set off from a structure that had been specially built in Hyde Park opposite the house. Elizabeth's lowlier guests – tradespeople and the like – watched from two tiers of seats in the courtyard, while the quality were indoors in an unlit room, where they stayed for two hours. As Horace Walpole commented, 'If they gave rise to any more birthdays, who could help it?'[48]

The display was a great success, and ended with a 'fine and pretty' illuminated painted scene to represent the royal family, with mottos in Latin and English for each of its members. To general amusement, the Dowager Princess of Wales' eldest daughter Princess Augusta was represented with a bird of paradise and the words '*Non habet parum* – unluckily this was translated, *I have no peer*. People laughed out, considering where this was exhibited', and the fact that the Duke of Kingston was there in a frock coat, which men tended to wear only in their own homes. There were more fireworks to come, for after the ball – led off by Elizabeth and the Margrave of Anspach – and a supper Walpole described as 'most sumptuous', there was a surprising finale. 'Behind the house was a cenotaph for the Princess Elizabeth,* a kind of illuminated cradle; the motto, *All the honours the dead can receive*. This burying-ground was a strange codicil to a festival; and, what was more strange, about one in the morning, this sarcophagus burst out into crackers and guns.'

The evening did not go entirely to plan, however. A few days later, Elizabeth wrote from Chudleigh House to one of her guests about the bad behaviour of a member of his household:

I am extreamly sorry to be obliged to make a complaint of one of your servents who willfully set fire to an eluminated scene and throwed it down – which might have indanger'd the life of many and have fired my house . . . The damage is very considerable the scene having cost several Hundred pounds and I am not certain it can be repaired – what is still more mortifieing is that not having finished one intended to be painted by myself borrow'd this center

* The second daughter of the late Prince of Wales and the Dowager Princess of Wales, who had died in 1759 at the age of eighteen.

peice I would not agravate his fault (already too bad) but must add that he & one more amongst upwards of four hundred livery servents was the only two who commited any outrage.[49]

When she was not spending the Duke's money on lavish receptions, Elizabeth shared quieter pleasures with her protector. That autumn, the pair toured the relatively new British Museum in Montagu House. At that time, the fledgling institution admitted only sixty visitors a day, who were shown through the rooms in groups of ten. That one-hour guided visit seems to have piqued Elizabeth's interest and, to the undisguised amazement of the Trustees, she applied for use of the reading room for study,[50] one of the first women to do so. Her request was granted for the standard six-month period, for as an acquaintance of the curator Thomas Birch remarked, 'I am sure, you cannot omit so favorable an opportunity of cultivating an Acquaintance with Miss Chudleigh, & of directing her to those Parts of the Collection, which may give her most Amusement'.[51] How much Elizabeth availed herself of the museum's facilities is unknown, however, although she did not reapply once the six months were expired.

Another of Elizabeth's enthusiasms was rather less scholarly. Through her friendship with Sir John Fielding, whose 'Brave Fellows' were the forerunners of the first police force, she and the Duke 'seldom missed the examination of any felon brought before the magistrate'.[52] Much to Thomas Whitehead's obvious disdain, 'Miss C——'s carriage and the Duke's were as well known in Bow-street as any of Sir John's thieftakers. Even the coachmen were ashamed to attend them, waiting so many hours amongst a nest of thieves and thieftakers.' Perhaps the interest was not completely inexplicable as Elizabeth's own mother had been attacked by highwaymen and there had been two fairly recent attempted break-ins at her house in Knightsbridge.

Unfortunately, the petty villains who could make life in London such an unpleasant ordeal were not always complete strangers. The following May, 1764, the *London Chronicle* reported an alarming episode at Chudleigh House. Elizabeth had apparently been so tired coming home one evening that she had allowed her maid to lock up her jewellery for her. She went to bed at once, 'and dismissed her servant, but letting the chamber-bolt fall with intent to fasten her door, she found it would not bolt'.[53] Someone had jammed a piece of wood in the mechanism to prevent it working, so Elizabeth removed it and bolted the door. Shortly after, 'she heard a rustling at her door, and soon after several violent pushes to get it open; she determined to lay quiet, and to discover who was the author of this unaccountable disturbance, which, to her great surprise, she found was her own man and maid-servant: upon his not opening it, the woman advised him to break it open; to which he said, No, 'twill disturb her – Never mind that, says she, if she wakes murder her, while I secure the other affair, meaning, as 'tis supposed, the jewels', which the maid had, in fact, merely put in their cabinet without locking it. At this point, Elizabeth thought it wise to summon help, and after ringing her bell for some time, managed to rouse the other servants. The maid and man-servant appeared before the magistrate the next day but, the *London Chronicle* complained, 'such is the nature of our laws, that as no real act was done that amounted to a possibility of commitment, they escaped the punishment'. In later years, it was said Elizabeth kept a loaded pistol by her bed to safeguard her jewels; if true, her servants' treachery would certainly explain why.

But soon it was summer, and London's less pleasant memories were left behind as society decamped to the seaside, the spas, the race courses or the country estates. By August, Elizabeth was in Nottinghamshire and had probably been staying at Thoresby with the Duke, for she and Mr Thoroton, MP for Newark, opened the grand ball in Nottingham's Assembly Rooms that month by dancing a minuet. The local reports noted, 'The assembly was remarkably gay and splendid, including the Duke of Kingston, and other leading members of the aristocracy.'[54] Elizabeth seemed more assured in her position than ever before, especially when that winter one of the witnesses to her marriage died, breaking another link with that spectacular error in her past. Unfortunately, Aunt Hanmer chose to be buried at Lainston, and a few days later Mr Merrill decided her death should be officially recorded. Thoughtlessly he broke open the seals on the register that Elizabeth had put there nearly six years before and gave it to the new rector, the Reverend Stephen Kinchin to make the entry, asking him to ignore the one before of his cousin's marriage with Augustus Hervey. One more person had been let in on Elizabeth's unhappy secret.[55]

CHAPTER 7

The Baths of Bohemia

The RED PILLS, six in a Box, 6d.
They are very efficacious in Rheumatic and
other Pains in the Limbs.
Public Advertiser, 3 January 1765

M iss Chudleigh's guest lists at Knightsbridge were not restricted to her fellow countrymen. According to Whitehead, 'There was not a foreign ambassador at our court, but Miss C—— provided an entertainment for, at some time or other.'[1] Listening to them describe the pleasures of their own countries – and doubtless having also heard tales of the Grand Tour from the men in her circle – had given her an irresistible urge to see Europe for herself. Her opportunity came when Count Bruhl, the new representative for Saxony, sent back a glowing report on his hostess to the Electress. Maria Antonia, not long widowed and in need of distractions, promptly issued an invitation to Miss Chudleigh to visit her in Dresden.

The invitation was accepted, and Elizabeth formed a plan to travel through the German states to Carlsbad* in Bohemia, famous then and now for its healing waters. The idea of such a trip appealed not only to her curiosity but also to her love of grandness, for it was a luxury few could afford. With help, however, Elizabeth's funds would allow her to do it in some style. Rather than trusting to hired transport, as most travellers did, she commissioned a bespoke coach from Mr Wright of Long Acre in Covent Garden.

* Now Karlovy Vary, in the Czech Republic.

This . . . was to hold four or five persons on occasion, to be made very strong, without a box; instead of which, a large trunk was contrived to hold her clothes, with a seat on the cover, having elbows, and a back like an easy chair: it was fixed on the spring of the fore-carriage . . . Part of the seat of her carriage was ordered to be made in the form of a night-stool, but open at the bottom, for the convenience of letting in fresh air: the other part was used as a case for holding a few bottles of her favourite liquor Madeira, with some other cordials equally necessary to her comfort on such long stages.[2]

London society was amazed. It was unheard of for a woman to make such a trip alone, except by dire necessity, so there had to be some scurrilous reason for it. The wags spent a happy December saying she and the Duke had quarrelled, and that the Duke had taken a pretty milliner from Cranborn Alley to Thoresby in her place.[3] As for the idea that she was going to Carlsbad to take the waters, 'They will be very famous', sneered Lady Mary Coke, 'if they can cleanse her from all her disorders.'[4]

Preparations for the Continental trip took up the first few months of 1765, for a coach could not be built overnight. There were also financial arrangements to make, for it would be disastrous to run short of money on her travels. Accordingly, she borrowed £1,400 from the Duke of Kingston's attorney William Feild in February, and a further £1,000 from her banker Mr Drummond in late March;[5] and another £720 in cash found its way into her account with the Bank of England. By late April, she and her entourage – for 'alone' in this context meant without a male of equal social standing such as a husband, brother, father or son – were ready to leave. On 22 April, the Duke saw her off from Harwich, but he was either so unhappy or so scrupulous in maintaining the decorum of which Lord Chesterfield approved that he did not even kiss his mistress on the lips in farewell.

The details of Elizabeth's first Continental journey are a little hazy for, although her executors' papers suggest she kept a diary of her journey, it has not been possible to trace it. From her bank statements, it seems she travelled through Hanover and on, as the *London Chronicle* had predicted, to Brunswick where she was to pay a visit to the Princess of Brunswick. Here Casanova claimed to have encountered her once more in entertaining circumstances (though he must have 'adopted' the story from someone else, as he was not there that year). The event was a review of the troops in pouring rain from which Miss Chudleigh, unlike the other ladies, refused to take shelter under the elegant tents provided. The result was that her fine Indian muslin dress became soaked through, clinging to her body in such a way as to leave little to the imagination, a fact which appeared not to embarrass her in the least.[6]

Miss Chudleigh and her party – her paid companions Miss Bate and Miss Penrose, an apothecary, a musician, a male servant and one of the Marquis of Granby's hussars who had served in Germany and knew the country well – now bumped and rattled their way over the bad roads to Berlin where they arrived on 11 July. Here Frederick the Great, the bellicose ruler of Prussia, had his first glimpse of the curious English traveller during the lavish celebrations for his nephew Prince Frederick William's marriage to Princess Elizabeth-Christin of Brunswick. In a letter of 22 July, he described 'an English lady, a Mrs Chudleigh, who, having drained a couple of bottles, wobbled around the dance floor, and was on the verge of falling over'.[7] The Prussians found the sight hilarious; a woman travelling alone was already a novel sight, but one with such a love of wine was even more extraordinary. The *London Chronicle*, however, confined itself to informing its readers that Miss Chudleigh had been presented to the Queen, and that the marriage ball 'which continued till late at night was performed by torchlight to the sound of two choruses of trumpets and kettle-drums',[8] which must have been deafening.

From Berlin, Elizabeth presumably travelled on via Leipzig to Bohemia, where she went shooting,[9] the countryside around being very famous for wild boar. By early August the Electress of Saxony was writing back to Frederick that she had heard from the 'Carlsbad water drinkers' about the curious Englishwoman, whom they thought might pass through Dresden, 'but perhaps she will fear not finding any Hungarian wine here'.[10] Lack of wine notwithstanding, however, Elizabeth must have reached Dresden soon after. Here she would have found a city still struggling to recover from the recent war with Prussia. Frederick the Great had invaded Saxony in 1756, and the exiled ruling family were not able to return to their country until six years later. When they did, they found it in ruins, ravaged by the

Prussian troops. To add to the desolation, the Elector's death in October 1763 was followed two months later by that of his heir Frederick Christian, leaving his widow Maria Antonia, now the Dowager Electress, sidelined from political life.

In this subdued and financially depleted court, Elizabeth was a welcome infusion of vitality, and the Electress took to her at once. She admired the Englishwoman's courage and wit, and Elizabeth returned the compliment with her respect for the Electress's creative talents, particularly in the musical sphere, for she adored music, too. It was the start of a lifelong friendship, as was evident from the affection of Elizabeth's first letter to the Electress, written as soon as she reached Carlsbad on her return journey to England.

It would be as difficult for me to show my gratitude as it would be to express the true judgement that your talents merit, I would not dare to trouble you with my thanks for the delight you have given and favour you have shown me in giving me your Opera if I did not have the pretext of asking you for a List of your English Books so I do not send you a duplicate of your Library.

I am extremely happy to have been given this Commission, and I would be truly delighted if there was anything else from my country worthy of appearing before the fine eyes of Madame the Electress; I have never regretted anything more than that now when I know so little French I have to write to the most polished and witty princess in the whole universe, and that I can do justice neither to her mind nor my feelings, for I must admit I have not written more than four letters of French in my life I lay myself at your feet to ask forgiveness for my mistakes, even that which I cannot cure myself of, which will be the liberty of repeating at every possible opportunity how much my Heart feels your favour.[11]

Lord Chesterfield, like many of Elizabeth's compatriots, was still puzzled by her motives for the trip. To his son, Britain's representative in Dresden, he wrote, 'Your guest, Miss Chudleigh, is another problem which I cannot solve. She no more wanted the waters of Carlsbad, than you did. Is it to show the Duke of Kingston that he cannot live without her? A dangerous experiment! which may possibly convince him that he can.'[12] But Chesterfield need not have worried. While his mistress jaunted around Germany, the Duke moped in England. He paid his customary summer visit to Weymouth for the sea bathing, something he took great pleasure in, but 'he much regretted the absence of Miss C——, being a very shy man, and not fond of new faces'.[13] In an unfailing daily routine, he would take a morning swim, ride until dinner time, and in the afternoon take tea with Elizabeth's cousin Isabella, who with some other ladies was also on a visit there from Chalmington. Given that Bell was at least as reserved as the Duke, these occasions must have been painfully quiet.

Much to the shy Duke's evident relief, Elizabeth landed back at Harwich in mid October. 'It was a dangerous experiment that she tried, in leaving him so long', commented Lord Chesterfield, 'but it seems she knew her man.'[14] After a brief stay in Chalmington, Elizabeth returned to London for the remainder of the year, spending Christmas and early January at Pierrepont Lodge with the Duke as usual. Unfortunately, the first few months of 1766 were marred for her by an eye complaint which was uncomfortable enough to stop her writing any letters or doing any banking business.[15] By April she had recovered, and was able to catch up on her correspondence, such as writing to the Duke of Portland to solicit a place in the royal household for her apothecary Mr Evans, who had accompanied her to Germany: 'I must confess I believe I owe my life to his care & skill.' She was also ready to spend with renewed enthusiasm, borrowing a staggering amount of money in the process; in the middle of the month she took out a mortgage of £4,000 against her Knightsbridge property from the obliging Mr Drummond, to add to the £1,000 she had borrowed from him the previous year – a total of around £300,000 in modern terms.

Whatever the Duke may have thought of Elizabeth's extravagance – and, in an age when conspicuous consumption was perfectly acceptable, he was not backward about spending money himself – he must have been looking forward to passing a much happier summer in her company than he had the previous year in her absence. It began promisingly enough with his usual visit to Thoresby, where Elizabeth joined him as she often did at that time of year when she was not needed by the Dowager Princess of Wales. Unfortunately, Whitehead remembered, 'She had not been there more than a week, before she received a letter from the Electress . . . informing her, that her

Highness was taken ill of the small-pox, and could not die in peace, without once more beholding her dear Miss Chudleigh, and begging she would immediately set out for her palace.'[16] The news threw the whole household into turmoil, as Elizabeth made haste to obey the desperate summons and set out that same night for London with Miss Bate for company. She left at midnight – 'a very dark night, and not one mile of turnpike road' – and, as she later reminded the Electress, made for Dresden as fast as possible, 'without going to bed even once'.[17]

If anything, the Duke was even more dejected in her absence than the previous year, not only because it was unexpected but because, as even his valet could see, 'Miss C—— so hung on his heart'.[18] He remained at Thoresby for another three weeks, where even the company of his old friends Colonel Litchfield and Captain Brown failed to lift his spirits. In August he headed, once more, to Weymouth. Here at least he could indulge his love of sea bathing, and there was the novel distraction of a group of visiting Indian chiefs who, at a ball in the new Assembly Rooms which the Duke was asked to open, 'appeared highly delighted with the dances, and afterwards danced according to their manner, with the war whoop'.[19] From Weymouth, the Duke stopped at Chalmington for a visit to Elizabeth's cousins, before returning to London. Elizabeth, meanwhile, had already reached Dresden, for at the beginning of August Lord Chesterfield was writing to ask his son, 'Is the fair, or at least the fat, Miss Chudleigh with you still? It must be confessed that she knows the art of Courts; to be so received at Dresden.'[20] For the Electress, in her overwhelming gratitude for her friend's presence, had showered her with valuable jewels, everything from a portrait in miniature of the giver set with diamonds to amethyst earrings and string after string of pearls.[21] As Lady Mary Coke remarked, 'One must say her Royal Highness bestows her favours with *judgement*.'[22]

Elizabeth presumably continued at Dresden at least until the Electress was out of danger, returning to England some time in the autumn. Life fell back into familiar patterns: entertainments at Chudleigh House, where she no doubt enjoyed showing off her glittering bounty from the Electress; Christmas and the first weeks of 1767 at Pierrepont Lodge; back to London to rejoin the social whirl. There were occasional disruptions – Elizabeth's cousin John Merrill, almost the last witness to that long-ago marriage at Lainston, died in the February – but, on the whole, it was a determinedly quiet year. The main diversion was that the Duke had finally turned his attention to the long-overdue rebuilding of his house of Thoresby. Plans were commissioned from an architect called John Carr for what was later described as 'rather a comfortable house than a magnificent seat',[23] and by January 1767 labourers had already set to work digging up the old foundations. Building progressed quickly enough for decorative work to begin on part of the interior by early summer, though it would be several years before the house would be finished, and then at a cost of £17,000, rather than the £11,000 of Carr's original estimate.

While Thoresby rose steadily from its foundations, the Duke and Elizabeth carried on with their usual routines of town socialising and country sports, and 1767 ended as usual with a few weeks at Pierrepont Lodge. The following year dawned with Elizabeth continuing to play the great hostess at her London home, with entertainments such as 'a great dinner to several of the Foreigners, Ld & Lady Hertford, the Duchess of Portland, & some others',[24] including the Spanish ambassadress. As Lady Mary Coke continued bitterly, 'Who may not have Company that will give a great dinner?'[25] Unfortunately, Elizabeth's menus have not survived, but it is possible to get an idea of a typical meal from some of the recipe books of the time. Elizabeth Raffald, author of *The Experienced English Housekeeper*, offered her readers a representative January dinner, served fashionably at four in the afternoon. After the 'remove', usually a bowl of soup, Raffald suggested twenty-five dishes for the first course, among them 'Pigeons comport', 'Harrico',* 'Fricas'd Chickens', 'Lambs Ears forc'd', 'bottled peas' and 'larded oysters'. The emphasis was firmly on meat; only four vegetable dishes were included. The second course, another twenty-five dishes, included more meat and fish – snipes in savoury jelly, roasted hare, potted lampreys – but also sweeter fare such as 'snow balls', which were apples baked in a pastry crust and iced, and the classic burnt cream, an English invention despite its modern name of 'crême brulée'. This was not the end of the meal, however, for a dessert of 'things extravagant',[26] as Raffald called it, rounded off the feast: sweetmeats,

---

* Haricot beans.

fresh and dried fruit, nuts and four or five flavours of ice cream. Not surprisingly, supper, served at around ten at night, was usually a very light meal of meat and cheese.

But the untroubled flow of the social year was about to be interrupted by the return to England of the journalist and radical John Wilkes. On the March night that he was elected MP for Middlesex, there was rioting in the streets of the capital, and each successive event in his life – his surrender to the courts in late April, the reversal of his outlawry, his sentence of twenty-two months in jail in early June and more – brought fresh trouble. Elizabeth was not the type to let such uneasy times bother her or make her change her plans, however. In May, it was noted that, although London was 'very unquiet' and many people 'full of melancholy apprehensions from all these bustles', the irrepressible Miss Chudleigh, 'willing to divert people's gloomy thoughts from these uneasy times, gives a great Ball this Evening at her House at Knights Bridge'.[27] Whatever it may have done for general morale, the occasion obviously did not help Elizabeth's finances, for a few weeks later she borrowed £500 from the Duke of Kingston's attorney William Feild.[28]

With the coming of fine weather, Elizabeth made plans to go to the seaside '250 miles from London',[29] as she told the Electress. Before she set off, however, there were important arrangements to be made. As Chudleigh House would be full of workmen all summer, most of the servants – including the stable hands – would be going into the country, too. Her horses, consequently, were to be put out at great expense to a livery stable. Among them was one belonging to the Electress, which her friend now urged her to send someone to collect as soon as possible. Elizabeth had already paid one set of livery bills for both this horse and one belonging to the young Elector for which, she pointed out, she had not yet been reimbursed. Elizabeth adored giving presents – this letter was accompanied by a gift of a much-loved greyhound – but being saddled with other people's bills was a completely different matter.

A few days later she was writing again about some private business of the Electress, but her mind was still on horses. This time, it was a special collection of rare butter-coloured ponies that she had been putting together as a coming-of-age gift for the Saxon Elector, which she had intended to present to him in person. 'But the state of my health, and my family affairs will not permit me to enjoy the pleasure of seeing you for several years to come.'[30] The man she had hoped would take them to Dresden on her behalf could only go as far as Calais, but if the Electress was sending someone to collect her own horse, perhaps they could also take the ponies. With the problem presumably sorted out to everyone's satisfaction, Elizabeth finally left London in the middle of June, although she was back by the start of August to check on the progress of the work at Chudleigh House. From here, she took the opportunity to write a rather flowery letter to Lord Bute, whose health had been at a low ebb for some time:

> Accept of the sincere offering of my good wishes for the return of health to your mind and body. My singularity need not surprise you, you have known me upwards of twenty years, always disinterested, loving merit, but disdaining to court it while sycophants follow'd its smiling fortune; contented to know you was happy without once telling you my sentiments on that subject. The fickle turns of fortune which we all experience shows itself in depriving you of health, and the society of your friends the tell tale sorrow breaks from my pen that prudence commands your absence yet every faithfull friend must commend your obedience to her call, your enemies (if it is permited that one who always meant so well should have any) will lament it eternally. Where will they now blunt their arrows? on whom load their faults? each leaden head will open their heavy sockets to conviction, and in your absence Envy may sleep, untill the promis'd minerals have restor'd your stomach to its usual tone Justice by that time will assert her power, and do honor to your Fame, and that your social spirits may resume their usual throne drink a large draught of Lethe to Mans ingratitude.[31]

Whatever Lord Bute's problems, however, Elizabeth was soon to find herself with more pressing concerns closer to home. For, as August opened, the gossips were gleefully spreading the news that Hervey was planning to sue her for divorce or, as he put it, 'unfortunately plunging myself in a very troublesome, disagreeable, yet I think (for me and my family) necessary business, which has long employed more of my thoughts and time than my health could bestow, but to my astonishment a few months' labour (and great labour) have given me what many years I could not obtain'.[32] As early as May, Hervey had consulted an attorney, Mr Barkley, with the intention of gathering the necessary evidence;[33] now that he had enough to proceed, he wrote to Elizabeth to let her know his intention. The town reported that she had 'return'd this answer: that if he proves the marriage, he will have sixteen thousand pounds to pay, as She owes that sum of money'.[34] This last bit, however, was invention, for it was some time before Elizabeth could bring herself to respond at all to Hervey's message.

For Elizabeth was deeply unhappy about this new development, to widespread surprise 'as it was the general opinion that if She was at liberty the Duke of Kingston wou'd marry her'.[35] The first sticking point was that, over time, she had come to believe that the long-ago ceremony she had gone through was not a marriage at all.[36] To the Electress, who was having her own problems with the opposite sex, she wrote bitterly about the way men only fell for those who were not interested in them – thinking of the youthful Hervey, no doubt. 'I am convinced the only way to win Men round is to be totally indifferent to them . . . and despise them all; that is about all they deserve',[37] she added.

Worse, however, was the fact that Hervey planned to sue for divorce on the grounds of 'the criminality of her conduct'[38] – adultery, in other words – of which, he explained through a mutual friend, he had 'the most ample and abundant proofs', the most scandalous of which he would nobly suppress if she did not put up any obstacles to the cause. Elizabeth was furious. 'Was she to make herself a whore to oblige him?' she told one confidant. Behind her anger, however, was a real fear, for it was being whispered that the fastidious Duke – who had retreated to Thoresby – would not after all be so keen on a wife who had been dragged through the courts. Divorce might suit Hervey, whose own many infidelities were of no account in law, but Elizabeth was determined to find some other method of separating herself permanently from him, one that would leave her honour intact.

Her hope was that somewhere in the lumbering, ancient machinery of the ecclesiastical courts, whose jurisdiction over all matters moral was increasingly being challenged by the more modern civil courts, there might be a loophole that could be exploited. Here she was in luck, for the lawyers she consulted informed her there was such a thing as a Jactitation of Marriage, which put the onus on the person who claimed a wedding had taken place to prove it. If they failed, the court's verdict would be that the marriage had never happened at all; the slate would be wiped clean. To the friend who had put her in touch with such obliging lawyers, she wrote excitedly, 'My heart is too full to say more than that my gratitude to Heaven for the Dawn of hope your letter brought of liberty possesses me so intirely that I can give with difficulty a thought to my Guardian friend the good Dr Collier . . . Pray call of Dr C sometimes of a morning tell him I dare not write to him untill he gives me leave he order'd me silence upon bussness, and to be easy'.[39]

As a preliminary step, Elizabeth filed a caveat in the ecclesiastical court on 18 August, which effectively barred Hervey from proceeding in any matrimonial cause without first warning her proctor. She was now able to send an answer to Hervey, thanking him for the polite parts of his message but – the events of nine years before conveniently slipping her mind – 'wishing him to understand that she did not acknowledge him for her legal husband'.[40] She was, she informed him, about to institute a suit in the ecclesiastical court to that purpose, and it would be up to him to prove that a marriage had taken place. Tartly, she added that 'as he had promised before, that he would act upon the line of a man of honour and a gentleman in his own intended suit, she hoped that he would pursue the same line now, and that he would confine himself to the proofs of legal marriage only, and not to other proofs of connections or cohabitations'. Despite his misgivings, Hervey agreed to Elizabeth's demands, saying that he had no more desire to be the focus of scandalous conversation than she did. Letting his honour and gallantry get the better of him, he added that 'if he could not establish the proof of legal matrimony . . . that he was too much of a gentleman to bring anything before the public relative to other connections with the lady'.

The lady, buoyed up by the promising turn of events, flung herself into the social torrent with renewed energy. London had been far fuller than usual since August, thanks to the visit of the King of Denmark who was lavishly feasted and fêted for several months, and Elizabeth went everywhere. In this season of crowds and pickpockets, she was spotted dancing at the Queen's Ball, where the King was in great spirits and did not go to bed until four in the morning; playing 'whisk' at the Princess's Ball with three Secretaries of State, Lords Weymouth, Rochford and Hillsborough; and being one of Lady

Ailesbury's party for a game of loo at the magnificent dance at Syon House.[41] Her spirits were so high that even when some ruffian – no doubt stirred up by Wilkes's latest speech – threw a squib into her coach, burning part of its lining and a fine lace ruffle, she was able to make light of it. At last, she was beginning to believe that she might achieve the status she had so long desired – and society was beginning to agree with her. Lady Mary Coke, who could never understand why people liked her less than the shameless Miss Chudleigh, wrote sourly, 'I make no doubt of Miss Chudleigh being Duchess of Kingston: infamy seems to prosper, while virtue appears under a cloud, neglected and oppressed.'[42] The cultured Mrs Montagu added, 'I suppose the Ladys noble Lover will marry her, and she will gravely tell her acquaintance it is lucky for an <u>old maid</u> to get such a match.'[43] Hervey was not left out of the matrimonial speculation, either. As he told a friend, 'I find this town has made me a much more intrepid person than I really am, for they have already given me another person for a wife, and such a one as I am sure I should never have thought of'[44] – a doctor's daughter from Bath, no less.

While the town talked, the legal machinery of the ecclesiastical court began to creak into action. In early November, Elizabeth's lawyers – Doctors Collier, Calvert and Wynne – filed a complaint against Hervey to the effect that his false and malicious claims of being married to their client had 'greatly injured, aggrieved, and disquieted'[45] her. Now would come the laborious and time-consuming business of accumulating evidence and witness statements; all Elizabeth could do was wait. To add to the anxiety, she was also having financial troubles. The Electress had still not reimbursed her for several bills Elizabeth had paid on her behalf, and the situation was becoming serious. Drummonds, who had been informed more than a year before that the money was on its way from Dresden to their client's account, had already paid out against it. Not surprisingly, they were now rather unhappy about its failure to appear and there was a danger that the whole business could become deeply embarrassing, at a time when she had enough problems already. As she pointed out to the Electress, 'If I was able to, I would give the money back to my Bankers, and tell them I received it another way, but I cannot as my court case will be very expensive.'[46] As to that, she would write a full account soon, reassuring her friend, 'there is not the slightest thing that can dishonour me, on the contrary'. Her lawyers were optimistic for success, had promised it, in fact.

By December, the carefully selected evidence had been accumulated, ready to be presented to the court: deeds for the Hill Street house, manor court records for Knightsbridge, her warrants as Maid of Honour, mortgage documentation, and family wills and letters, all referring to 'Miss Chudleigh'.[47] Towards the end of the month, Elizabeth's lawyers began to take written statements from servants, business connections and the like, who likewise swore they had always dealt with Elizabeth Chudleigh. Even her cousin Isabella was roped in to state that she had 'for fifteen years past . . . lived almost constantly with her during which time she the said Elizabeth Chudleigh hath always been called & known by her maiden name'.[48]

Christmas brought an interruption to the legal proceedings, and Elizabeth spent it as usual at Pierrepont Lodge with the Duke – who had finally come down from Thoresby a fortnight before – and close friends such as Isabella Chudleigh, a distant relation called Alice Yeo and the extremely useful Doctor Collier. The 'sweet warbler'[49] Miss Bate was on hand to provide musical entertainment when it was too wet to stir outdoors, for it was a particularly rainy winter that year. What should have been a happy time, however, was marred by the fact that several members of the party fell ill, were 'all dying with violent colds' as Arthur Collier put it. Among the joke epitaphs he composed on the occasion was an irreverent one for Miss Chudleigh:

> What have we here! a Maid upon her Back!
> Why that is as she should be, is it not? Good lack.

Back in London, the lawyers continued to collect statements: from two of John Merrill's former servants, and from William Craddock, who had been Hervey's servant when they had visited Lainston all those years before. All insisted they had heard rumours that a wedding had taken place, but nothing more. None of it constituted the 'proofs of legal marriage' that Hervey had so rashly agreed to confine himself to, and by letting gallantry win over common sense and consequently putting up only a weak defence he laid himself open to damaging suspicions of collusion. As another lawyer later put it, 'a great variety of witnesses was called, whom it would have been very rash to produce without some foregone agreement or perfect understanding that they should not be cross-examined. Many of them could not have kept their secret under that discussion, even in the imperfect and wretched manner in which cross-examination is managed upon paper and in those courts.'[50] This was slightly unfair, for Hervey's real problem was that there was little to prove absolutely that a marriage *had* taken place. The only person whose evidence could have had any real bearing on the case was Mrs Hanmer's former maid Ann, who had since married Hervey's servant Craddock. But when Hervey's proctor William Barkley asked her to appear as a witness for his client, she refused, saying 'that she was old and very infirm that the affair happened a great many years ago and that she could not . . . at such a great distance of time remember anything of the matter'.[51] It was a lie, but no doubt she thought that a grateful Duchess of Kingston would be more generous than a mere Honourable Augustus Hervey.

In the absence of the only surviving witness to the shabby, scrambling ceremony in Lainston Chapel, the case of Chudleigh v. Hervey was duly heard without any surprises. Even Elizabeth's concern at discovering that she was expected to make a positive oath that she was not married, which she assured a friend she could not go through with, was allayed by the fact that 'what had been offered her had been so complicated . . . with other things that were certainly not true that she could and had taken the oath with a very safe conscience'.[52] On 11 February the court finally decided in favour of the lady. Elizabeth was ecstatic, free at last to correct the wrong turn her life had taken so long ago. She dashed off a note to the Electress to tell her the happy news that she had not only won her case 'with all honour',[53] but that Hervey was to pay all the legal costs and to refrain from calling her his wife in future on pain of excommunication. Most importantly, she was free to marry whomever she chose and had full control of her finances. 'Our laws do not allow child marriages', she told her friend in a triumph of conviction over fact, for only Hervey had been a minor in 1744. She continued:

> The person in question [Hervey] is ill it is believed he will die, I hope not for I bear him not the slightest ill will, and although this gentleman made me miserable for twenty five years I forgive him with all my heart and I hope he will live to repent all the wicked things he has done Goodbye my very dear friend, I am overwhelmed by all the congratulations that I have received these past

two days I am shaking so much that I cannot write, I have so many things to tell you why not come to see me when the Elector is married the trip will be better for you than the Carlsbad waters.

Hervey was considerably less happy about the result – especially about being landed with both sides' costs, but without Ann Craddock's testimony there was nothing he could do. The fourteen-day time limit for launching an appeal passed. The sentence would stand, for now.

CHAPTER 8

Her Grace

Wedded to one, intriguing with another,
This same Miss, Wife, Mistress, Maid & Mother,
Profuse, bold, perjur'd, arrogant and vain,
Unwives herself, & next Day weds again:
The Gentleman's Magazine, April 1776

Elizabeth had long ago convinced herself that her marriage with Augustus Hervey was nothing of the kind; now she had also convinced the ecclesiastical court, and to general shock it appeared she had also persuaded the Duke. 'Miss Chudleigh has taken an Oath that she is not Mr Hervey's Wife; & tho' every body knows She is, as the witnesses to the marriage are all dead She intends marrying the Duke of Kingston',[1] wrote Lady Mary Coke who, like the rest of the town, could talk of nothing else that early March but the 'Chudleigh farce'. ''Tis indeed wonderful, but such encouragement does vice meet with that I'm persuaded She will be visited by half the people of Fashion as soon as ever he [the Duke] calls her Duchess of Kingston.'[2] The Duke, however, was not quite as persuaded as society seemed to think. Even while the jactitation case was progressing, he had walked nearly every morning with James Laroche to Doctor Collier's offices at Doctors-Commons to consult him. These visits continued after the sentence in Miss Chudleigh's favour, for the Duke was concerned there might be something else to prevent the marriage. Once the appeal was revoked, however, Doctor Collier was able to assure him, 'You may safely marry Miss Chudleigh, my Lord, for you neither offend against the laws of God nor man.'[3]

A few days afterwards, the Duke of Kingston applied in person for

a special marriage licence, and a rumour sprang up that the
Archbishop of Canterbury had turned down the application. However,
Frederick Cornwallis plainly overcame any supposed moral objec-
tions, for five days later, on 8 March, Elizabeth's forty-eighth birthday,
the Duke walked once again with James Laroche to Doctor Collier's
offices to collect the licence, planning to dine afterwards at the
Thatched House Tavern. Unfortunately, as Mr Laroche later remembered, they found no sign of Doctor Collier, who had decided to
deliver the licence in person to the Duke's house. They did not return
to Arlington Street until five in the afternoon, and at once 'all the
footmen and chairmen were dispatched to different parts, for lawyers,
clergymen, &c. &c. and in two hours they were all assembled',[4]
Whitehead later recalled.

Despite the fact that it was Lent, when marriages were officially
discouraged by the Church, the ceremony was performed by the
Duke's chaplain the Reverend Samuel Harpur that same evening in
the Duke's Arlington Street house[5] 'before 40 persons',[6] a select group
of friends such as the Yeos, James Laroche and, of course, Arthur
Collier. Lord Masham, who had been granted leave not to attend the
King to the Oratorio that night, played the part of the father and
gave Miss Chudleigh away. Whitehead, without explaining why,
thought it 'the worst ceremony I ever saw in my life',[7] but it was a
distinct improvement on the last one Elizabeth had been through,
for not only was it to someone she truly cared for, it also made her
a Duchess at last. It was the best birthday present the Duke could
possibly have given her.

Two days later, 'their Graces' – a phrase that must have sounded
sweet to the new Duchess's ears – set out for Pierrepont Lodge to
prepare for their presentation at court. As Whitehead remembered,
'We set off, accompanied by Miss Bell Chudleigh, Miss Bate and
servants. The only person that seemed pleased with this journey was
the Duchess; as at every inn we stopped, the landlord or landlady
complimented them with, "God bless ye both, my Lady duchess, and
my Lord Duke! May you long be happy!" '[8] In all the bustle and
excitement, Elizabeth found the time to dash off a brief note to the
Electress to tell her the happy news that 'In the end my dearest friend
your wishes have been accomplished . . . I find myself under the
protection of the most perfect gentleman in the world'.[9] They had
the blessing of the Archbishop of Canterbury and of the court, who

were all doing them the honour of wearing the wedding favours – which, she explained, were rose-shaped brooches of silver lace – that the Duke had sent them to mark the event. The Dowager Princess of Wales had even made her a gift of 'superb diamonds', which was gratifying. But there, at the bottom of the letter, was the present that meant the most to her: signed with a flourish, her new name, 'Elizabeth Duchess of Kingston'.

The sudden marriage – even Elizabeth said it was 'a little in haste' – provoked a great deal of scandalised or amused comment among the beau monde. Hervey's sister Lady Mary Fitzgerald was heard to say that she felt she, too, as a member of the bride's family, should have had a wedding favour, and the *London Chronicle* was pleased to report a story then going the rounds that 'a certain Duke, previous to his marriage, had ordered two Jewellers to wait on his intended bride, to take her orders for eight thousand pounds worth of jewels, which the Lady refused, assuring his Grace, that she had sufficient quantity, having received a present from her dear friend the Electress of Saxony, of jewels, to the amount of forty thousand pounds, these added to her own, it is supposed that her Grace has the most of any Lady in England.'[10]

After several days at Pierrepont Lodge, where they hosted a 'grand entertainment'[11] for some of the smart set and kept open house for their tenants, as well as giving 'great quantities of meat, bread, and strong beer . . . daily to the neighbouring poor', the Duke and Duchess returned to London. The Duke was presented at court on 17 March, but it was the new Duchess's presentation two days later that everyone was longing to see. On that Sunday St James's Street and the court-yard of the palace were packed with curious spectators, who saw Elizabeth walk from her carriage, across a carpet of flowers strewn by the women who sold nosegays at St James's, into the palace itself. Inside was just as crowded, for people had been speculating about what she would wear and how she would be received for days. In the event, the 'embroidery of orient pearl'[12] she had commissioned was not finished in time, so the new Duchess wore a white and silver dress 'and pearl lappets, which were the most curious piece of work-manship that were ever seen; they looked like the finest Brussels point'. Pinned to her left shoulder was the jewelled miniature of the Electress of Saxony given to her several years before, a new idea that soon caught on in fashionable circles.[13]

As for how the new Duchess was received, the perception was distorted by whether the commentator disapproved of her or not. The Countess Temple and Lady Mary Coke – like many of the women – piously reported that the King and Queen had barely spoken to her: 'It wd have vexed me if they had been more gracious,'[14] added Lady Mary. Lord Buckingham, however, thought the King was in a good mood, smiling at everyone, and others saw their Majesties talking with the greatest civility to the new peeress. At least all the stories diverted everyone's attention from the latest bout of civil disturbances, though the mob could sometimes be surprisingly good-natured; the mud-throwers who set upon the Duke of Kingston's coach a few days after his presentation, mistaking it for someone else's, wiped the dirt off as soon as they realised their error and even gave him three cheers.

The newlyweds now settled into Chudleigh House, which was promptly renamed Kingston House, where the Duchess prepared to receive visits from society ladies. There was just one problem. Despite Lady Mary Coke's gloomy predictions, not even half the 'people of Fashion', particularly not the female half, came to call. As Whitehead saw it, 'Her Grace was not much troubled with staying at home, to receive the compliments of the nobility and gentry, as usual on such occasions. Not a single lady of quality or fashion paid her a visit – perhaps they were anxious to avoid close scrutiny of their *own* indiscretions – except the Duchess of Queensbury and Lady Marsham.'*[15] For, while society could stomach many things, such as adultery, illegitimate children, fornication and the like if discreetly done, such blatant bigamy – to the extent of denying in public that your past marriage had even taken place – was another matter entirely, no matter how indulgent the royal family chose to be to their favoured former Maid of Honour.†

Moreover, many of those who had gone to Miss Chudleigh's in the past had gone as much out of curiosity as anything, and always with the hope she might say or do something they could laugh at later. To have to call her 'your Grace' and give precedence to her – and having waited so long for it, she was inclined to be overly particular about

* Lady Masham; as Miss Dives she was Maid of Honour to the Princess of Wales.
† Her post became vacant on her marriage.

being paid all the honours due to her new rank – was more than they could bear. In the face of such social disapproval, and amid rumours that Augustus's younger brother, the Bishop of Derry, was preparing an action to have the marriage annulled, the Duke's earlier misgivings seem to have returned, for it was claimed that he was seen getting drunk every day with Lord Masham, and Whitehead reported he was 'sighing and thoughtful'.[16]

All the same, their Graces soon settled back into a way of life that differed little at first from that of the previous years. The social frost was not universal; for though many of the fashionable ladies would not pay visits to *her*, though she might never hobnob with all her fellow duchesses to the tinkle of teacups, there were others – though more men than women – who liked them both or respected him enough to continue to include them in social events, expecially those involving the royal family. Their Graces were seen at Lady Ailesbury's party at the Tower on the night of the King's birthday, enjoying the magnificent fireworks with everyone else; and at court a few days later one indignant diary-writer observed that the King was as nice to the Duchess as to any of the other ladies there.[17] When London was quiet, they headed as usual to the seaside at Weymouth, to the Duke's house and private hot-springs at Bath, to the nearly completed Thoresby. When they came back to town, they were seen at court almost as often as usual – though Elizabeth had ceased to be a Maid of Honour on her marriage – and were the subject of as much gossip as ever, the most ludicrous example of which was the rumour that circulated in June that the Duchess was pregnant. It was a story surely only the most idiotic could have believed, for Elizabeth was forty-eight, her child-bearing days almost certainly behind her. Still, some people thought a baby would be produced one way or another as a fraudulent heir to the Kingston title and estates, for by now they had convinced themselves that Elizabeth was capable of anything.

Elizabeth herself, however, was more concerned with news from Dresden, where the Electress was recovering slowly from a bad bout of measles, which had laid her low that spring. 'I am very angry to learn from your letter that you have been ill for such a long time,'[18] she told the Electress. Measles, after all, was a serious disease that could move to the lungs and leave one with a dreadful cough, even consumption. She recommended purgative medicines, which were effective as long as one took enough – it was a miracle anyone who

could afford doctors ever recovered from *anything* – and then a trip
to England. 'You promised me that when the Elector came of age
and married you would come to England so come incognito, you will
be received with as much honour as the King of Denmark, and more,
so dear friend make arrangements for next spring I will meet you in
Calais to cross the sea with you and when you leave I will escort you
back as far as Paris.'

By now the Kingstons were beginning to spend more and more
of their time away from shallow London society. Sometime that
summer they headed to the West Country, where the Duchess,
'covered with diamonds',[19] was spotted in Bristol at the theatre with
the Duke and Mr and Mrs Laroche. From here, they went down to
just beyond Plymouth to visit a recently widowed friend, Alice Yeo,
who had been at their wedding. Despite Mr Yeo's recent death it
was a happy few weeks; even the Duke's valet Thomas Whitehead,
whose reminiscences were often soured by later disappointments,
clearly thought so. The 'neat palace, clean and compact'[20] was in a
delightful situation overlooking the sea; its owner was attentive and
hospitable, diffusing 'a spirit of love and harmony through the whole
house'; and the surprisingly fine weather added to the pleasure. Even
when a trip to the Eddystone lighthouse had to be abandoned halfway
when the tide turned, it did not spoil the mood. Their captain –
actually an admiral – ordered his men to put out fishing lines while
he talked about the lighthouse. 'He said, two or three men were
stationed there for a month, though sometimes it would be two or
more before they could be relieved, on account of the difficulty of
getting near the rock,' Whitehead remembered. 'While the Admiral
was thus entertaining us, our men had drawn up some few mack-
erel, and before we landed they caught about three dozen: some of
them were split open, salted, and laid on the deck until we came on
shore, when they were broiled. I never ate them in such perfection
before, or since.'

But it was 'Thoresbys inchanted castle',[21] as Elizabeth called it,
that from 1769 began to claim more and more of the Duke and
Duchess's time, for the new house was progressing well.[22] James Carr's
classical three-storey structure, with its rusticated basement, Ionic
portico and, inside, a wide staircase leading to an unusual elliptical
hall on the first floor lit by a skylight in the dome above,[23] was
complete; all that remained was the decoration and furnishing. While

Elizabeth amused herself with choosing wall coverings for the 'Green Damask Bed Chamber' and 'India Paper Bed Room', and green Venetian sunshades and crimson damask festoon curtains for the ground-floor drawing room,[24] the Duke settled happily into the life of a country gentleman. There was his fine collection of black pointers and spaniels – generations of Floras and Plutos and Waggs – looked after by the dogkeeper in the large, elegant kennels about a mile from the house. Then there was his stable of racehorses – eighteen or more – which were paraded in the park every Sunday, the Duke's public day when the park was open to visitors, their riders dressed in his Grace's colours of crimson trimmed with white. There was also fishing near the house, and plenty of opportunities for shooting game in the grounds.

These grounds were widely regarded as some of the most beautiful in England, more worthy of comment than the 'neat and compact villa',[25] as one visitor called it. One Russian traveller praised 'the paths shaded by dense foliage, waterfalls whose gentle babble tempts one to daydream, meadows carpeted with the best turf, fallow deer, red deer'.[26] Another thought the lake was 'a Noble peice of Water',[27] with its steps at one end where the water cascaded down to form 'a pretty River through the other part of the Park, near the end of which there is a handsome Brick Building with four Turrets, composed in an elegant and simple Gothic style'. The lake itself was huge, about a mile long and a quarter of a mile across, Whitehead thought. Its most notable feature, however, was not its size but its boats. These included a flat-bottomed yacht with a cabin large enough to seat twelve people to dinner, a small half-decked sailing boat and another Dutch-style one, all of which were – like the horses – dressed up on Sundays in their crimson and white colours. Most impressive, though, was the scale model of a fifty-gun frigate, fifteen feet long and perfect in every detail down to its miniature brass guns: truly a rich man's plaything. It had been commissioned by James Laroche as a present for the Duke from a maker at Jacob's Wells, near Bristol, at a cost of around £1,600 and conveyed on a specially made carriage to Thoresby. There it provided entertainment for guests such as Sir John Fielding, who, though blind, would happily clamber all over it, as high as the yard-arm, 'for an hour at a time or more'.[28] Whitehead noted, 'Besides these vessels, there were several Scarborough cobbles, boats, and canoes. When they all moored near the house, at the bottom of the lake adjoining the little battery, they had the appearance of a fleet.'

While the Duke pottered happily round his domain, his wife set herself to the task of running an aristocratic household with its battalion of servants: among them a housekeeper, clerk of the kitchen, butler, under butler, brewer and baker, two musical footmen and maids of all descriptions from personal to laundry.[29] According to the Duke's valet, her Grace took particular interest in her personal maids – maids of honour, as she rather grandly called them – for when she hired one, her advice to them was, 'Take care of the men; they will first squeeze your hand, next kiss you: growing bolder, they will attempt your bosom; which gained, they will soon try for something else: now be you a good girl, and remember my advice.'[30] It was a sensible approach, both for their own future prospects and for the smooth running of the household. Even with the housekeeper Mrs Coats taking most of the responsibility, it would have been a quite tedious enough business finding and hanging on to reliable, hard-working and honest staff of either gender without the young women having to leave in disgrace because they were pregnant.

Whether Elizabeth was a better or worse mistress than others is hard to tell: the Duke's ex-valet cannot be considered an objective commentator on this particular issue. He accused her of all sorts of meannesses – not letting the servants have enough wine with their meals and complaining if they sat up late 'guzzling', the fact that there was nothing left over to give to the poor after his Grace's public days as there used to be – but these suggest she might in fact have been rather a good manager, who hated waste (here her 'careful' childhood showed) and drunken servants. Many of her servants were with her for years, unlikely if she were really such a harridan. If she finally tired of Whitehead, however, it is perhaps not surprising; though he claimed 'I always paid her proper respect', he gave himself away by adding, 'indeed, rather more before than after she was Duchess'.[31] It was bad enough being looked down upon by the neighbouring peeresses; the Duke's servants could hardly expect to get away with doing the same.

For according to Thomas Whitehead her Grace was no more troubled by visits from the 'ladies of fashion' at Thoresby than she was at her London house. The Duchess of Norfolk led the chorus of disapproving peeresses, declaring emphatically she would *never* visit her. However, it is doubtful if she really missed out on female company; some of the Duke's close friends had wives, there was her cousin Bell Chudleigh, and her companions such as Miss Bate and Miss Penrose, good but perhaps rather too quiet women who both went on to marry clergymen. In fact, Whitehead contradicts his former assertion when he describes how when the Duke and Duchess expected company to tea and cards – plainly not a rare event – her maids of honour would 'usher the ladies into her presence, being at those times ranged in a row, according to precedence'.[32] So there were female guests at Thoresby, but perhaps not always of the quality Whitehead thought such a place ought to have.

Still, even the disgruntled valet was not always so harsh on his former master's wife, and at times he paints a picture of domestic harmony and even offers up some grudging praise. On wet mornings, for instance, Elizabeth would usually listen to music played by her band of servant-musicians. To this melodious background – harpsichord, two violins, cello, three horns and the soprano of Miss Bate, who sang 'The soldier tired' and 'I know that my Redeemer liveth' particularly well – she would dictate several letters at a time in both English and French, and also discuss alterations to the house with Mr Simpson, the architect in charge of carrying out James Carr's design. The valet, who sang the tenor parts, noted that despite this she would 'yet be very attentive to the music; would often cry, "Bravo! bravo! Miss Bate, do me the favour of singing that again . . ." This was all done by her with the greatest ease and perspicuity imaginable. I never heard of her equal; she being endowed with an uncommon share of sense, though too often it was applied to very bad purposes.'[33]

Music, in fact, was an important part of Elizabeth's day, for she loved it and when she was merely Miss Chudleigh she had often had private concerts at her London house. At Thoresby, even her after-dinner doze on the sofa in the afternoon took place to the sound of Mr Siprinhi's cello, though it was usually overpowered by her snoring, which was surprising loud given how quiet her voice was. Not all of Elizabeth's traits, however, were as attractive as her love of music. Apart from anything else, she was horribly greedy. At dinner, in company, she would overeat to such an extent that she would have to retire to an adjoining room, 'leaving the door open, where after violently cascading in the hearing of all, a glass of Madeira was sent as a bracer: she would then return to her company smiling, and say, "I beg your pardon; a fit of gout just took me in the stomach; but I am now much better."[34] She would then be persuaded to have perhaps a glass or two of Madeira to do her good, and something to eat to settle her stomach. Dinner over, she would retire to snore on the sofa next door until tea-time, when she would re-appear with a white handkerchief tied round her now aching head. Not surprisingly, the rather plump Elizabeth often suffered from pains in her stomach and head, for she spent much of the morning eating, too: Whitehead remembered, 'Between breakfast and dinner-time, while airing in the park, I have known her order the carriage home five or six times, and take tea, chocolate, sweet cakes, and Madeira, or some other damper, every time she returned.'[35]

The Duke and Duchess were now almost permanently at Thoresby; they may even have spent Christmas 1769 there instead of at Pierrepont as they usually did, for the following February they were still there; 'they have not yet fix'd upon a day for going to Town I believe at soonest they will not go 'till the latter end of next week. Her Grace wishes most heartily to remain here, for many reasons I believe,'[36] someone told the Duke of Newcastle. By later that spring, Elizabeth had another reason for staying in the area: the presence of her cousin Susanna, whose husband the Reverend Nathan Haines was given the living of St Mary's, Nottingham. The Duke gradually began to cut his links with the capital, starting with the sale of his Arlington Street house in May for £16,850,[37] for the countrified Kingston House was a more congenial London residence. If he wanted a break from Thoresby, it was not far to his estate at Holme Pierrepont, near Nottingham, where generations of Pierreponts were buried, and which also had fine shooting thanks to its two gamekeepers (Thoresby had one). Elizabeth visited the house just once, the year after her marriage; but after only a day she announced that she could not stay there any longer, 'the church being so near the house, she said, it put her in mind of her mortality; to think her remains must lie there, made her very unhappy'.[38] The gentlemen stayed on, and probably had a far more relaxed time without her.

By late spring 1771 the Duke had disposed of another house, this time Pierrepont Lodge in Surrey.[39] It had been a much-loved country bolt-hole before the rebuilding of Thoresby, so its sale suggests that the Duke and Duchess were spending so little time in London that a handy retreat from it was no longer necessary. They were not always in Nottinghamshire, however. In late May, they spent several days in Bath where, the Bishop of Salisbury wrote, 'the Dutchess was ill three or four days before they went, but was recovered enough to go to ye Rooms the last Evening'.[40] From here they passed on to Exeter, and then to Plymouth, of which they had many happy memories. Later that year the Duke also attended the investiture at Windsor of several new Knights of the Garter, including the Prince of Wales. But wherever else the Duke and Duchess spent time that year, by mid November they were back at Thoresby, where a young Russian, Prince Alexander Kurakin, encountered them and came away well pleased with the experience.

He was full of praise for the park and the clean and tidy house – 'furnished with an elegant simplicity',[41] much of it the work of Thomas Chippendale – but also for the gracious and unexpected hospitality his party received from the Duchess in particular. 'You have to have travelled yourself', he wrote, 'to understand how flattering such a kind welcome is when it comes from someone who has nothing to gain by it.' Their Sunday morning visit was, after all, unexpected; they were not invited guests, merely tourists on a trip round the country who hoped, in the custom of the times, to be shown round a grand house. At first they were thwarted in their aim; the Duke and Duchess were at church and the servants did not dare to let them in without their master's permission. When their Graces returned, 'not content with making us a thousand apologies for keeping us waiting such a long time, [they] lent us their carriage, so that they could organise the house during our drive. After we had toured the living quarters, we were shown into a room, where a magnificent table well stocked with all kinds of refreshments met our gaze. It was a very agreeable surprise, especially to travellers who were known to no one.'

The picture of elegance and ease that Kurakin paints is in such sharp contrast to the grossness of many of Whitehead's reminiscences that it is tempting to believe that one of them, probably the angry former servant, is lying. Yet it was precisely these contradictions in her character that made Elizabeth so remarkable in the eyes of her contemporaries. While Whitehead was undoubtedly selective in what he chose to write down, even he is unable to avoid praising her excellence in some areas. So much for the Duchess; as for the Duke, Kurakin merely noted that 'the current Duke does not mix in government matters. He likes peace and quiet and his little pleasures, and he never deviates from the way of life he has fixed for himself.'

This unchanging, harmonious way of life continued through the rest of 1771. The Duke and Duchess spent Christmas at Thoresby, and to the delight of both their near neighbour the Duke of Newcastle, with whom they were always on the friendliest terms, returned to his estate at Clumber for the festivities:

> The Duke and Dutchess of Kingstons Compliments to his Grace the Duke of Newcastle and desires to know how he does: they wish to hear that his Grace is return'd to Clumber in perfect health, and that he has not forgot his friends at Thoresby. Their expectation of the honor of his Graces, and all his company from Clumber, to pertake of their chearfulness on the last day of this year, and the first of the next, is to compleat ye [yr], and prognosticate a happy continuation of the good neighbourhood for the year 1772.[42]

Unfortunately for Newcastle, however, the new year brought with it some bad news from his second son, who was in Italy. The foolish young man, having sat down to a game of chance with a professional gambler called Primislas Zannowich, had ended the encounter a staggering 12,000 guineas the poorer[43] – something like three-quarters of a million pounds in modern terms. Elizabeth immediately put pen to paper, trying first to tease the Duke gently both into a better humour and into accepting a dinner invitation to Thoresby, and then offering sympathy and philosophical consolation:

> To persuade you to do what you do not like, is not friendly. But to persuade you to do what is good for you is to be so in a supreme degree, and is my pleasing business for this morning. Your Graces plausible excuse for not dining with us yesterday was accepted for the first reason . . On the second and persuasive part, we add our claim to you as our due for this days dinner, and tho' you make light of disapointing my Ld, yet I dare say you will borth agree, that it is a heavy offence to disapoint a Lady; nor can I think of any good reason for yr Graces not keeping an appointment at a

good dinner at four oclock, when you would make it a point of conscience, to be at a garden gate, as Woodward says, at the hour of eight, where you might meet a vixen, or catch a cold: but joking apart, life is too full of vicissitudes and cares to dwell too much upon the common accidents in life. Mr Addison sweetly and justly observes, 'that these are not Ills, else would they never fall upon Heaven's first Favourites, and the best of men,' but through the mirrour in which you see this little errow of your sons, you may not be in a disposition to hear me say, what I realy think in that subject: an opinion, that prehaps, in a more chearful and unbiass'd hour, you may willingly adopt. In the mean time make reason to your self, from Sr Francis Bacon's opinion 'That Fortitude Will Conquer Fortune;' and a very little philosophy will teach your Grace that the misfortune you lament so much, is not so terrible as you first thought. I am quite certain, if you consult your cool reflection, that you would have given twice the sum in question to have been sure that the . . . author of the charming letter possess'd so much reflection, filial affection, good sense, and spirit to confess a Fault with frankness, and Honor and Reason sufficient to renounce an Error as soon as perceived. A heart so formed, can never essentially go astray . . .[44]

To the Kingstons' grief for their dear friend's problems was soon added another sorrow: the death in the early morning of 8 February of Elizabeth's former mistress the Dowager Princess of Wales. She was fifty-two. The *Annual Register* reported her peaceful end, for after saying goodnight to her son George III 'she remained very quiet all the night, and gave no tokens of death till a few minutes before she expired, when she laid her hand upon her heart, and went off without a groan. His majesty was then informed, and he came and took her by the hand, kissed it, and burst into tears.'[45] The great bell of St Paul's tolled for an hour from eleven to twelve that same morning, to herald a period of sixteen weeks of public mourning starting eight days later that would close the theatres, opera house and other places of entertainment. A week after, on 15 February, Augusta was interred in the royal vaults in Westminster Abbey with all the solemn ceremonial befitting her position as mother of the King, her coffin draped and canopied in black velvet and flanked by countesses, with a great line of members of the royal household before and after. Although

Elizabeth was not an official mourner, it is hard to believe she was not among the many peeresses who attended. The two women, only two years apart in age, had been close friends for many years and the former Maid of Honour must have felt the loss keenly.

In need of its restorative waters, the Duke and Duchess headed to Bath for a short stay that spring. In mid April, Elizabeth was 'at Bristol Wells in a very bad state of health',[46] the Duke being in Newmarket at the time. Sometime in May they were back in Bath for what seems to have been a prolonged stay in the West Country, for by July they were both down in Plymouth, where the Duke had some business to sort out. As it happened, so did the Duchess, for she had been made an offer for her small Dartmoor estate (though, of course, technically it now belonged to the Duke, for married women could not hold property in their own right). She wrote to her Devon neighbour Sir John Rogers to ask if he might also be interested in buying Hall, which his own lands nearly surrounded:

> if I am offer'd what I think it is worth it will never be put up to Sale by Auction but on the Contrary if the offers are very small they shall not have my little Hall and then it may go to the best bidder after a survey is call'd. I wish you may have it, if it contribute to your Health or happiness. I hope to have soon an opertunity of laughing when at Blanchford at the great bustle people make about nothing, at the same time pray observe that I do not deny my sex when I desire a great deal for a small matter, these small things have ruin'd many a man and made many a woman.[47]

Her opportunity for laughing with Sir John was delayed, however, for she was prevented from waiting upon him that same day 'being much indisposed with the Headack & the weather is so very bad that she does not dare to venture out'. In the end, however, the 'great bustle' came to nothing, and Elizabeth left Devon without having disposed of her 'Fairy land'.

Back at Thoresby, life continued as before, with occasional diversions such as a three-day musical festival in Nottingham in October, attended by all the leading local families, with performances of oratorios such as the *Messiah* in the daytime 'and in the evening, musical entertainments were given of a miscellaneous character, concluding with a ball at the Assembly Rooms'.[48] At the end of the year, there was a house party at Thoresby with all the usual suppers and dances, the pleasure of the Duke of Newcastle's return to the neighbourhood with his friends and family, and even a broken engagement between two of the guests to provide a little drama at the beginning of 1773.[49] His Grace of Kingston was always pleased to have the Duke of Newcastle so near, and when he threatened to go to an estate of his in Lincolnshire he was teasingly urged to change his mind:

> The Duke and Dutchess of Kingston desire leave to wish the Duke of Newcastle a good journey and a quick return to dry healthy land not so <u>near a Fen as Bamber</u> & better for the spirits. The Dutchess takes the liberty to say that she hopes his Grace will consider the great Rains may make any place damp, the Duke of K groans so much about it, & as chief phisician at Clumber he absolutely orders an intire diffirent plan from the intended one. instead . . . of sighing at Bamber, laugh with the Dutchess, and play at whist in Nottinghamshire rather than cough in Lincolnshire.[50]

It was clear to all who cared to see that the Kingstons were supremely happy with their way of life. Settled in the country with the man she had loved for more than twenty years, and who adored her in return, the Duchess seemed to have lost any appetite she may once have had for the froth of London society. As for the Duke, he had never cared for town life in the first place. At Thoresby, he had everything he could want: his wife, his hobbies, his friends – in short, all the ingredients for a relaxed and contented old age.

CHAPTER 9

The Beginning of Sorrow

But cruel death, thou tyrant, grim,
No mortal can withstand thee,
Thy darts thou hast display'd at him,
That once doated upon me.

Ballad

Unfortunately, the Duke of Kingston *did* lack one thing vital for a long and happy life: good health. Sometime in the summer of 1773, he had a series of strokes which affected him badly. In the hope of finding a cure for his 'paralytick disorder', Elizabeth accompanied the Duke to Bath, taking the family physician Dr Thomas Raynes to look after him. As if the Duke's poor health was not worrying enough, August brought the terrible news that Elizabeth's cousin Susanna, Bell's younger sister, was dead. Almost incoherent with misery, Elizabeth wrote to the Duke of Newcastle:

My trembling nerves are agitated with the distressing scene of my dear Lds sickness has aded to its burden the loss of dear Mrs Haines one of my most near & dearest relations poor Miss Bell Chudleigh still a paralytick object befor my eyes dying with apprehendsion that her sisters illness may prove fatal is on the point of setting out for Chalmington to comfort her aged mother with the hopes that her dead darling may recover. I have not fortitude sufficient to tell her she is no more, to my dear friend and affec^t Husband all ties all friendship must give way, and I must see her go without the relief of one single tear, for my dear friend consults my Countinence to raise or fall her spirits . . . The Duke must be left in ignorance of this calamity, for he loved her affect[ly], untill his nerves are restored to their former tone. My Ld your Graces affectionate friendship for my dear Ld and your Graces solicitude & compasion for my sufferings demands my most grateful returns of thanks, but do not let your pittying Heart give one sigh to my sufferings, Trained in a school of sorrow I have learn'd to submit to that power who can give, and can take away; in his wrath he has remember'd mercy, and the Duke seems to recover into his usual Health Strenght & Spirits Can walk sleep & eat well, can move his Hand, but it is not yet become usefull, Mine & all of me is willingly devoted to him & he takes food & medicines from my hand only, Night & Day. I bless God that he has given me strenght to attend him as I do. Your Grace does me the honor to inquire after my health – my anxiety is not to be described, My Ld I fear you know that a feeling heart in this Life is a Life of Suffering, Bodily pains I have many, they are so far friendly but they attack me with the greatest severity when my Ld is sleeping, the Rheumatism has fixed in my Hip, and the ague in my Head borth these complaints come by too long watching on my knees by his bed side, and when through fatigue nature has been almost exhaus[t]ed I have slept a little on the floor.[1]

Fear and tiredness made her restless, as she tried everything she could think of to improve the Duke's chances of recovery and make him more comfortable. The first set of lodgings she rented in Bath, Mrs Hodgkinson's in the Orange Grove, were not right, so she moved the Duke to his own Abbey Bath-house, and then to a tall, elegant Palladian townhouse in South Parade. Others fussed around the Duke as well, all with their own ideas of what would lead to his Grace's recovery. None of it seemed to help; in the middle of August the Duke of Newcastle was told of the severity of his friend's latest stroke, which had left him paralysed. 'I am sorry to say that he has faln a Sacrifise to the <u>Obstinacy</u> of the Dutchess and the <u>Ignorance</u> of Dr Raynes; as they both were resolutely determined to depend solely on <u>this</u> Physicians skill, nor could any remonstrance or Persuasive Argument that I could make use of invite them to call in any assistance, till the last <u>Fatal Relapse</u> obliged them to it.'[2]

By mid September the prognosis was even less encouraging. Despite everything, the Duke showed no great signs of improvement. His agent Sam Shering kept Newcastle informed of his friend's lack of progress: his sudden spells of lethargy, the violent spasms in his lame arm that left the muscles in knots as big as hazelnuts, his lack of appetite and uncomfortable attacks of hiccups. 'Every body, physicians and all, seem to dispair of his recovery excepting the Duchess: she does not see with the same eyes as other people.'[3] Refusing to give up hope, with the Duke's consent Elizabeth called in a new doctor, 'Dr Delacour, a physician who practis'd in London, with great reputation; retir'd from thence to this place for his own Health; is much sought and respected in these parts: His plan of opperations is different from the others, by Emeticks, and will obtain, if possible, Evacuations by warm nervous Glisters, and not by weakning physick – I pray God give a blessing to his Endeavours!'[4] Miss Bate added as a postscript: 'The Dutchess is inconsolable, not only with grief, but with surprize; for the Drs have kept her in ignorance of the Dukes danger allways telling her his Graces pulse was good; and as he Eat and slept well, she flatter'd herself that there was not that immediate danger.'

On 22 September 1773, it rained heavily and the wind howled round Bath's elegant streets: 'tempestuous night and day',[5] the *Gentleman's Magazine* called it. By the time the storm blew over the following morning, the Duke was dead. The Duchess would not, after all, be able to take her beloved husband to Carlsbad and Dresden the following year, as she had promised the Electress she would do if he recovered.[6] She would be the one in need of their healing powers now. First, though, there was all the dispiriting business of the funeral arrangements. Until it could be taken to Nottinghamshire the Duke's body was deposited in the parish church of St James in Bath, with four chairmen to keep watch over it; the quaintly named Messrs Jelly and Palmer supplied 'Coffins and furniture'[7] at a cost of £43.11s. – presumably one for immediate use and a more lavish bespoke one for the funeral itself. Various dressmakers and milliners were set to work making mourning clothes and hats for the servants and the housekeeper Mrs Wilkinson, with rather grander ones for her widowed Grace.

The world of gossip, which had ignored Elizabeth for several years, turned its distorting lens on her once more. It looked on with amazement as it took her five days to travel from Bath to London, making as many stops on the way, Walpole commented, as Queen Eleanor's corpse: 'I hope for mercy she will not send for me to write verses on all the crosses she shall erect where she and the horses stopped to weep.'[8] Mrs Delany piously commented, 'her widow'd Grace fell into fits at *every turn* on the road from Bath: – *true* affection and gratitude surely cannot inhabit such a breast?'[9] There was, so it seemed, a right way to mourn, which was not too much or too loudly, presumably to spare the blushes of those whose grief might otherwise be unconvincing. Elizabeth's noisy, extravagant sorrow must therefore be an act; it never even occurred to the tattlers that she might have truly loved the Duke and that the past few months worrying about him and caring for him might have left her physically and emotionally drained. Not everyone was quite so cruel; Lady Ossory, one of Walpole's correspondents, was gracious and perceptive enough to say 'that much will be said that she does deserve, and more that she does not'.[10]

When the Duchess eventually reached Kingston House, her companion Miss Bate contacted the Duke of Newcastle, who had custody of his late neighbour's will. 'Her Graces Health and Spirits are eaqually bad',[11] she wrote, adding 'that the Will shall be Open'd when ever your Grace will appoint the time'. Elizabeth scrawled her own postscript, the handwriting ragged and unclear: 'I am my good Ld Duke the most comfortless & the most meserable of Beings.' It was several days before the Duchess – 'so ill (*of grief*)', said one disbelieving letter writer[12] – could bear to have the will opened, though the whole world was desperate to hear what it contained. Eventually the Duke of Newcastle said he could not put it off any longer, and all the interested parties were summoned to Knightsbridge. For most of them, however, it was to be a disappointment. The Duke had left all his personal wealth to his wife for ever; he had also bequeathed her the income from his estates for life, as long as she did not remarry. Only after her death would the estates pass to his sister Lady Frances Meadows's second son Charles and his heirs, failing which it would pass to the third, fourth or fifth sons. Nor would their cash legacies be paid during the lifetime of the Duchess. The eldest son Evelyn was cut out of the succession completely, with just £500 left to him in a codicil.

The Meadowses were shocked by the news. Evelyn's father left the meeting in tears, so upset that he was unable to speak. The family had somehow convinced themselves that they would be the main beneficiaries of the will, in spite of the fact that the Duke had made it clear during his lifetime that he disliked all of them. As for Evelyn Meadows, Thomas Whitehead said 'the porter had particular orders never to let in the Captain on any account whatever'.[13] Despite this, he had been so sure of his inheritance that in the previous ten years he had borrowed more than £6,000 from his younger brother Charles on the expectation of it,[14] and probably more elsewhere. The Duchess, at least, had a good idea of what Evelyn had done to earn his uncle's contempt. As she later wrote:

> The eldest Nephew for many Reasons was disinherited. The principal cause was, that when he had the Advantage of being an Aid de camp to Duke F. in the late war & in immediate Service, he quited that Post of Honour & immediate Service to retire into a marching Regiment unemploy'd, & afterwards without any Property quited the Army intirely living extravagantly, on the Hopes of Succession, which was in the Duke's Power to give to his more worthy Brothers.[15]

To the Duke, that would have been bad enough, but there was more, for 'poor Lady Francis Medows in her intervals of Sense told the Duke that her Unhappiness proceded from the ill Treatment of this Son & her barbarous Husband'. The barbarous husband's treatment of his own sister had been even more shocking, for both she and her husband 'the most amiable Mr Camil son' had died of a broken heart thanks to his unkindness.

In a classic example of self-delusion, however, the furious Meadowses came to the conclusion that their pecuniary disappointment was all Elizabeth's fault. In fact, it is possible that they would have received even *less* from the Duke without her intervention, for she claimed that 'it was to my own Generosity the Family hold the Benefit of succeeding to me. For his Love & Friendship was such, that had I not resisted by Prayers & Tears to his Request, he would have given it to me for ever.' If the Meadowses derived so little benefit from the Duke's death, much of the blame for that rested on their own shoulders; it was at least partly their years of unsubtle manoeuvring, grasping behaviour and sheer presumption that had been their downfall. Elizabeth, however, had been the Duke's companion for nearly a quarter of a century, and he had been devoted to her. The will, so carefully written in his own hand to make it all but impregnable, was the clearest sign of his love. He had willingly done all he could to make sure that when *he* was no longer able to protect her from the malice of society – so evident in the days after their wedding – his money would protect her instead.

Society, of course, saw none of this, for it had decided long ago that Elizabeth was no more than an unscrupulous gold-digger; it was impossible that the couple could have loved each other. They gleefully spread the story that the Duke had named his wife by all her aliases in the will, before paying their shilling to go and read for themselves that he had actually called her 'my wife Elizabeth Duchess of Kingston'. They hinted that the Duke had been bullied by his wife into making his will in her favour. How much better it would have been, someone later said, if she had been content with the £4,000 a year settled on her at her marriage and had allowed the Duke to leave his estates to his family.[16]

In the midst of all the slanderous gossiping, on 13 October the Duke of Kingston's coffin left Bath to the solemn sound of church bells, for the long journey to Holme Pierrepont, the Nottinghamshire estate that had put the Duchess in mind of her own mortality. The procession was headed by six mutes, the newspapers reported, followed by:

First Coach with the Archdeacon and three other Clergymen
The Coronet on a crimson Velvet Cushion borne by the Duke's
Gentleman on horseback, attended by
Two Grooms and Two Pages
The Plume of Feathers
THE HEARSE
Adorned with Escutcheons on his Grace's Armorial Ensigns
Five Coaches with Mourners, Physicians, and Attendants.
A great Number of Horsemen, chiefly composed of his Grace's
Tenants and Tradesmen, Two and Two.[17]

This great cavalcade moved on slowly towards Nottinghamshire, stopping at the main inns along the route where the Duke's corpse could lie in state; the Mayor and Corporation of Leicester came out to meet the procession, as did the dignitaries of all the main towns they passed through, 'endeavouring', the *Public Ledger's* reporter put it, quite carried away, 'by every mournful Attention to prove their sincere Veneration for the Memory of so benevolent! so good a Man!' After six days' travel, they reached Nottingham, where they were met by huge numbers of mourners – the local nobility and gentry whose line of coaches was more than a mile long, the Duke's tenants and many others – ready to accompany the hearse on the final leg of its journey to Holme Pierrepont. The roads were so thickly lined with well-wishers that the carriages could barely squeeze through.

They reached Holme Pierrepont at noon, where they rested for a while. Three hours later, the procession had swelled to vast proportions to escort the coffin, draped in crimson velvet, from the house to the church. There were twenty constables, the doctor Thomas Raynes, and seven Reverends including Nathan Haines; the pall-bearers, including the Duke of Newcastle and his sons and the Duke of Portland; the chief mourner Samuel Shering with his assistants, followed by various gentlemen, among them Thomas Whitehead, in deep mourning and many of the Duke's tenants and employees. At the end of the service, the Duke's body was deposited in the family vault; minute guns at Thoresby were fired sixty-two times, once for each year of the Duke's life, and 'the Colours of the Vessels on the Lake were struck half Mast, and the Bells were muffled and tolled'. The *Public Ledger's* reporter noted that 'among all Ranks an universal Murmur of Grief prevailed; and in every Countenance were strongly marked, the Impressions of a Sorrow that spoke the Loss of a most dear Relation, an honoured Friend, a noble, an universal Protector, and Benefactor!' Yet even among all this sorrow, one peeress could not help sneering, 'The Dss of K——! (alias Mrs H.,) must have been struck wth a whim for ye D. to apear a Grand Seignior before he died. She and her six women attending with all humility gives me an idea of a seraglio.'[18]

The heartbroken Duchess now had to decide what to do next. There would be no more jolly notes to the Duke of Newcastle asking for his company and a little coffee, only letters to him from the jeweller asking the size of his finger for a mourning ring. Elizabeth's happy world was shattered. She had lost her best friend, her devoted companion, the man who had protected her for so long. Without him she was not only bereft but vulnerable; exactly how vulnerable, she was soon to find out.

CHAPTER 10

The Warmth of Rome

After a sleepless night, I trod, with a lofty step,
the ruins of the Forum; each memorable spot where
Romulus stood, or Tully spoke, or Caesar fell.

Edward Gibbon

E ngland in the dank, gloomy days of winter was hardly the ideal place for Elizabeth to recover from her terrible loss. Not only was there the dismal weather to cope with, but it was also becoming increasingly clear that many of those who had tolerated her for the Duke's sake no longer felt obliged to continue now that he was dead. In fact, she complained to one of her acquaintances, 'she had been so ill-treated since her worthy lord's decease, that she was determined to quit this vile country'.[1] While society assured itself that she would go and live in Saxony with her dear Electress, the bereft Duchess decided to head south to Italy instead to escape the chill, both climatic and social, possibly at the suggestion of that same Electress who had passed an agreeable few months in Rome two years before. Before she went, she sat for her portrait* 'in her weeds, looking at a picture of the Duke, her Robes carelessly behind her on a Chair, & an Hour glass & Scull on the Table, all her own device – she wd have had some bones at her feet, but Hoare wd not comply with *that*'.[2] By early January the heartbroken Dowager was ready to set off on her journey overland, finally arriving in Rome in the middle of February.[3]

The city was one of the main stops on the Grand Tour, without which no young English gentleman's education was considered

* Not found.

complete and which a growing number of women were also experiencing. Having studied the classics at school and university, the men came to Italy to dig for antiquities, admire the architecture and have their portrait painted, and there was 'a very grand show of British Nobility & Gentry'[4] that year in Rome enjoying the special favour of the Anglophile Pope. Clement XIV – a brave, witty man with a passion for practical jokes, though detested by the Jesuits whose order he had officially dissolved in 1773 – was so fond of the English that he had given them permission to give musical entertainments twice a week, despite the fact that it was Lent. Many were shocked by this concession, but went along to the concerts anyway. The Duchess, however, kept her distance from her countrymen and, more particularly, her country*women*, who were industriously and rather smugly spreading their stories about her to the Italians. She stayed in deep mourning and carefully saw only a select company, thereby depriving the more self-righteous travelling Englishwomen of the gratification of snubbing her as they had planned.[5]

Instead, she found solace in the presence of various members of Rome's large religious community. She was particularly kind to the Irish Franciscans of St Isidore's, and when she suffered a fit of convulsions only a couple of weeks after her arrival she 'would have the Father Guardian to be always near her'.[6] So Friar O'Kelly became an almost permanent guest at the Duchess's table, and when she went out to look at the sights he was always within her sight or hearing.[7] Her connections with the Church went higher than that, however, right to the very top. Not long after she reached Rome, she was presented to the Pope at the Church of La Vittoria where 'she told his Holiness that she could not come to Jerusalem without adoring; he raised her up & received her ve[ry] graciously'[8] – in fact he was charmed with this sprightly friend of the Electress. To show his appreciation, His Holiness sent her a fine snuffbox decorated with his portrait; she returned the compliment with 'a rich present'[9] to the Pope's favourite friar Bontempi who, not surprisingly, was afterwards noted to be paying 'assiduous attendance'[10] upon the Duchess.

Elizabeth, too, was charmed by almost every aspect of Rome. There was plenty to distract her thoughts and keep her spirits from sinking too low, and she spent lavishly – around £1,600 passed into the hands of her Roman bankers in a few months.[11] There was the sightseeing, of course, and private concerts, for her entourage included a small band of musicians.[12] There were public spectacles, too: in honour of the visiting Duke and Duchess of Cumberland, the Pope ordered the illumination of the dome of St Peter's and the colonnades in front; all Rome gasped at the beautiful vision produced by a staggering number of paper lanterns.[13] Elizabeth was also having language lessons with an Abbé Turner, and studying Russian under the poet Vasilii Petrov with the intention, so the British representative in Florence Horace Mann thought, of later visiting that country.[14] Like many of her countrymen, she was also buying 'a great number of wretched paintings, most of them not worth the carriage & duty': it was noted 'that she chuses all pious subjects except a Venus & two or three such like pieces'.[15]

As she slowly recovered a little of her zest for life, the Duchess began to widen her social circle so that, by the end of April, one English priest could write to his noble Catholic employer in England: 'her conversazione is very brilliant, much frequented by the gay Prelates, young noblemen, & the Pope's favorite friar Fra Bontempi. She sometimes has somewhat like litterary Academies, wherein each one of the company makes a short discourse upon some interesting subject. The sprightlyness of her character & the singularity of her sentiments make many curious to see & converse with her.'[16]

The late Duke was never far from her mind, however, and she finally decided to commission a memorial to him in marble, an idea she had initially rejected because 'there was not a Michael Angelo to execute it, & no other artist was ever able to do justice to the noble figure of her dear Duke'.[17] The design she came up with was – like Hoare's mourning portrait – characteristically unsubtle and over-the-top: 'In the upper part she puts the Eternal Father amidst all the glories of heaven, somewhat below is the Divine Son, comed [*sic*] down (pity the impropriety of her Grace's notions) to receive the Duke, & place him amidst the highest Angels.'[18]

A woman whose thoughts were apparently fixed firmly on religious matters must, so many of the English at Rome thought, be not far from converting to Catholicism. It was not a rumour that pleased the Duchess. The ambassador at Naples reported back to his masters in London that 'Her Grace is much offended at a report of her intending, to change her Religion, being determined to live and die a good Protestant.'[19] This did not prevent her from having another long conversation with the Pope, during which 'He held her by the hands a long while, & as he kept his gloves on, he turned to one of his Prelates, & bid him remember the italian proverb, That <u>Love does not pass the glove.</u>'[20]

With such pleasant company, and a climate that suited her, it was not long before the Duchess decided to spend all her remaining winters in Rome. She told the Duke of Portland, a neighbour in Nottinghamshire, that 'my sorrow knows no end, but at Rome I have found Rest, sleep has restored me to a better state of health than when I left England'.[21] Late in April, she decided to make an offer for the Villa Negroni, an elegant late-Renaissance building which had once belonged to Pope Sixtus V, set in large grounds on a hill overlooking the baths of Diocletian towards the north of the city. A courier was dispatched at once to Genoa, where the Negroni family lived, to make an offer on the house of 62,000 crowns, or about £15,000,[22] though some reports put the figure as high as £16,000 or even £20,000.[23] However, the family 'raised some difficulty'[24] or other, perhaps hoping to push the price higher, for the English were generally regarded in Italy as big spenders. Elizabeth abandoned the idea for the present,[25] and concentrated instead on preparing for her departure for England, where she intended to pass the summer.

By the middle of May she was in Florence, where she was entertained by her childhood playmate Horace Mann. They dined together, then Mann took her for some fresh air to the Cascine 'which delighted her much till their resemblance to some of her own parks, where she had passed such delicious hours with the Duke, produced a flood of tears'.[26] Late that same night she set out again, travelling overland to Lerici to pick up a boat – or rather, three feluccas – for Genoa.[27] Here she paused for a few days, having once again changed her mind about buying the Villa Negroni, for not only did it have a fine garden but its spacious rooms with their scattering of antiquities would be the perfect backdrop for her more modern furniture from England.[28] But the negotiations went badly; the owners had a fit of greed and raised their price so high that the Duchess was forced to give up any idea of ever owning the elegant villa.[29]

The pause at Genoa had at least given the Duchess a chance to recover some of her strength, for, as she wrote to the Electress on 28 May, 'I have been ill, and I am still not completely recovered, and

I embark this evening or tomorrow morning, for Antibes.'[30] Moreover, she explained, she had been unable to pay her compliments to the Electress's niece the Archduchess on her way through Florence, as the children had only just been inoculated against smallpox and the court was consequently in retreat. She had, however, received 'a very gracious message' from the Archduchess, and promised to stop again in Florence on her return to Rome in the autumn.

By the end of June she was in Paris, about to leave for England and trying to sort out a few business matters regarding the sale of the late Duke's horses, despite her 'infirmities and great afflictions which still render me unequal to business, and unworthy of society'.[31] Luckily, she would not have to suffer the discomfort and inconvenience of a packet boat for her Channel crossing; a few days later, Captain Harden sailed her own ship the *Minerva* from Calais across to England.[32] The Duchess was soon back in her house in Knightsbridge, but her stay was to be an unpleasantly short one. For, while she had been meandering slowly northwards through Italy and France, hampered by a painfully swollen leg,[33] the Meadows family had launched a devastating attack on her at home, one they had been working on for months.

Almost from the moment he had discovered the contents of the Duke's will, Evelyn Meadows had been delving into the Duchess's past to see if he could find any solid evidence of the rumoured first marriage. He had travelled to Bath, where the Duke's former valet Thomas Whitehead was now eking out a living as a music master. The impoverished, disgruntled Whitehead obliged him with damning gossip to the effect that the Duchess had used undue pressure to get the Duke to alter his succession in her favour – that 'he had no will to act as he pleased'[34] – and then put him in touch with the Reverend Amis's widow, now Mrs Phillips. She, too, was in a mood to help, for her husband was a former steward of the Kingstons, whom the Duke had been obliged to fire for misconduct.

It was a good start, but better was to come. Evelyn Meadows kept his horses at a livery stable at Hyde Park corner, owned by John Fozard, yet another ex-servant of the Duke, as his wife was of the Duchess. He told Meadows that 'his own wife had heard Mrs. Craddock say, that she saw them married and bedded. And a Mrs. Bird, who lived with Miss C—— at the same time with his wife, could prove something material.'[35] More importantly, he also knew where

Ann Craddock could be found. This was exactly what the Meadowses had been waiting for. Fozard wrote to her at once on their behalf and, though she would later deny it, offered her a financial inducement in return for her cooperation.[36]

The offer came at just the right time for Craddock. Two or three years before – exactly when is not clear – the Duchess had apparently offered this one surviving witness to her long-ago secret marriage an income of 'twenty guineas a year to go and settle in the country, and a choice of three different counties':[37] Derbyshire, Northumberland and Yorkshire. Craddock, reluctantly, chose the last, but got no further north than Thoresby, claiming she was too unhappy at leaving her friends. As a result the annuity had never been paid and the Duchess, refusing to submit to what she chose to see as blackmail, had made it clear that Craddock could expect nothing in future from *her*, at least. Fozard's letter offered a new possibility, and Ann Craddock agreed to tell the Meadowses everything she could remember.

Armed with this vital account, on 17 May Philip Meadows and his wife Lady Frances had filed a Bill of Complaint in the Court of Chancery – which heard civil cases, rather than criminal ones – with the aim of overturning the Duke's will. The Bill contained shockingly scandalous allegations against both Elizabeth and Hervey: that they had been married secretly, that they had colluded to deceive the Duke, that the Duchess had used 'threats and menaces'[38] to force the Duke to leave his money to her instead of to his next-of-kin Lady Frances Meadows. This was soon backed up by Ann Craddock's damning eye-witness account of the first marriage given before the court examiner.[39] It was a disaster for the Duchess, and on her long journey home, she had missed her lawyer's letters warning her of what awaited her in England. In a panic, all she could do for now was turn tail and hurry back to Dover with undignified speed. As she later recalled, there were no packet boats, so she was rowed out to an Ostend merchant ship that was about to set sail for Calais. She arrived in the French port 'with only a Young Lady and not Even a Change of Cloaths or linnen'.[40] From here, she at once wrote bitterly to the Duke of Portland:

> I depended upon being in England, Alas! I have been there! and the first melancholy object that presented itself to my view, was

the Atacvement.* It is true, I did not want that memento to tell me, that all was wanting from wither, that wound bleeding again afresh, and all kinds of opposition to my completion of business, from Mr Medows and his eldest son, with variety of sorrows, which will soon end my wretched life; which tho' I am well apprized that is their aim in all their proceedings: weakened by sickness, as well as sorrow, I have not philosophy enough to support me. I was obliged to submit, after twenty four hours being in my house, to be put into my Coach, one more to embark for France. I wait at Calais to settle some business with Sherring, my Steward, and proceed by advice to the German Spaw, and intend to pass the Winter at Rome. But as Mr Addison says 'while I yet live let me not live in vain'.[41]

The news of the Duchess's flight was picked up with glee by every gossip and letter writer in Britain, many of whom had long had severe doubts about the validity of her marriage to the Duke. Horace Walpole joked about her becoming a nun, and Mrs Delany and Lord Bruce both had something to say about the matter. Even the Queen herself, as Lady Mary Coke was thrilled to be able to report, 'said that things always came out at last, & did not seem sorry, as I thought, that all that infamy was brought to light'.[42] George Selwyn, though he was hardly a model of probity himself, called her 'execrable', and added happily, 'Nobody doubts of her felony . . . All expect some untimely death.'[43] There were rumours that the Duchess had bribed a man with £10,000 as hush money, who had promptly betrayed her for a bribe of the same amount from Evelyn Meadows.[44] The writer, however, had muddled the facts; it was Evelyn Meadows that the Duchess was trying to offer money to, as she later wrote: 'You well know I have incontestable proofs that You would have Accomadated the disputes between us . . . for ten thousand pounds.'[45]

Back in Calais, Elizabeth was bewailing her fate and complaining bitterly about the Meadows family to anyone who would listen, 'saying

* It is not entirely clear what Elizabeth meant by 'atacvement', though the handwriting, at least, seems unambiguous. It may be based on the French for 'vehement attack', or she may have meant 'attachment', as in 'writ of attachment', essentially a legal device to ensure that the defendant appeared to answer the charges against them on pain of forfeiting property.

how cruel it was of them to interrupt her peace of Mind', as the acid-tongued Lady Mary Coke complained, continuing nastily, 'If, with all her Crimes, her peace of mind is only disturb'd by the Meadows Family, 'tis extraordinary indeed.'[46] Elizabeth wrote again to the Duke of Portland: 'Mr Meadows has broke the bruised reed and nature yields to my great affliction; my life is all my enemys desire; for the affection I bear my friends I would fain be justified, and death will not than be terrible.'[47] She was feverishly busy from early morning till late at night, consulting lawyers, studying law books, writing letters until she was almost blind. Even if it should all come to nothing, her reputation would be damaged beyond repair, and not just in Britain. The European news sheets had all picked up on the story, and the scandalised talk stretched from Russia to Rome.

There was only one friend who could help her, one woman whose own standing in European society was beyond reproach. Elizabeth took up her pen and wrote to the Electress. 'My very dear friend, To spare me the distress of seeing the respected character of several of my friends ripped to pieces in the gazettes; I have been well advised never to read them, by that I have escaped seeing the malicious gossip being spread about me.'[48] Unfortunately, she had also missed reading about the Electress's recent accident, which had left her with a broken leg.* Elizabeth grieved for her friend, and was unhappy that her present circumstances prevented her from rushing to her side in Munich, where the Electress was visiting her brother, as she had done in 1766. With a well-judged amount of flattery, the Duchess wrote of the Pope's high regard for the Electress, before concluding: 'I know myself to be full of faults, but do not believe all the bad things said about me in the gazettes, I assure you I know how to defend myself, and the good Lord will not allow the envious and the wicked to destroy me.'[49]

If she were to defend herself successfully, however, she would need all her strength. Rome had had a tremendously restorative effect earlier in the year, so the Duchess made up her mind to stick to her proposal of once more spending the winter there. After all, Chancery cases could drag on for years. By early September she had started to make preparations for her departure. She apparently informed Mr

---

* She had been injured on a visit to the Elector Palatine at Mannheim, when the gallery of his new manege collapsed.

Jenkins, her banker and art dealer in Rome, that 'the Physicians advised her to quit England so speedily, but many say that she ought to have written Lawyers instead of Physicians'.[50] Then she wrote to the Duke of Portland to ask if he could do her the favour of sparing her some of his pineapples, for she had an opportunity to send some to the Pope and her own hot house had failed.[51] No doubt she also wrote to Cardinal Albani to see if his previous offer to lend her his fine villa – described by one Rome resident as 'rather in a brilliant than in an ancient taste'[52] – until she could buy somewhere for herself was still open.[53]

But at the end of September came dreadful news from Rome. Pope Clement XIV, who even in April had been in fragile health,[54] had taken to his bed on 10 September where he had died two weeks later. The newspapers, pointing the finger of blame at the Jesuits whose order the Pope had abolished in 1773, hinted at unnatural causes. It was said that the post-mortem showed signs of poisoning and that the Pope's chief food taster was ill with the same symptoms. Elizabeth, on the eve of her departure from Paris, realised at once how this would affect her plans for the future. Without her exalted friend and ally, Rome would no longer be such a congenial refuge. She shared her sad thoughts with the Electress in a letter from Dijon, dated 8 October, though her sorrow at the Pope's death was largely for its consequences for herself:

> Unhappy news! my bad luck continues; Since the death of my dear husband my country, & everything in it, have only added to my woes. The Duke's nephew's persecution, and all the malicious gossip that, thank God, I do not in the least deserve, has given me a feeling of distaste for everything in England; and I went away with the intention of buying the Villa Negroni, for which I was on the point of paying 60,000 ecus, and the favours his Holiness would have given me would have made this visit for six months every winter very enjoyable.[55]

Certainly, the Pope had apparently made her some valuable concessions: no import or export duty on her goods, no restrictions on what she could buy or sell, and permission for her ship to sail up to the last bridge over the Tiber without being inspected. No wonder she called his friendship 'a fortress against all my enemies'.[56] She was now inclined to settle permanently in France instead, and hoped the Electress would be able to send her a letter of introduction to that country's court. In the meantime, however, she was on her way to Rome as planned, with her servants and copious luggage travelling separately by sea in the *Minerva* – 'a shipload of plunder',[57] as someone called it.

She passed through Genoa towards the end of October, and headed on towards Florence where she kept her promise to the Electress and paused for a few days to pay her compliments to the Archduke and Archduchess. By 11 November she had reached Rome, where, the newspapers confidently predicted, she was to stay in a hotel for a while before moving into the Villa Albani on Porta Solara street.[58] She was in a defiant mood, determined to put her troubles behind her and enjoy what might be her last visit to Rome. Her health was more robust than on her first sojourn, and she was in a mood to entertain and be seen. A pilgrimage to the Holy Land which she had clearly talked of making was now given up.[59] Instead she began making preparations for two nights of receiving visits from the Roman ladies, helped by her friend La Marchese de los Balbases. On 8 and 9 December, 'The curious Romans visited her during two nights & she had forty soldiers about the avenues of her house to prevent desorderly people from giving any trouble, & to escort the Visitors up stairs. The soldiers had their bandoleers flung over their shoulders, & instead of muskets, had large wax torches in their hands.'[60] The Duchess was inadvertently providing entertainment for the Romans in other ways, too. Her black and white coach, its box decorated with white bear skin, was like something out of Carnival, an effect only increased by her servants' new mourning livery trimmed with silver which made them look 'like so many Pantalones'.[61] Here, the Romans felt, was someone extraordinary, who would provide them with far more to smile at and talk about than the usual dreary tourist on the culture trail or the Conclave's seemingly eternal quest for a new Pope.

They were right; there would soon be more, *much* more, to talk about. The day after the Duchess's reception, the English newspapers all carried the news that, even as the Roman ladies had been preparing to swish upstairs to meet the curious English Duchess, the Grand Jury for the County of Middlesex at Hicks's Hall had been considering a Bill of Indictment against 'a Lady, for felony, in marrying a late Nobleman, at the Time she was actually the Wife of another person'[62] and had decided there was a case to answer. Below was another short item: 'A celebrated Lady has disposed of all her moveable effects in this kingdom, with a design of ending her days on the Continent; on which account it is expected an outlawry will take place without opposition.' The Meadowses had struck a second and far more serious legal blow for, unless the Duchess took the hint offered by the second item and settled for voluntary banishment and the goods she had already taken abroad – which she was unlikely to agree to – she faced a humiliatingly public criminal trial at the Old Bailey. Her loyal agent at Thoresby wrote in agitation to Sir Richard Heron, one of the Duke's trustees:

> What a scene doth this event open to my mind? I can remember what you once hinted <u>might</u> be done, & could never get it out of my mind, tho' I tried to forget it. Alass the time is come! Good God! how will the Dtss bear the shock when she is first made acquainted with this criminal process? It will require more firmness and fortitude than she is mistress of, I fear, to support herself under the tumultuous passions this injurious Treatment will raise within her throbbing Breast. She can lay no blame but on herself. It has been all of her own seeking . . . This looks to me like the beginning of sorrows.[63]

An accusation of bigamy was, indeed, no laughing matter. As a felony, this particular crime, 'so great a violation of the public oeconomy and decency of a well ordered state',[64] had once been punishable under common law by hanging. In the reign of James I, however, it had been made a lesser felony, under what was called 'benefit of clergy'; the sentence was effectively reduced to transportation or imprisonment – which would have been of precious little consolation to the Duchess. Nor would her frantic reading of Blackstone's learned *Commentaries on the Laws of England* have provided her with much solace. There was, it is true, a glimmer of hope in the fact that where one of the parties to the first marriage was a minor at the time – as Hervey had been – the contract was, as Blackstone put it, 'voidable by the disagreement of either party'[65] and there would be no charge to answer. Unfortunately, by having a child together *after* Hervey had reached the age of consent of twenty-one, he and Elizabeth had implicitly completed their marriage contract. At any rate, even if this had not been the case, Elizabeth's cherished second marriage would still have been decreed void.

There was the Chancery case to deal with, too, which rumbled on. The Meadowses were clearly worried that Elizabeth might – before they could get their hands on it – sell or export all the personal estate, 'consisting principally of a great quantity of Gold & Silver Plate Jewills Magnificent furniture and valuable Pictures a Stud of very valuable High bred Horses a great number of Horses in training and Carriages of various Sorts a very Large and valuable live & Dead stock in and upon his parks and Farms in hand'.[66] On 14 December, they applied for an injunction 'to stop the Payment of a sum of money in the Hands of Mr Tattersall, from being paid to the Trustees of the Duchess of Kingston, which arose from the Sale of the late Duke's Horses, Dogs etc on the Ground of being an Executor by false Pretences, & being now indicted of Felony'. The Lord Chancellor was having none of it, however; according to the newspapers, he pointed out that the indictment had been issued not against the Duchess of Kingston but against Elizabeth Chudleigh, who did not exist. He ordered the money to be given to the Duke's trustees so they could pay the Duke's debts and funeral expenses.* The Meadows family had not had their way this time, but they had not finished with the Duchess yet.

* The indictment for bigamy was re-presented in January, omitting the name 'Elizabeth Chudleigh'.

CHAPTER 11

The Last Days of Rome

A Meteorological Diary of the Weather for Jan. 1775
3 . . . heavy, churlish, moist day.
The Gentleman's Magazine, January 1776

I t took time for the report of the Meadowses' second attack to reach Rome, and in the interim Elizabeth continued to live the life of a wealthy duchess dowager. She had found somewhere to live: the Palazzo Rufo, owned by a Neapolitan prelate of the same name, which she was furnishing with everything she had brought from England in the *Minerva*; this included a quantity of paintings that were swiftly adjudged to be just as bad as the ones she had bought in Rome on her previous visit. There were regrets, of course; there was still the Chancery case to be dealt with, although she had already managed to put off replying to the charges twice. Her husband's absence was a daily sorrow, and she spoke so often of her sadness at ˙ the death of her favourite Pope that the Roman wits joked that her coach and servants' liveries – still in their mourning colours – were for him and not for the man 'whom she calls her dear Duke, whose death is now at too great a distance, & was too profitable, to be mourned'.[1]

But the dreadful news from England could not be kept away for ever. Barely three weeks after the indictment – an astonishing speed, the courier can have hardly slept *en route* – Elizabeth learnt of this latest attack by the Meadows family. The agitated Duchess immediately dashed off a brief note to the Electress: 'My dear friend weep not for my misfortunes because I have not deserved them and I know how to bear them with a steadfastness equal to the malice of my enemies which is unfailing farewell continue with your friendship I will never dishonour it farewell I will be your faithful friend to the grave.'[2]

It was clear the Duchess would have to cut short her trip to Rome, and though she continued to protest her innocence – seemed, in fact, to believe in it – she also started thinking of ways to prevent it being put to the test. Her first thought was to apply to the King to stop the proceedings, though her advisers thought it unlikely to succeed for 'the Crown will not I fear think it prudent to interpose'.[3] As far as the lawyers were concerned that left her only two options: to stand trial and bear the consequences, or come to some arrangement with the Meadowses. 'Tho' I know this Measure will be very ungrateful to your Grace, I venture to advise it; The greatest Princes in Europe are obliged to pay for Peace, and there does not seem to me, the likelyhood of your Graces enjoying any without submitting to purchase it by a Treaty.'[4]

Alone in Rome, with no one to confide in – no one she could trust, at least – the Duchess struggled, and failed, to maintain her spirits. Even the power to impress seemed to have deserted her (though, in truth, it had always been more a power to provoke curiosity rather than admiration), for although huge crowds flocked to see her ship sail up the Tiber they returned disappointed, saying it was 'only a model, & . . . a pretty thing to put upon the Lake of Albano, & be a pleasure boat for the late Pope'.[5] Even the Roman ladies neglected her. The one person she *could* rely on, whose friendship she said was the only source of happiness she had left, was the Electress. In two long letters that forlorn early February she poured out her feelings: of gratitude for the affection the Electress still showed her in spite of everything; of loss for a husband who was so 'tender, faithful and worthy of being loved' and whom she would miss for the rest of her life; of resentment for the Duke's malicious relatives who, having failed to destroy his will, were now trying to destroy *her*. This latest case was the most barbarous imaginable, she told her tender-hearted friend, for if she did not return to answer the charges by the end of June she would be declared an outlaw and thereby automatically deemed guilty. 'The disgrace will pierce my soul. Alas! Can you believe that in a free country like ours, that the testimony of its lowest subjects, which can be bought for a louis d'or can summon a person from Rome to London.'[6]

Her misery was all too clear as she told the Electress that it was a journey she was dreading, because in winter it was dangerous by sea and almost impossible by land, and would probably kill her. This was an exaggeration, although not much of one, for parts of the journey could be more than usually difficult. The roads in Italy were poor, and there were none at all across the Alps, so overland travellers had to be carried in a chair along a perilously narrow track through the passes at Mount Cenis or Brenner; heavy snow did not make the crossing any easier. Storms and Barbary pirates from the north coast of Africa caused serious problems for those who preferred to travel between Italy and southern France by boat. The trip was only part of Elizabeth's worries, however, as she told the Electress. She was, she wailed, all alone in the world: no father, mother, brother, sister or beloved husband. Her only hope was that the King might intervene to stop the trial but, if she asked him – and here she hinted as much as she dared – it might look as if she feared its consequences. By the second letter a week later, however, desperation had got the better of discretion, and she appealed directly to the Electress for her to petition the King on her behalf, and to ask her brother, son and the Holy Roman Emperor to do the same. 'Consider dear friend, that although it is a lot to do, it is for a cherished friend, who would give her last drop of blood for you; it would be a sign to everyone of the strength of your friendship and the nobility of your sentiments.'[7] The only proviso was that it should be made to look as if it was the Electress's own idea, one that her friend had no inkling of; just as importantly, therefore, the plan had to be kept secret.

All she could do now was wait to see if the Electress would agree with her suggestion, and to make preparations for her departure from Rome. But even here there were difficulties, for the Court of Chancery had issued an order to prevent her from receiving any more money from the Duke's personal estate until she answered the original complaint.[8] As a result of this and the Duchess's rampant spending – nearly £5,000 left her account in a month – the panicking Mr Hoare had cut off her supply of money and she was 'reduced to sell my trinkets & jewells in a City where I was treated like a Sovereign to get a way with credit'.[9] For this, Mr Hoare was never forgiven; as soon as she could Elizabeth closed her account with him and returned to Drummonds, her bankers before her marriage to the Duke of Kingston. Far racier versions of her financial dealings spread, though, for it was said that having gone to her Roman banker's house on several occasions to retrieve various valuables as well as money and found him either out or deliberately avoiding her, she had resorted to waiting at his door armed with the two pistols she kept to protect her jewels, which did wonders to make him more open-handed.

With her finances on a slightly better footing for now, she could make her final preparations to leave Rome and face her fate. Her jewels – which she had apparently used as security for a loan and *not*, in fact, had to sell – and furniture at Rome were left under the immediate protection of the Pope, whoever he might turn out to be, to be released only by an order signed by her and witnessed by a lawyer.[10] She penned a few last letters; one to the Electress, to let her know how happy she was at the thought of seeing her friend briefly in Munich on her way north and to pass on the news that the Conclave had finally elected a new Pope. Another, longer missive, nearly as melodramatic as the ones she had written to the Electress, went to one of her advisers, Richard Heron:

> I am armed for every evil that can befall me in this transitory passage to a better world, one of two things will be my fate God will fight my Cause protect my inocence & I shall not need to fear a host of foes, or he will with great mercy give me strength to bear this Load of afflictions he suffers to be lay'd upon me –
>
> I will stand Tryal & you shall never blush for me tho' humanity will sigh for my distress, & if I am Conquor'd the Victor will be ashamed I recommend delay because my iron Constitution gives way & I can not travel fast The country is Cover'd with snow & the post makes long delays I have asthma even in this fine clime, as I drew near to France last year I could not lay down in my Bed a Rhumatis attacks my Right side and a threaten'd palsy on my left side such numness as terrifies the imagination of those that so lately has had the dismal object befor the sight my two women in there Beds borth light Headed one with an appoplectick fitt the other Cover'd with St Antonys fire.[11]

Delay was impossible, however. The Duchess discovered that it was vital that she met her lawyers in Paris on 26 March, in order to respond at last to the Meadowses' Chancery bill of complaint. It meant giving up her visit to the Electress, 'the only expectation I had of passing one day happily before arriving in my own country',[12] for the detour via Munich would add five days to her journey. She travelled as fast as possible, though the roads between Rome and Florence were so bad that an abscess in her side burst and, in agony, she had to be carried in a litter from Florence to Bologna.[13] Despite this, she made reasonably good time, and by 22 March she had reached Paris, where someone noted that she was 'so melancholy she cannot bear the sight of anybody'.[14] Her lawyers were not there, so after two days' rest – for, as she told the Electress, she was 'fatigué a Mourir'[15] – she set off for Calais. Her legal advisers were not there yet, either. All that frantic hurry on the road had been for nothing, except to make her even more ill.

There was, however, one good piece of news, for the Duchess at least. Two days before her arrival in Paris, Hervey's older brother George had died at Bath, four months after suffering a stroke that had had 'taken away the use of all his limbs'[16] and affected his speech. Augustus was now the Earl of Bristol, so that whatever happened Elizabeth was definitely a peeress. But in her weakened, depressed state, she continued to worry about her fate, unaware that her now indisputable rank could provide her with privileges such as being allowed bail. That was why she hovered at Calais, unwilling to venture across the Channel until she was completely sure it was safe to do so, convinced she would be thrown in jail the moment she set foot on English soil.

For Elizabeth – still protesting her innocence – had finally resigned herself to standing trial, especially as the Electress had given her opinion that an application to the King for a pardon from any quarter was unwise. Her hope was now to be tried by the House of Peers. 'I must not be afraid for I am not in the wrong but I have been led to believe that the great men of the Ecclesiastical law and those of the other laws are at odds and that the latter are determined that they shall be the ones to have jurisdiction over all disputes. . . and as they are the stronger I may be the sacrifice.'[17] She was buoyed up, however, by support from an unlikely quarter, for apparently she had received a flattering note from Frederick the Great of all people, whom she had met briefly on her travels in Germany, and to whom she had once sent a present of an English plough about which he wrote a flattering poem.[18]

Her time was devoted almost entirely to legal matters. In the middle of April, three weeks late, the Duchess's lawyers reached Calais and she was able to reply in writing to the charge that Philip Meadows and his wife had put before Chancery the previous May. With that pressing task out of the way, her attention turned to the criminal proceedings and in finding people willing to stand bail for her. Here there were a few disappointments: the Duke of Rutland, her neighbour in Knightsbridge and old friend of her late husband, refused,[19] and the Duke of Portland dragged his heels so much that, doubtless to his relief, she had already found someone else by the time he replied.[20] Fortunately the kindly Duke of Newcastle, along with Lord Mountstuart who was Lord Bute's handsome oldest son, Mr Laroche, an old friend of her late husband, and Sir Thomas Clarges, Baronet, was more enthusiastic about standing bail.

With her health improved, and her fears of being flung in prison allayed, the Duchess began to recover her spirits. Though she might have to stand trial, she was 'arm'd with inocence',[21] as she told that Duke of Portland whose 'many professions of friendship' had yet to translate into more concrete support. Her legal worries no longer preoccupied her, and she turned her attention to other matters such as sending to Thoresby for venison and pineapples, as well as 'a Draft of the Barge that stands in the Boat House the one that is most fit – Her Grace thinks there is one that is better than that which belongs to Her Ship now in the Medetiranean'.[22] The faithful *Minerva*, about which the Romans had been so disparaging, was obviously in danger of being replaced with something grander.

This moment of relative calm was about to come to an abrupt end, however. 'I leave for my own country at midnight on 17 May,' Elizabeth scribbled to the Electress. 'I only received the news four hours ago that I have to be in England in two days.'[23] Unfortunately, the elements were against her. She was held up for nearly thirty-six anxious hours by stormy seas and contrary winds, and when she set sail at last conditions were still so rough that it had taken 120 men to haul her vessel safely out of the harbour. She eventually arrived in London early on the morning of 20 May 'after a Dangerous and fatigueing Passage from Callais to Dover'.[24] The fact was briefly noted by the press among lengthier reports: a recent duel; the death of the King's sister, the Queen of Denmark; and a masquerade at the 'winter Ranelagh', the Pantheon,* with the dome of its fabulous rotunda

* Opened in January 1772 in Oxford Street; demolished in the 1930s.

decorated with silver lamps to look like a starlit sky, and under it two thousand of the dullest people in fancy dress – which included a remarkable number of nuns' habits, invariably worn by those beauties with the most tarnished reputations.

As the Duchess had waited nervously in Calais for the wind to change, the process had begun to transfer her indictment for bigamy from the Middlesex Sessions at Hick's Hall to the higher Court of King's Bench, the highest common law court in England and Wales.* Accordingly, four days after her arrival, in weather so unseasonably warm that gardeners were complaining of a plague of caterpillars that threatened 'the total destruction of the leaves of the gooseberry and currant bushes',[25] the Duchess made her way to the Duke of Newcastle's house, which backed on to Westminster Hall. The law courts had been housed in the venerable old Hall, part of the old Palace of Westminster, since the thirteenth century, and five hundred years later the building continued to bustle with lawyers, witnesses – many of them, it was said, for hire – and bystanders. When the legal business became tedious, there was even the diversion of a spot of shopping at the stalls along the walls, which sold books, toys and prints among much else.

After a few preliminaries, the judge, Lord Mansfield, asked for the Duchess and the men standing bail for her to be called in. To the delight of a packed court, her Grace – looking well but 'somewhat thinner than she was before she left England'[26] and not in the least embarrassed or terrified – emerged from the ante-chamber, attended by the Duke of Newcastle, Lord Mountstuart, Mr Laroche and Sir Thomas Clarges. She was received with great respect and, in a change to the usual procedures, invited to sit down between Mr Justice Aston and the Duke of Newcastle. The indictment was read by the Sheriff of Middlesex, and the Duchess pledged the sum of £8,000 – half from her and £1,000 each from her four supporters – to appear in person to answer the charge when called upon by the King and her peers. That done, 'Her Grace then, in a very polite manner, took leave of

---

* According to Blackstone's *Commentaries*, there were various reasons for such a transfer to the superior court: to plead the King's pardon there, to consider the validity of indictments and quash or confirm them, or where the defendant was abroad and the lower court felt to have insufficient powers to force them to return to face the charges.

the court, and retired.'[27] It was all over in ten minutes. The world could now turn its attention back to other matters, such as mourning the Queen of Denmark, or the great cricket match at the Artillery Ground in London.

Not surprisingly, the Duchess's attention remained fixed firmly on her own concerns. Despite knowing how it had been achieved, she continued to put her faith in the ecclesiastical court's judgement, a translation of which she had already sent to the Electress. 'It is impossible for any other Court to try me after the sentence passed in the Ecclesiastic Court',[28] Elizabeth reassured her friend, a belief that received a boost the following month when the Court of Chancery accepted that same sentence in their own proceedings and found in her favour in the case brought against her by Lady Frances Meadows regarding the Duke of Kingston's will.[29] Though it was barely noted by the newspapers, it was far more significant for Elizabeth than the mere formality of her appearance before the Court of King's Bench. If the church court decision held firm in a civil court, after all, it seemed certain the same would be true in the criminal courts. The tide seemed to have turned at last. Relieved and happy, the Duchess wrote at once to the Electress.

My dear friend! It is with the greatest pleasure that I tell you the news that I have obtained complete victory, over my enemies. On Tuesday 27 at around ten o'clock, in the morning, my cause came on before the Supreme Court of Chancery. The following day every ruse imaginable, that the quibblers could think up, was used against me. Nevertheless, the Court strongly and obviously convinced of my innocence, decided in my favour. This Decree pronounced by the Lord Chancellor is so complete and so decisive: that I find myself out of Danger from the Malice of my enemies, from now on. Added to this Decree which confirms me in possession of my goods: which, in truth, is a lesser object, for a well-meaning soul. There is another Consideration which is: that by this Solemn and public Declaration, my honour . . . and my innocence are affirmed.[30]

If it seemed that one humiliation would be avoided, another was about to appear from a totally unexpected quarter. Samuel Foote – and the singular surname was apt, for he had only one leg, as well –

had made a living for years by writing and acting parodies of the great and the good which frequently landed him in legal trouble. He now turned his satirical pen upon the Duchess, writing a play called *A Trip to Calais*, which he planned to put on that summer. However the Lord Chamberlain, Lord Hertford, refused to licence the piece, a decision praised with spirit in the press by a succession of the Duchess's supporters. Foote, angry and determined to 'bully 'Em into a License',[31] as fellow thespian David Garrick put it, wrote a public reply to Lord Hertford, printed in all the papers early that August. In it he talked of how Lord Mountstuart had come to see him and had taken a copy of the play to the Duchess. 'Her Grace saw the play, and, in consequence, I saw her Grace. . . Her Grace could not discern', wrote Foote disingenuously, 'a single trait in the character of Lady Kitty Crocodile, that resembled herself.'[32] This was highly unlikely, given cruelly pointed lines that referred among many things to Iphigenia, a Lent wedding, her husband's recent death, and her attachment to mourning clothes, 'and no wonder, for it is a dress vastly becoming, especially to people inclined to be fat'.[33] However, the Duchess had certainly refused to fall for Foote's ruse of asking her to mark those passages which she felt applied to her own situation. She had also refused to comply with Foote's suggestion that, to compensate him for the loss of revenue the play's suppression would cause, the Duchess might like to offer him a small recompense of £2,000 – though Foote maintained she was the one who had tried to bribe *him*.

Foote's public letter produced a flurry of responses from anonymous members of the Duchess's camp. 'Verus' accused him of betraying 'that malicious revenge which generally attends a vain, an indolent, and a disappointed man. . . You have drawn Kitty Crocodile . . . as a very infamous person; and though there is nothing in the character like the Duchess of Kingston, yet you have given the former situations similar enough to force the audience to apply the character to her Grace.'[34] 'A Friend to Justice' joined the fray, expressing it as 'a matter of surprize that a man so susceptable of injuries as Mr Foote, should, with the hand of profusion deal them to others',[35] and accusing him of trying to prejudice the Duchess's legal case.

Foote's riposte was deadly and humiliatingly public, for he wrote to the Duchess herself and then sent his own letter and her reply to the newspapers. His announcement that he intended to publish *A*

Trip to Calais, the public learnt, had earned him a visit from the Duke of Newcastle, who explained to him 'what I did not conceive, that the publication of the scenes in "A Trip to Calais" at this juncture, with the dedication and preface, might be of infinite ill-consequence to your affairs'.³⁶ Of course, he intended no harm to the Duchess and would not publish the play, 'upon condition of her putting an end to the attacks which at her instigation, he says, have been made upon him in the papers; intimating that she had made pecuniary offers to him which had been rejected'.³⁷ Impetuous to a fault and clearly extremely angry, the Duchess replied at once, though it would have been more dignified and a great deal more discreet, given her rank and gender, to have allowed others to deal publicly with Foote on her behalf. It was a bad letter, pompous and a little ridiculous, for she called Foote a 'subservient vassal', declared that she 'scorn[ed] to be bullied into a purchase of your silence' and described herself as being 'cloathed in my innocence like a coat of mail'.³⁸ It made her look a fool in the eyes of the public, and a vulgar one at that.

A witty but savage answer from Foote only sank the Duchess's fame lower. 'I can't help thinking but it would have been prudent in Your Grace to have answered my letter before dinner',³⁹ he wrote a few days later, insinuating she had been drunk when she wrote it. 'Instead of begging relief from your charity, I rejected your splendid offers to suppress the "Trip to Calais" with the contempt they deserved . . . I am happy, Madam, however, to hear that your robe of innocence is in such perfect repair. I was afraid it might have been a little the worse for the wearing; may it hold out to keep you warm this coming winter.'

'Foote has thrown the Duchess on her back', wrote Garrick, 'and there has left her, as you or I would do – She is Sick & has given up the Cause, & has made herself very ridiculous, & hurt herself much in the struggle.'⁴⁰ Even the printing of an affidavit from the Duchess's chaplain Mr Foster, that the playwright had indeed offered to suppress the play for £2,000, could not prevent her ending up the loser in this ill-judged paper war. Whether through fear or pride she had allowed herself to be drawn into an undignified public slanging match. Walpole, not in the least surprised by this act of folly, wrote to friends: 'The Pope will not be able to wash out the spots with all the holy water in the Tiber. I imagine she will escape a trial – but Foote has given her the *coup de grâce*.'⁴¹ Not for the first time in her life,

Elizabeth's impulsiveness had led her astray, for on reflection she fully understood how much harm she had done her fragile reputation by descending to a public battle with Foote. Months later, a country squire who met her on the road from Thoresby to Grantham, and spoke of the episode with her travelling companions, was advised, 'Pray no mention such matter to her Grace, her Grace no bear hear of it.'[42] It had ruined her summer, and now other matters were brewing to make it a difficult autumn, too.

CHAPTER 12

Approaching Doom

Dame fortune to me's been unkind,
From good to bad is ranging,
By death's most fatal dart I find,
She's like the weather changing.

Ballad

The Chancery case might have been dealt with, but there remained the criminal charge of bigamy to answer. Elizabeth pinned her hopes on having this heard by the House of Lords, where her rank would protect her from the harsher punishments of the law, such as transportation or imprisonment. In early November she asked to have the indictment transferred there from the Court of King's Bench. 'I have sent the Petition to the Chancellor', she informed the Duke of Portland, 'but should it be necessary to be moved by any other Peer, I entreat that Favour from your Grace.'[1] Fortunately, Portland's help was unnecessary; Mansfield, her unfailing supporter, did as he was asked. Her petition was duly presented to the Lords but, as Walpole noted, 'they seem neither eager to acquit or condemn her. Nobody would mind the first, and she would not mind the second, as it would go only to infamy, which she has shown she can digest.'[2]

Unfortunately, the Lords seemed to have little choice in the matter. When the Meadowses' counsel Mr Elbro Woodcock was interviewed in the House a fortnight later, he made it clear that, despite the rulings of the ecclesiastical court and of Chancery, the family intended to pursue the prosecution. Lord Mansfield, however, argued against trying the case, for it 'was instituted, not really at the suit of the Crown; it was the prosecution of private individuals . . . It was simply before their Lordships as a matter, although of a criminal complexion, yet entirely of a civil nature. It was connected with other disputes about property. The indictment was to be pursued in defiance of the sentence obtained in the ecclesiastical court, which sentence to this house remained in full force.'[3] There were other considerations, too. Even if she were tried and convicted, the Meadowses were no more likely as a result to succeed in overturning the late Duke's will. Neither would any conviction act as a deterrent to the general public, because as a peeress she would escape punishment entirely: 'She makes your Lordships a curtsey, and you return the compliment with a bow.' Many of the other Lords were not of the same opinion, and the trial was fixed for 18 December.

Even before the date had been set, the strain was beginning to tell on the Duchess. In November, one of her household was writing to the Duke of Portland that she 'has been and still is verry ill in a fever and inflamation in her bowells is wore allmost to death with sorrow & fatigue'.[4] Early in December, as it began to be whispered that the ecclesiastical court's verdict might *not* be final after all, she was taken ill during a service at the Chapel Royal in St James's, 'seized with a fainting . . . and carried home speechless'.[5] She had depended on the trial being called off – and there was still talk of a *nolle prosequi** – but now it seemed that she had hoped in vain.

While all London was diverted by another trial, that of a Mrs Rudd – 'a woman of spirit, sense, and intrigue'[6] – for forgery at the Old Bailey on 8 December, of which she was sensationally cleared, the Lords started to discuss arrangements for the trial, anything from the seating to whether the Duchess should be imprisoned in the Tower for its duration. It was not the kind of suggestion likely to improve her state of mind, so it was hardly surprising that a few days later Elizabeth petitioned to have the trial postponed for two months on the grounds that for several days she had been 'confined to her Bed by a very severe Illness; and her Physicians are of Opinion it is impossible she can be able to appear before their Lordships, and take her Trial at the Time appointed'.[7] Her spirits, as well as her health, were now at a low ebb. In desperation, she resorted to a course of action

---

* Literally, 'refuse to pursue'; formal notice by the prosecution that they intend to give up the case.

that both the Electress and her legal advisers had counselled against; she wrote to the King to ask him to stop the proceedings:

> I am, my Lord, by this malicious prosecution detained in England at the hazard of my life. My memory is so impaired with want of rest, sorrow, and sickness that I am not capable of even recapitulating half the sorrow I daily experience . . . Our Lord Chief Justice, in the House of Lords, has publicly declared that the law stands in my favour; and as he is the greatest judge and the ablest lawyer that this country ever boasted of, His Majesty is justified to all nations in not suffering an unhappy woman to die under persecutions when the prosecutors can only be benefited in gratifying an inveterate malice . . . Your feeling heart, I flatter myself, will enforce my plea, considering how every woman in every station who has the misfortune to survive a good husband stands exposed, and my fate may be that of every individual's wife or daughter . . . His Majesty . . . will not surely now suffer a peeress to be disgraced with a trial, and break the heart of a most faithful and loyal subject, when every mouth will speak his praise for having rescued me from the hands of my enemies without doing an injury to any mortal. Be persuaded, my Lord, that I will not dishonour your friendship, for good actions are the best contradiction to bad words.[8]

His Majesty, however, clearly thought it wiser not to intervene at this stage, perhaps because such favouritism might play badly to the general public at a time when the money they contributed in taxes was needed for the costly war in America. The trial would not be called off for the moment. It could, however, be delayed. The Duchess's three physicians were summoned to the House, and explained that their patient was 'in a bad State of Health . . . her Memory is disordered . . . her Illness is in consequence of a Fit of a Paralytic Kind . . . and a Debility of the Nervous System, whereby her Faculties are impaired and her Memory'.[9] The proceedings were put off until 24 January, which had the benefit of also giving the Lords longer to make necessary arrangements. There was still plenty to decide, including where the trial should be held. Lord Mansfield continued to maintain that it ought to take place privately in the Lords' chamber, but others thought a public spectacle in Westminster Hall more fitting for, as one peer put it, 'I am far from thinking the offence so trivial, or the consequences so uninteresting, as his Lordship has been pleased to represent them. I think the offence an offence of the most atrocious nature, immediately tending to dissolve the great bonds of civil society; and, in my opinion, a crime of the blackest dye; for I know of none that exceeds it in guilt.'[10] He was far from alone in his view. More prosaically, however, the Lords' chamber was simply too small for the task. Visitors described, with some surprise, how narrow it was, and how poorly it compared in 'grandeur and magnificence'[11] even with Ranelagh. Worse, there was not enough seating, so that when all the Lords were in attendance many were forced to stand and the King faced an undignified struggle through the crowd of disgruntled aristocrats to reach his throne.

The Duchess was appalled by the prospect of the proceedings being moved from the confines of the Lords' White Chamber in Parliament to the vastness of Westminster Hall. 'I have no fear from my cause', she explained to the Duke of Portland in a lucid moment, 'but surely you would not have your friend and the widow of your relation a publick spectacle . . .'[12] This was precisely what she had been trying to avoid in having the case transferred to the Lords from the Court of King's Bench in the first place. Even now, there was far too much publicity over her case, including the press reports of the Lords' debates in which she was 'condemned unheard' and 'insinuations made of farther accusations to embitter and aggravate the opinions of my judges'. Every half-remembered piece of unlikely gossip about the former Maid of Honour was excavated and embellished, and many found their way into the newspapers. 'There is hardly a crime upon earth for which she may not be tried,'[13] wrote George Selwyn smugly; certainly, there were very few of which she was not accused in the tittle-tattle of that winter. The moral high ground was becoming an extremely crowded place.

More ominously, the tide of events in the Lords was also turning against the Duchess. Despite Lord Mansfield's arguments against it, the trial was moved to Westminster Hall. Instead of just the peers, there would be an audience of thousands to follow the courtroom drama. The only silver lining for Elizabeth was that preparations for such a large event would take longer than for a private hearing; on 20 December the trial was accordingly postponed again, this time to 28 February. Two days later, the Duchess's last real hope of a permanent reprieve was dashed; her petition to the King for a *nolle prosequi* was argued before the Attorney-General Thurlow in his chambers by the fourteen lawyers she had appointed and turned down by him, on the grounds he did not have authority to override penal laws.[14] She was not the only person to see no way out of the 'terrible labyrinth'[15] she was in.

The new year started as 1775 had ended, with a committee of peers busily working out all the necessary arrangements for a Westminster Hall spectacle. Not everything here went to plan. Towards the end of January, they interviewed Mr Shakespear, master carpenter to the Board of Works, who in the time-honoured fashion of builders everywhere informed them 'that the fitting up Westmenser Hall for the Trial of Elizabeth calling herself Duchess Dowager of Kingston, will take up Five Weeks, or Thirty compleat working Days, and that they cannot undertake to do it in less Time at this Season of the Year'.[16] The trial was delayed again, this time to 15 April, but it could not be put off for ever. All the same, the Duchess's friends made one final attempt to get the Lords to drop the charges against their fellow peeress. At the end of February, the Earl of Hillsborough put it to the House that there were real doubts as to whether they were legally competent to try the case. He added that 'he saw no other effect that the trial would produce but a public *spectacle*, which every body seemed now-a-days to be particularly fond of'.[17] Moreover,

> the noble Lord could not forebear mentioning, . . . it appeared to him a measure calculated to answer a vindictive purpose. The Jury who had found the bill were men of as unpleasant a cast as the refuse of human nature could produce. Many years had elapsed since the commission of the supposed offence; during these years the marriage of the unhappy Lady with the Duke of Kingston, had been notorious; her title had been formally recognised; her rank universally admitted: Why therefore had the commission of this offence been connived at for so long a time? Why was it now arraigned, unless to answer some latent purpose?[18]

It was a brave attempt of Lord Hillsborough's, and much of what he said was true, but sadly his last-ditch effort was unsuccessful.

The question of where the noble prisoner should be held during the trial now reared its ugly head again, and once more the Tower was mentioned as a suitable place of confinement. Perturbed, Elizabeth wrote to the Duke of Portland for his support as 'this intended motion to put the Dutchess under the care of the Constable of the Tower and to be ordered a few days before the trial to appear at the House seems to be intended only as a mortification and persecution and which in the bad state of health the Dutchess is in the changing her house and going by the water side will very probably kill her'.[19] Even the newspapers teased her that 'an apartment in the Tower is fitting up in a very splendid and elegant stile fit for the reception of a Lady',[20] which provoked more anxious notes to Portland. The issue was only resolved two days before the trial itself, when after a debate in which Lord Cathcart had 'urged the cruelty of rendering that offence capital in its consequence, which was not so in its nature, by committing a person to the Tower in so infirm and ill a state as the Dutchess was at present'[21] it was agreed she should be allowed to return home at the end of each day in the custody of Black Rod – a form of house arrest.

Meanwhile, a battle had been in progress for months in the news sheets between the supporters and foes of the Duchess. Naturally, there were earnest debates on the letters pages on points of law and other aspects of the case. In addition the Meadows camp planted stories designed specifically to frighten her, such as the Tower one just quoted. They were helped by the fact that the outbreak of war in America had made transportation of convicted criminals impossible, so that the anxious Duchess was likely to stumble across unsettling reports such as the one that 'a regulation respecting the punishment of felons within the benefit of clergy, is to be the most early attention of the next meeting of parliament. A number of modes are already adopted, among which 'tis said, that working in the Lead Mines is to be applied to the most atrocious cases.'[22] Other items were more wittily sympathetic to the Duchess's cause, one declaring that the female 'Members of the Coterie . . . insist, that one Husband is Punishment enough in all Conscience, and that it is the Height of Cruelty to add to the Misery of her who is under the Misfortune of having two . . .'[23] Much was made, too, of the Duchess's generous £50 donation in March to the newly established fund for the relief of the clergy in North America.[24]

With so much advance publicity, it was hardly surprising that the scramble for tickets should be so intense. The peers had each been

granted seven for every day of the proceedings, and as 15 April drew
near every delivery of post brought letters from friends, neighbours
and acquaintances asking the favour of one of the coveted pieces of
paper.[25] To add to the mounting excitement, the seating for the spectators in Westminster Hall was finished by the start of April, and
enormous crowds of people flocked to see the splendid structure with
its lining of crimson baize. According to the *Daily Advertiser*, the
Hall's lucky overseer 'who had the power of opening the different
doors' collected more than £500 in fees from visitors in one week.[26]
However, they assured their readers, the Duchess herself had not
been among the crowds: 'This like many other reports to her Grace's
Disadvantage, was maliciously propagated by her Enemies.'[27]

Those of the Duchess's friends and acquaintances who had been
summoned as witnesses against her were understandably much less
enthusiastic about the approaching hearing. Lord Barrington had
received one of the dreaded letters from the Meadowses' counsel Elbro
Woodcock, who was 'convinced that it is in your Lordships power to
give most material evidence in support of the prosecution',[28] and
requesting his presence on the opening day of the trial. Barrington, to
whom 'Miss Chudleigh' had confided many secrets in the past, was
loath to betray her confidences. His first reaction, apart from staying
out of London for the present, was to see if there were any grounds
on which he could avoid complying with Woodcock's request. Another
potential witness went to much further lengths, and distances, to escape
the summons. To the scandal of his home town of Winchester, 'Our
Chief Magistrate of the City the Mayor is absconded and gone to
France in order that he sho[d] not be summons'd to give Evidence ag[t]
the Dutchess of Kingston it is supposed he is Bribed high upon the
occasion'.[29] Yet the evening before Mayor James Spearing had left, his
doctors had sworn his health was too bad for him to travel up to London
to draw the Lottery, of which he was a Commissioner. Spearing was
important for he had, in 1759, been the lawyer in whose presence the
register for Lainston chapel, with the entry regarding the marriage of
Elizabeth Chudleigh and Augustus John Hervey, had been created.
Another potential and reluctant witness was the Reverend Mr Cotton,
'who was in London last week for the Dutchess but as his Evidence
wo[d] be prejudicial he return'd to the Country and since has been served
wth an Order on behalf of the Medows's he was always very intimate
with the Dutchess and is now a very Violent friend'.[30]

Though Lord Barrington, Spearing and the Reverend Cotton might be able to avoid taking the stand in Westminster Hall, for the Duchess there was no such escape. Resigned to her fate, she wrote once more to the Electress.

There are only four days until the beginning of the Trial. How it will be resolved, only God knows. As for me, I have come to terms with it. In Philosophy I have all the resources that I could hope for in this Life. I risked dear friend a tedious journey in a thankless season, overwhelmed with grief and given up by the Doctors, I crossed the sea in a Tempest; for twelve hours, we thought we would be shipwrecked. I risked everything for my honour and if I lose my Case there is no Law or Justice in any Country. My Enemies, who have gone through all their Fortune want to make good their loss with mine, but I cannot believe that the Laws are entitled to allow my marriage with the Duke and then take away from me my Fortune, my honour and everything that is most dear to me in the world. False Witnesses in this Country have brought about everything and my adversaries have neither honour nor Fortune.[31]

Two days before the trial, the tickets were available for collection from either the Prince's Chamber or the Lord Great Chamberlain's house in Berkeley Square. Though the *Morning Post* might describe them as 'meaner than those generally delivered for a puppet-show',[32] those lucky enough to lay their hands on one could congratulate themselves. The trial of a peer, let alone a peeress, was a rare event; the two most recent had been that of Earl Ferrars in 1760, who was hanged for murdering his steward, and Lord Byron in 1765, who had killed a friend in a drunken duel but was found guilty only of manslaughter and escaped punishment entirely. Such an occasion was definitely not to be missed.

The day after, the Duchess 'attended divine service at the Chapel-royal, St. James's, and received the sacrament'.[33] While all of London – those going to Westminster Hall, anyway – fussed and fretted over what they were going to wear tomorrow, the Duchess offered up her prayers to the God who was now her only hope of escaping the earthly judgement day that awaited her the following morning.

CHAPTER 13

Trial By Her Peers

They as a felon would me try,
Or enter an outlawry,
I in my native land can't die,
Which makes me very sorry.

Ballad

It had been one of the main topics of conversation for months and now, despite all the Duchess's desperate attempts to put it off, the day of her trial[1] had finally arrived. By eight o'clock on the morning of Monday 15 April, the judges and some of the nobility and gentry began to gather at the Lord High Steward's house in Great Russell Street, 'where an elegant Breakfast was provided for them; his Lordship's Attendants breakfasting on cold Tongue, &c. with choice of rich Wines'.[2] At the same hour, on the other side of London, the Duchess of Kingston was climbing into her chair for the half-hour journey from Knightsbridge to the Duke of Newcastle's house adjoining Westminster Hall. She was dressed simply, in a plain black silk polonaise – a dress with a ruched overskirt, like an Austrian blind – trimmed with black flowers, and a black hood over her unpowdered hair.[3]

Shortly after nine, the Lord High Steward set out for Westminster, with all the pomp and circumstance that could be mustered: 'five new Carriages, four painted green, and the fifth white, with the Arms of the Family of Bathurst, and the Motto, "Tien ta Foy"; all the Coachmen and Footmen having new Liveries. Next followed the State Coach in which was the Lord High Steward.'[4] It was, the newspapers agreed, a marvellously grand and solemn occasion; it was also a terrific crush. The crowds along the route and around Westminster had been growing all morning, even though the sky was heavy with clouds which threatened rain, and it took a regiment of foot guards and two of cavalry to keep them under control. In the pressing mass of humanity one unfortunate man was pushed forward by the crowds and fell under the wheels of a cart, which crushed his skull. The jostle was not confined to the ground; every window with a view of the procession had been rented out for as much as a guinea,[5] so there seemed to be eager faces everywhere.

Those privileged souls with tickets for the proceedings had been at the entrance of Westminster Hall in all their finery well before the Duchess had left Kingston House, determined to obtain the best seats they could. As soon as the doors opened at eight, a bustling, chattering flood of people poured into the vast, ancient building, clambering noisily on to the dizzying tiers of crimson baize where they were to sit. Most, especially the women, had been up for hours, assuming that they had managed to sleep at all the night before, for everyone was anxious to look their very best on such an occasion.

Their efforts, and those of London's harried hairdressers and maids, were not in vain, as the newspapers were quick to note. 'The ladies seemed to outvie each other in the richness of their dresses and the brilliancy of their ornaments',[6] commented the *Gazetteer and New Daily Advertiser*, and it was widely reported that the value of the jewels they wore exceeded four million pounds. An impressed James Boswell 'did not think there had been so many fine women in the Universe'.[7] In one area, however, the ladies had been made to sacrifice fashion to practical concerns; strict instructions had been issued banning feathers and other such ornaments for fear that these additions to the towering hairstyles so in vogue would obstruct the view of people behind. These were obviously not scrupulously observed, for Boswell 'thought the mode of dressing, with a deal of hair and feathers and flowers of various colours, more beautiful than what I had ever seen before'.

The occupants of the Hall – up to 4,000 of them according to the papers – had plenty of time to drink in the magnificence and glitter. The Lords were delayed in their chamber by one final debate on whether they could go ahead with trying the Duchess, given that she had been indicted in the name of 'Elizabeth, wife of Augustus John Hervey'[8] and was thus implicitly deemed guilty in advance. The audience began to grow restless, fidgeting on their hard seats. Two women, hearing a noise that they thought announced the arrival of the peers at last, went to the edge of their gallery for a better view. Unluckily for them, there was a crucial floorboard missing. One of the unfortunate women tumbled right through the gap and, as the *Morning Chronicle* solemnly noted, ended up with 'her bare bum squatted on a gentleman's head'.⁹ As she fell, her heel grazed the cheek of the fashionable lady below her and collided with her towering headdress, 'dissipating the mock grass, flowers, fruits; uncasing the wool; and, by a separation of the several component parts, shewing to every beholder the simple and absurd materials which had helped to support the fabric'. As for the other woman, 'she harmed no one but herself', for she became wedged in the gap and hung there, legs dangling, revealing considerably more of her lower half to the public gaze than she would have wished.

But at last, just after ten, having settled everything to their satisfaction, the Lords emerged in their long ample red robes, edged with ermine and trimmed from shoulder to elbow with bands of gold and more ermine,¹⁰ to add the finishing touches to a scene that the *Morning Post* described as 'one of the most splendid and at the same time awful that fancy could design'.¹¹ The sole person missing from the drama was the accused, but there was another pause before she could be summoned; there were royal commissions, indictments and writs to be read out, and some solemn ceremonial involving the White Staff, Black Rod and the Purse-Bearer. Only when all that was done was the Duchess called to the Bar.

This was the moment everyone had been waiting for, and as the Duchess entered the huge, medieval hall thousands of eyes were turned upon her. In her simple clothes, the short and rather plump woman on the verge of old age, accompanied by two female attendants in white satin, made a striking contrast to the glitter and finery all around her. She looked, one eye-witness thought, 'very pale and a good deal agitated as well she might, at the first view of so tremendous a Court'.¹² Under the implacable gaze of the huge wooden angels carved into the buttresses of the soaring oak ceiling, the Duchess approached the Bar where she curtsied three times and fell upon her knees. 'Madam, you may rise,' said Lord Bathurst, the Lord High Steward. The charges against her were read, to which she pleaded 'not guilty'. It was now time for the lawyers for the defence to launch into their arguments.

It was at this point that the spectators began to realise an important truth about legal proceedings. As one reporter commented:

A portrait miniature on a snuffbox lid of a youthful Elizabeth Chudleigh,
painted by Samuel Finney in the mid 1740s.

Augustus Hervey in 1750, at the age of twenty-six, after the final breakdown of his marriage. Detail from a group portrait at Ickworth.

A nineteenth-century engraving of Elizabeth Chudleigh, after a now lost painting by Joshua Reynolds from the mid 1740s.

Elizabeth Chudleigh, in her thirties, painted by Francis Cotes, probably in the late 1740s or early 1750s.

A Perspective View of the Grand Walk in Vauxhall Gardens and the Orchestra, 1765.

Elizabeth Chudleigh as Iphegenia: one of many prints – and interpretations –
of her infamous masquerade costume of 1749.

Evelyn, 2nd Duke of Kingston, painted in 1741 after he had been awarded the Order of the Garter. He was then thirty, and one of the most handsome men in England.

Evelyn Pierrepont. 2nd Duke of Kingston

Kingston House, as it appeared in the mid nineteenth-century, its plain façade having been embellished in the Regency period.

A Prospect of Thoresby Hall with the Duke and Duchess of Kingston on Horses in the Foreground,
painted in the short interval between the completion of the house and the death of
the Duke in 1773.

(*Above left*) A 1763 pastel of Elizabeth Chudleigh, aged forty-two:
by now an established society hostess.

(*Left*) *The Duchess of Kingston, full length, in a White and Pink Dress*: the Duke apparently commissioned a matching pair of portraits of himself and Elizabeth after their marriage in 1769.

Westminster Hall, bursting with people during the Duchess of Kingston's trial, from a contemporary engraving.

A detail from the last-known portrait of the Duchess of Kingston, a tinted drawing by Richard Cosway made in 1786, about two years before her death.

The trial of a Peer is certainly one of the most splendid spectacles which can be formed by the human imagination; but it is one
of the dullest also. Neither the pleadings, nor any other parts of
the process, are heard by nine tenths of the company; so that when
the eye has been fatigued by the magnificence of the scene, the
spirits immediately flag, curiosity gives way to languor, and in a
little time people discover that the fatigue is by much too high a
price for the gratification.[13]

Moreover, as another eye-witness thought, 'There was. . . a great deal
of nonsense: they adjourned upon the most foolish pretences imaginable, and did <u>nothing</u> with such an air of business as was truly
ridiculous.'[14] At least those seated in the Duke of Newcastle's gallery
could, when their spirits flagged, withdraw to an adjoining room
where there was 'a very fine cold collation of all sorts of meats and
wines, with tea, etc'.[15] Everyone else had to rely on whatever refreshments they could bring with them; how they dealt with other, even
more basic needs, however, is not reported.

While the Duchess's counsel talked their way through arcane arguments in support of the finality of the ecclesiastical court's decision
in 1769, the audience found it more interesting to watch the Duchess
herself. For some, who had built her up into a grotesque figure of
fun in their minds, there was disappointment, for she failed to live
up to their expectations. Indeed, it was generally agreed she behaved
extremely well, considering the circumstances. She 'seemed cheerful
and composed after the first shock',[16] said the *Gazetteer and New Daily
Advertiser*; 'Her Grace discovered through the whole of this day's
trying scene, a fortitude, and dignity of deportment, that commanded
great admiration,'[17] echoed the *Morning Post*; she 'behaved with the
spirit of an heroine',[18] agreed the *London Evening-Post*. 'She was dignified, without arrogance', the reporter continued; 'collected without
audacity; and humble without any of those sycophantic arts which
characterise the vulgar.' The only person to create a drama was one
of Elizabeth's attendants, Mrs Barrington, who 'was so fatigued by
standing, that . . . she was seized with violent hysterics, and continued
indisposed for a considerable time'.

The following day promised to be even duller, for it was the turn
of the prosecution to knock down all the arguments the Duchess's
lawyers had built up so carefully, and with great effect, on the first

day. The heavily pregnant Queen, who with several of her children had watched some of the opening day from the comfort of the Duke of Newcastle's gallery, felt this brief visit was enough to satisfy their, and her, curiosity.[19] Given the likely absence of the royal family, many of the nobility also decided to spare themselves another boring day, boosting an already brisk trade in tickets indicated by advertisements such as that in Monday's *Morning Post*: 'Any Lady or Gentleman wanting a Peeress or Peer's ticket for Tuesday's Trial may be supplied by applying to Mr. Spier's, Goldsmith, No. 30, Coventry-street.' No price was given, but the sums demanded were reported to be high.

Those who *did* attend the second day of the trial – including the Duchess of Devonshire and Lady Derby, with their workbags full of food and drinks – were rewarded with a show of 'beauty and magnificence'[20] that nearly equalled that of the day before. There was as much of a crush, as much of a bustle to find seats and the same solemn command to the audience for silence on pain of imprisonment, 'which, however, was very ill observed'.[21] This second day was much more worrying for the defendant. With great skill, the Meadowses' counsel turned the tide of opinion against both the Duchess – who this time was in a black silk sacque with crape trimmings, with 'her hair modestly dressed and powdered' – and the ecclesiastical court. James Boswell, for instance, who had a far better seat this time, thought Mr Dunning spoke well 'and was pleased with his shrewdness and vivacity'.[22] Someone else commented, 'Dunning's manner is insufferably bad, coughing and spitting at every three words; but his sense and his expression pointed to the last degree; he made her grace shed bitter tears.'[23] He and his colleagues argued cleverly, and at length, about the follies and weaknesses of the ecclesiastical court, until at last Lord Talbot called for an adjournment, saying weakly, 'I think we have already heard more than we can retain, at least I honestly confess for my part I have.'[24]

While the Lords collected their thoughts in their own chamber, the Duchess, who had been looking increasingly pale and agitated, had collapsed in floods of tears and was being blooded* in the apartment reserved for her. Her illness provided just the excuse the Lords needed, and it was decided that the trial should not continue until the Friday. This would at least allow the House of Commons two

* Blood-letting was still generally accepted as being beneficial to the health.

undisturbed days in which to continue an important debate on events in the American colonies, for the MPs had been dreading having to battle their way through the vast crowds of a trial day. Luckily, the Duchess soon rallied; on the Thursday, she was well enough to go to the chambers of one of her advocates, Mr Wallace. The *Morning Post* noted that her appearance 'drew together a vast number of people, who attended her return to her coach . . . many of whom expressed their hearty wishes for her deliverance',[25] which must have been comforting.

But when the trial resumed the following morning, Elizabeth's deliverance seemed considerably less likely than on that promising first day. After more dull legal arguments, her plea that the ecclesiastical court sentence was final, and that therefore she could not be indicted on the same matter, was at last disallowed by the noble judges. To the relief and excitement of the spectators – who had restlessly waited for an hour and a half for the Lords to return from their chamber with their decision – the real business of the trial could go ahead.

It began with a damning introductory speech for the prosecution by the Attorney-General, Thurlow.* Never a man to mince his words, especially when dealing with a crime of such a 'malignant complexion and pernicious example', Thurlow launched into a merciless attack on the character of the woman before him. The evidence the court would hear, he said, would show that the Duchess's motive for committing bigamy was money: 'dry lucre was the whole inducement, cold fraud the only means to perpetrate that crime'.[26] Moreover, he claimed, it would demonstrate only too clearly that it was 'a matter of perfect indifference to the prisoner, which husband she adhered to, so that the profit to be drawn from this marriage or from that was tolerably equal'. It was not true – Elizabeth's reasons for acting as she had were, as we have seen, far more complicated than that – but that would be how the outside world would shortly view it.

Then came the moment the whispering throng in Westminster Hall had been waiting for: the witnesses for the prosecution. The first, and most damaging, was Ann Craddock, the late Mrs Hanmer's maid, who had been in Lainston's chapel all those years before and

---

* Edward, 1st Baron Thurlow (1731–1806), appointed Attorney-General in 1771.

seen the shabby ceremony with her own eyes. She now told every-thing: the events leading up to the wedding, the marriage service itself, the fact that she 'saw them put to bed'.[27] The woman who in 1768 had told Hervey's attorney that she 'could not . . . remember anything of the matter'[28] had clearly regained her memory with a vengeance now that she had fallen out with the Duchess. She was a little evasive, however, about whether she had been offered any finan-cial inducement by the Meadowses or their agents in return for coming forward – it eventually came out that she *had* – though during continued questioning the next day she mentioned the Duchess's own monetary dealings with her several years before.

With the real business of the trial in hand and the promise of more scandalous revelations, there was a splendid crowd of nobility and gentry in Westminster Hall for the fourth day. First, there was the conclusion of Ann Craddock's damning testimony: a tidying-up of loose ends. Next, the surgeon Caesar Hawkins was called to answer questions about the child born to Elizabeth and Hervey,* at whose delivery he had been present, and also to relate his role as a go-between in 1768 when Hervey had asked for a divorce.

Afterwards came the Honourable Sophia Fettiplace, a friend and confidante, whose mother had been one of Augusta's Ladies of the Bedchamber, and who, if she had anything interesting to say, was not prepared to admit it. Her reticence was as nothing, however, compared with that of the next witness, Lord Barrington, who had spent the past few days doing everything he could to avoid appearing, short of feigning illness or leaving the country. The lawyers he had anxiously consulted about whether he was bound to disclose 'private confidential conversation',[29] and if he refused whether that could 'in any light be treated as Perjury', had informed him that there was no escape.[30] Lord Barrington was not to be deterred that easily from sticking to his code of honour, however, and he proved an intractable witness. Although Elizabeth released him from any obligation of honour, he hedged and prevaricated so much before finally admit-

---

* There was some discussion as to whether, given the strict rules that required doctors to keep patient information confidential, Hawkins could break this trust, even in a court of law. It was eventually decided he was obliged to disclose anything he knew relevant to the case, setting an important legal precedent.

ting that she had mentioned an engagement of some kind that the prosecution gave up on him and called Judith Phillips, formerly Mrs Amis, instead.

Judith Phillips was much more forthcoming, and spoke at great length about the defendant's visit to Winchester in 1759 and the creation of a written record of her marriage with Hervey, which Elizabeth had reportedly told the Reverend Amis might be worth a hundred thousand pounds to her. The register was produced, with the traces of the seals that had once kept its contents private, and Phillips confirmed that the relevant entry was in her former husband's writing. Like Ann Craddock, however, she was less voluble when asked whether she had been offered money to appear against the Duchess, and denied – thoroughly unconvincingly – any knowledge of who might be paying for her and her husband to live at the Turf Coffee House.

That day's final witnesses were more straightforward: the Reverend Stephen Kinchin of Lainston, with some more information on the parish register, and the Reverend John Dennis, who confirmed that the handwriting in it belonged to the Reverend Thomas Amis. The session ended with the examination of several documents, such as the record of Elizabeth's marriage to the Duke of Kingston, and a couple of letters from the Phillipses to their Graces after Mr Phillips had been dismissed. Throughout it all, to the admiration of the spectators and the *Public Advertiser*, 'Her Grace . . . shewed herself Mistress of that Fortitude and Serenity so peculiar to Great Minds under Affliction.'[31] For one of the audience, however, it had all been too much; as the same newspaper reported, 'An elderly Lady who sat behind the Peeresses and their Daughters . . . fell asleep, owing to Fatigue; and it was with some Difficulty she was awaked when the august Tribunal broke up.'

Proceedings resumed on Monday, with 'a long & most curious speech'[32] by the Duchess of Kingston in her own defence. Her words, she said, flowed 'freely from my heart, adorned simply with innocence and truth'.[33] She talked of the persecutions she had faced; the attacks on her honour and that of her ancient family; of the injustice of the case against her, which had been brought out of greed. For, she asked, 'Had this prosecution been set on foot merely for the love of justice or good example to the community, why did they not institute their prosecution during the five years your prisoner was received and acknowledged the undoubted and unmolested wife of the late Duke of Kingston?' She next attempted to cast doubt on the crucial evidence of Ann Craddock and her mention of payments supposedly offered to her by the Duchess, though not received. 'Can your Lordships believe that if I could have been weak enough to have instituted the suit, with a conviction in my own mind of a real lawful marriage between Mr Hervey and myself, that I would not, at any expense, have taken care to have put the woman out of the way?'

That conviction, however, had been Elizabeth's problem all along. Her belief that the ceremony performed by Reverend Amis in the shadows of Lainston chapel could not be a legal marriage had led her to institute the case in the ecclesiastical courts. That had allowed her to wed the Duke of Kingston with 'the most perfect conviction that it was lawful', especially as her advocate Doctor Collier had assured her that the sentence of jactitation of marriage was final and conclusive. She finished with a plea that the Doctor's evidence should be heard. There was only one problem: Collier had been ill for months, and was still extremely weak. The Lords were still arguing over whether evidence given out of court could be admissible when Mr Barkley, Hervey's attorney at the time of the proposed divorce, offered his own recollections of the time. He was followed by a woman called Ann Pritchard, who mentioned several conversations with the chief prosecution witness in which Craddock had said she had not, in fact, heard the marriage ceremony. Next, Doctor Warren related his medical examination of the unfortunate Doctor Collier, who was suffering from 'a St Anthony's fire in his head and face, by which one side of it was so much swelled that the eye was almost closed up',[34] and who was consequently in no fit state to appear. The last witness for the defence was James Laroche, who had accompanied the Duke on many of his consultations with Doctor Collier.

As the trial drew closer to what now seemed its inevitable conclusion, the strain began to tell on the Duchess. She had, according to one newspaper, been 'exceedingly affected'[35] during several parts of her forty-five-minute-long speech; so much so that at its conclusion, she fainted or had 'an Hysteric Fit',[36] and had to be carried out of the court to recover. Sadly for Elizabeth, it had become clear that neither her passionate justification nor the handful of witnesses for the defence would protect her from the overwhelming weight of evidence against her – no matter how much she believed in her own innocence. There remained only the summing up, before the Lords adjourned to their own chamber to consider their decision.

Their absence was brief, however, for there could be no doubt over the verdict. When they returned, each was asked by the Lord High Steward: 'How says your Lordship? Is the prisoner guilty of the felony of which she stands indicted or not guilty?' To the great satisfaction of the audience and the surprise of no one, a hundred and sixteen peers rose in turn and answered, 'Guilty, upon my honour.' One other, the kind Duke of Newcastle, answered, 'Guilty erroneously, but not intentionally', though several peers – including the Duke of Ancaster and the Earls of Pembroke, Exeter and March[37] – retired without giving a verdict at all. Before he passed sentence, the Lord High Steward asked Elizabeth if she had anything else to say, to which she replied with a claim of benefit of peerage. This exempted peers from corporal punishment for certain offences, and would mean that Elizabeth would escape being branded on the thumb. Her request, the *Annual Register* noted, 'gave rise to a laboured speech of the Attorney-General, wherein he attempted to prove, that . . . Peeresses had not the least title to the same exemption'.[38] Fortunately for Elizabeth, he was out-argued and the judges unanimously gave their opinion that she was entitled to the same benefit as the men.

It had all turned out exactly as Lord Mansfield had predicted: 'She makes your Lordships a curtsey, and you return the compliment with a bow.'[39] Though she had been found guilty, Elizabeth would face no legal punishment – though, after forty-eight years as Miss Chudleigh and seven as the Duchess of Kingston, she would have to pass the remainder of her life as the Countess of Bristol. She was discharged on condition she paid her fees, the Lord High Steward adding only that he hoped her own troubled conscience would be punishment enough – which was unlikely – and reminding her that a second offence, even less likely, would not be treated so leniently. With a finishing flurry of pompous ceremony, the trial of the demoted Duchess was over and the satisfied spectators poured out of court, blinking as they emerged into the brightness of a warm and sunny spring day.

If the Lords could not make an example of Elizabeth, however, society was able and willing to supply the deficiency. 'Her guilt was so evident',[40] one man said, that those who had attended the trial could not 'feel any compassion for her, or attribute her disgrace singly to the natural frailty of a woman.' However, as someone else wisely commented: 'The invidious spleen of the peeresses, not the justice of the peers are her grace's untameable persecutors.'⁴¹ Fashionable women raced to condemn the 'unprincipled, artful, licentious woman'⁴² who had been *'undignified and unduchessed*, and very narrowly escaped being burned in the hand'. One remarked that 'greatly to the general satisfaction, the shameless Dss is degraded into as shameless a countess'.⁴³ Even some of the men joined in the condemnation, for it was said that Lord Camden was angry that Elizabeth had not been branded on the thumb: 'He says, as he was once a professed lover of hers, he thought it would have looked ill-natured and ungallant for him to propose it: but that he should have acceded to it most heartily, though he believes he should have recommended a cold iron.'⁴⁴ It was all too clear that life in England would be extremely uncomfortable for the new Countess from now on.

CHAPTER 14

A Trip to Calais

From hence, ye beauties, undeceived,
Know, one false step is ne'er retrieved,
And be with caution bold.
Thomas Gray

The Meadowses, having successfully turned a duchess into a countess in one court, were now rumoured to be heading back to another with renewed determination. Two days after the proceedings at Westminster had finished, it was reported that they had filed a bill in Chancery with the aim of setting aside the late Duke of Kingston's will 'as being obtained under false suggestions'.[1] At the same time, they apparently obtained a writ of *ne exeat regno*,* to prevent Elizabeth leaving the country.[2] In this, however, they were too late. The Duchess – for she clung obstinately to the title for the rest of her life – had already been alerted to their plans, and, unwilling to be condemned to remain in England to be ostracised, had set off on the Wednesday evening for Dover, from where she had sailed early the following morning for Calais.[3]

She reached France at noon on 25 April where, the moment her arrival was announced, 'she was waited on by the principal Persons in the Town, who attended her on Shore, and shewed her every possible Mark of Respect and Civility. The Cannon of the Duchess's Yacht were fired on her Grace's reaching the Harbour. Monsieur Cafferay,† in the politest Terms, complimented the Duchess on her landing.'[4] Gratifying though the warmth of this reception must

---

* Literally, 'let him not leave the kingdom'.
† Monsieur Caffieri, the King's land-tax collector at Calais.

have been, assuming she were in any condition to notice it, Elizabeth's first priority would have been to find somewhere to stay. The principal accommodation in Calais was at the Hotel d'Angleterre on rue Royale, owned by a Monsieur Dessein: 'a House of Surprising Magnitude',[5] commented one traveller, 'standing in a vast extent of Ground; He makes 120 Beds for Guests, without reckoning Servants, who are accomodated in the Offices'. Dessein also had a large number of carriages for hire, stables full of horses to pull them, and shops selling everything that the travelling, mainly English, public could need. Not only that, the hotel also boasted 'a Playhouse furnished with good actors a table de hotte and everything tolerable raisonable',[6] added another impressed visitor.

Much later, the story was told that Dessein, misunderstanding the result of the trial and believing that Elizabeth was not merely demoted but deprived of her money, offered her only a very small room that first night, explaining it was the only one available; that the following morning, by now aware of his mistake, he had rushed to offer her the best suite he had. It seems unlikely, however. If she needed accommodation, there was also the Silver Lion which, one newspaper correspondent commented, was 'equally as good a House; and now Mons. Dessain [*sic*] is become so rich, by much also the most reasonable'.[7] Then there was always the obliging Monsieur Caffieri, with whom she had lodged on a previous visit and who had greeted her so warmly this time. Wherever she stayed, however, it did not improve her turmoil of spirit after the events of the past ten days, as she told several of her European friends soon after her arrival in Calais:

I am writing to inform you that the Peers have decided that the Church Court sentence does not justify the marriage which I contracted with the Duke of Kingston. They have disgraced the Ecclesiastical Court whose dogmas have been inviolable for 1475 years. In destroying this court of justice I am the unfortunate sacrifice, but they cannot take away my fortune, my only punishment was to make them a curtsey. It was all done for public show, but to be honest with you, my dear friend, I confess that I am still in an unparalleled state of shock. The heart shudders at the injustice that has been done to me . . . I am therefore, my dear friend, known in the Ecclesiastical Court as Duchess of Kingston, and with the Peers as Countess of Bristol . . . greatness and riches are for me only a hindrance.[8]

In the circumstances, it was not surprising that the English newspapers were soon commenting that 'letters from Calais mention, that the Duchess of Kingston is greatly indisposed at that place'.[9] Despite this, she did not forget those few true friends she had left behind in England. She had been in France only a few days when she poured out her thanks to Lord Barrington, who had tried so nobly to avoid adding to the evidence against her:

> Alass my good friend why do I feel a Difficulty of Expressing to you the gratefull feelings of My Heart in your regard – thought flows too fast for Expression when I would Convey the Idea I have of your honorable and steady friendship, I have the Highest Veneration for Lord Hillsborow he is full of Virtue Generosity & Honor, and has been to me a true friend. I recommend Myself to both your rememberance.[10]

There were plenty of other letters to be written in those first months after the trial, not all to such true friends. The Duke of Portland had sent to ask if a Doctor Aldrich might take over a tumble-down cottage that she owned. Although his Grace had, in fact, been remarkably adept at doing nothing at all to help his neighbour in the period leading up to her trial, in June Elizabeth wrote him a far kinder answer than he deserved, thanking him for his repeated politeness:

> They cannot fail to make great impressions on my mind, for the respect that is justly due to you from all the world. The testimonies shown to me, since my affliction in losing the best of husbands, and your politeness still following me in my exile, when worldly beings might have forgot there was such a being existed as myself, draws opposite lines of delicacy in your character not to be described.[11]

Despite rumoured sightings of her in Paris,[12] Elizabeth remained in Calais for several months, trying to make plans for her future. Although her exile from her own country was entirely voluntary, there was no going back to England for the foreseeable future, for she would be snubbed by society and, what was worse, be snubbed as the Countess of Bristol, a title she refused ever to use. With this in mind, Elizabeth would need to give serious thought over the following months, and even years, to the thorny question of where she could live and continue to be welcomed as the Duchess of Kingston. This was not mere snobbery – though many of her contemporaries chose to interpret it in that light. At least as importantly, it was also the name bestowed upon her by the man she had loved for so long.

Not that Elizabeth had given up on returning to England, and to Thoresby in particular, at some point in the future, to live the agree-able life of a country lady. Writing to ask the Duke of Portland, a neighbour at Thoresby, for his help in preventing the estate from being overrun by poachers, she commented:

> I probably shall spend my later days at Thoresby, and can shoot very well, it is an amusement that I would choose to take within my own park. It is an exercise I took when in Bohemia, but the late Duke appeared fearful any accident might happen to me; it was no pain to refrain from anything he did not approve; his disap-probation was my safety; his will would be as much followed now.[13]

In the meantime, however, there were less complicated problems to tackle. One was that if the Meadowses were determined to pursue their quest of overturning the Duke of Kingston's will, she was equally determined there should be as little as possible left in England for them to lay their grasping hands on. Among the first requests Elizabeth made – in the first week of May – was for the removal of eight large paintings from Thoresby, to be packed up very carefully; 'the cases Must not be Made with green wood on any account, as the Pictures would be Mouldy and Entirely Spoil'd you must do it as Privately as Possible and you will oblige Her Grace',[14] instructed her companion Eliza Lapp.

Yet, while Elizabeth was bracing herself for the next attack from the Meadows family, it was actually her unwanted husband who made the first legal move against her, as a preliminary to divorce. On the afternoon of 26 June, two local notaries, accompanied by a London merchant Monsieur Morlet, went to the house of Jacques de Cocove Moyecques in the rue de l'Etoile, which Elizabeth had bought or was buying, and which she afterwards rebuilt into something more suitably grand.[15] Their mission was to deliver a letter from Hervey's proctors, regarding the reopening of the cause of jactitation and asking for her to appear 'to shew cause, why the Sentence obtained by you should not be revoked, by reason that he is now able to prove his marriage with your Ladyship to the satisfaction of the Court'.[16]

However, when they reached the house, they were told by one of the servants that 'the Dutchess was still in Bed, being indisposed, and that it was not possible to speak to her'.[17] While they waited to see the valet instead, the first servant returned and said 'that he had just acquainted the Chamber Maid of My Lady Dutchess that a Person had a Letter to deliver into the said Lady's own Hands concerning the Law Suit which was carrying on against her at London, that the Chamber Maid had informed her Mistress of it who had answered her that she received Letters from Nobody, that the Letters coming from London gave her so much uneasiness that she was resolved to live in Peace'. Despite their protests, the notaries had no option but to go, leaving the letter open on the kitchen table, their departure watched from an upper window by Elizabeth herself.

A week later, Hervey's motion came on to be heard at the ecclesiastical court in London, Doctors Commons. In it he asked the court to order a citation to be pinned up on the Royal Exchange – the usual way of citing peers and peeresses who lived abroad – requesting her reply to the setting aside of the sentence of jactitation. Doctor Bettesworth, chancellor of the diocese of London, however, was not immediately keen to grant the motion: 'As the marriage with Lord Bristol had been determined by a verdict, he could not see the reason for coming to that court; and, as everything was new, he was apprehensive of collusion somewhere; and therefore was cautious how he proceeded.'[18] The Duchess, after all, had not been the only one damaged by the Westminster Hall trial; the ecclesiastical court, too, had been made to look foolish at the very least. In the end, Bettesworth relented; the request was granted, moving Walpole to comment, 'the Ecclesiastical Court affects to be ashamed, and thunders against the Duchess'.[19]

Only now did the Meadowses make their next move, which was to revive their original bill of complaint in Chancery against Elizabeth, with a few technical amendments, but still including the Earl of Bristol.[20] Hardly surprisingly, there were rumours that July that Elizabeth – 'the poor, hunted Duchess', as one childhood playmate called her – had made a flying visit to London to consult her various lawyers.[21] However, they were able to reassure her, it was well known that cases in Chancery could drag on for years and years and, anyway, nothing could be transacted during the summer. The Duke's money was still hers to spend as she wished. Moreover, although Hervey might succeed in proving his marriage in the church courts, this was no more than repeating what had already been done in Westminster Hall. It did not guarantee he would find it as easy to then sue for a divorce, which was what Elizabeth feared most, for she believed it would make her more vulnerable to the Meadowses.

Though she must have been constantly aware of these legal challenges to both her marital status and her money, it was now the first concern of the Duchess to restore her energy and enthusiasm for life as best she could. Calais, 'a paltry place'[22] someone called it, was perhaps not the ideal setting for this. That September, Lady Harriet Vernon claimed to have seen Elizabeth in Paris, 'with a hat and feathers like Henri Quatre'[23] in the French fashion, where she was thought to be looking for property. However, it was probably no more accurate than the other stories about her that reached the newspapers in early October, which claimed that she was practically the 'gouvernante' of Calais, that her carriage was emblazoned with the Bristol coat of arms, and that 'two grenadier centinels are always mounted at her door, and salute her with rested arms, as she passes and repasses'.[24] For the readers, these silly stories – and amused comment on those fashionably effeminate dandies called the macaronis, those 'pretty, dear, he-she creatures'[25] who had taken to wearing beauty spots – at least provided light relief from the lengthy and gloomy reports about the war in America that had begun the previous year, the lists of dead, wounded and missing, and the mounting evidence that France was preparing to join the American rebels in battle against Britain.

With winter drawing closer, however, the limited charms of Calais began to pall, and Elizabeth decided to head again to the warmth and society of Rome – to stop her servants pawning any more of her possessions, so the gossips said – taking in Vienna and Venice on her way south.[26] She also planned to pause on the way in Bavaria for ten days or so to pay her respects to the Elector and, more particularly, his sister and her friend the Electress of Saxony, who was making a lengthy stay there. She was also hoping to renew there her acquaintance with a cultured, dashing though far from handsome Polish prince, Karol Stanislaw Radziwill, whom she had probably encountered in Rome on her second journey there and whose problems were at least as great as her own. The election of the Russian-backed Stanislaw Augustus Poniatowski, a former lover of Catherine the Great, as King of Poland in 1764 had led to a virtual civil war from 1768 to 1772, which was crushed by Catherine's forces. The patriotic Radziwill, who was on the losing side, was forced to flee to Munich, taking with him twelve statues of the Apostles in solid gold to support him in lavish style.[27] From there, on an estate given to him by the Bavarian Elector, he watched a weakened Poland lose a third of its territory to Russia, Austria and Prussia. Among the lands confiscated were large parts of Radziwill's extensive estates, which he was naturally keen to recover. Given her own fears of being deprived of her estates in England, it was a position with which Elizabeth could all too easily sympathise.

By mid October Elizabeth was ready to set out from Calais,[28] and she reached Munich on 9 November.[29] Some idea of the local ruler's taste may be gauged from the descriptions of an English traveller who passed through four years later during a trip to Italy, and stopped at Nymphenburg, the Elector's country palace, 'the bosquets, jets-d'eaux, and parterres of which are the pride of all the Bavarians'.[30] There he encountered a style of decoration that was the antithesis of the new classically inspired fashion then sweeping England: 'The principal platform is all of a glitter with gilded cupids and shining serpents spouting at every pore. Beds of poppies, hollyhocks, scarlet lychnis, and other flame-coloured flowers, border the edge of the walks, which extend till the perspective appears to meet and swarm with ladies and gentlemen in party-coloured raiment.' The following day, he visited the palace, 'which glares with looking-glass, gilding, and furbelowed flounces of cut velvet, most sumptuously fringed and spangled'. It was all rather obviously grand but, given the descriptions of Kingston House, probably exactly to Elizabeth's taste.

But if Elizabeth had hoped her time in Munich with the Electress would restore her battered spirits, she was to be horribly disappointed. For here she was to find out that the ripples from her trial had spread further than she had hitherto realised. Humiliatingly, despite Elizabeth's close friendship with his sister, the Elector of Bavaria refused absolutely to receive her as the Duchess of Kingston. Nothing could change his mind, and for months afterwards he continued to assure the British ambassador that he had too much respect for George III ever to do so.[31] It was the first, worrying sign that it was not only in England that the title Elizabeth had borne so proudly for the past seven years would in future be denied her. Not even the best efforts of the Electress of Saxony, it seemed, were enough to guarantee the Duchess of Kingston an obliging reception in all the glittering courts of continental Europe. Elizabeth had to content herself with spending her time in Munich privately with her 'dear friend' the Electress Dowager, and without the diversion of Prince Radziwill who had gone to Warsaw.

Elizabeth resumed her journey towards Italy in the middle of November as she had planned.[32] But, while the whole of Roman society waited the return of the Duchess with 'presents for Card. Alex Albani, who tho' blind is raising new Temples',[33] Elizabeth decided to go ahead with her proposed stop at Vienna on her way south. It was a curious decision, given her recent disappointment in Munich, for the court of the Empress Maria Theresa and her son the Emperor Joseph was generally regarded as not only the dullest in the whole of Europe, but also the most rigidly correct. Although a presentation there would certainly be a social triumph, that could be the only possible pleasure to be derived from the event. However, there was every possibility Elizabeth might not be received at all, let alone as the Duchess of Kingston.

If the Electress *did* try to smooth her friend's way with letters to her contacts in the Imperial city, it was all in vain. By the time Elizabeth arrived in Vienna on 28 November, the British ambassador Robert Murray Keith had already been asked by the court whether he would acknowledge Elizabeth's title '& assist her by my Intervention in obtaining an Audience of the Sovereign'.[34] As he told his superiors in London, 'Your Lordship already knows my Answer, for having been present in the House of Peers when the Nullity of her Marriage with the Duke of Kingston, was unanimously decreed, I could not hesitate a Moment to declare, that that name could in no Shape belong to her, & that I could never give the Countenance of my publick Character, to a Person, who came under a false Name.'

As soon as Elizabeth arrived in Vienna, Keith asked if he could call on her to discuss the matter, but she put him off and, in an attempt to bypass the usual channels, wrote to the Grande Maitresse instead to request the honour of being presented by her to the Empress. There was no reply, and the next day Elizabeth was forced to save face with a second note saying that, after all, she was obliged to withdraw her request as ill health made it necessary for her to go to a warmer climate at once. Keith, with a reluctant hint of admiration, informed London of his subsequent long interview with Elizabeth:

> It is sufficient to say, that <u>Her Part</u> of a very animated Conversation was supported, with Spirit, Address, Wit, & Perseverance; but as on my Side, I had Duty, Truth, Good-humor, and the most guarded Politeness, I need not say, how the contest ended. She has promis'd not to appear in Publick, & to set out for Rome by the Way of Venice, as soon as her Health will permit. – After offering her every Civility in my Power, I have assured her Ladyship that I leave full scope to her Ingenuity, to give to our little <u>Rencontre</u> whatever Colours she may think most favorable for herself.[35]

While Elizabeth lingered in Vienna – because of poor health, she later claimed – with a second social failure to her credit in the space of a month, her law business with Hervey got underway in London without her. On 24 January 1777, Doctor Bettesworth listened to four hours of arguments by counsel for the Duchess and for the Earl of Bristol, at the end of which 'in a clear candid manner'[36] he reviewed the position. Noting that it was not clear whether Lord Bristol had been in a position to provide, at the time of the original suit, the evidence of the marriage which had since come out, Bettesworth made his decision in his favour. It was now up to Elizabeth to provide evidence of why the sentence of jactitation should not be revoked, confirming her first marriage with Hervey in the ecclesiastical court and paving the way for a divorce.

The news took a little time to reach Vienna, but as soon as it did it became obvious that Elizabeth would have to abandon the idea of moving on to Rome and head back to Paris or Calais at once to consult her lawyers. This was a great nuisance, for there was a disturbing report from the Eternal City that Monsignor Rufo, the Neapolitan prelate who had let her have a whole grand apartment in his palace in the Piazza de SS Apostoli, 'tired with her delays has ordered her Agent here to quit it, and take away all her moveables'.[37] Poor Mr Hendrick was, not surprisingly, distressed by the sudden turn of events, for he had nowhere to put the things. Nor, it now appeared, was there any likelihood of his mistress arriving soon in Rome to help him resolve the problem.*

Elizabeth took her leave of Vienna, foiled in her attempts to be presented at its court, towards the end of January. Travelling 'in a deep snow & the worst of weather after a fever of seven weeks',[38] she arrived in Munich on 3 February, where she stayed one night. From here, she wrote to the still-absent Prince Radziwill: 'I am rushing with all possible speed to Paris to meet my lawyers, for they are intending to give me a husband without my consent and judge my case without hearing it.'[39]

She was back on the road the following morning at nine o'clock for the long journey back to Calais, while her lawyers tried to hold up the ecclesiastical court proceedings.[40] By 22 March, she was in Paris 'and will be at Callais soon'.[41] While she travelled, Thoresby was already being systematically stripped of its contents – damask chairs and four damask settees, a particular table, all the china flower pots – and when the Duchess finally reached Calais, probably towards the end of April,[42] the process only gathered speed. First she ordered John Williams, her butler at Kingston House, to send for the jack from the kitchen, then 'the two velvet card tables – and Likewise the sett of China that was bought about two year agoe and there was some China at Thoresby of the same sort before . . . all must come that is match and of the same sort – you will take care about the Packin of them'.[43]

There was a purpose to these seemingly strange requests. For some time, Elizabeth had been considering a journey to somewhere far more exotic and unusual than the regular haunts of the Grand Tourist. 'I think', she told Radziwill that March, 'that this summer I will go to Petersburg for a month,'[44] for she must have heard a great deal

* The problem must have been resolved, however, and another apartment found, possibly the one in the Palazzo Guarnieri that Elizabeth was renting at the time of her death.

about the city and the court of Catherine the Great from such acquaintances as Vasilii Petrov, the Russian poet who had accompanied her to Rome on her first visit, and her chaplain the Reverend Forster, who had travelled there more than thirty years before as chaplain to the British Ambassador Lord Hyndford.[45] A handful of British travellers had also been there and published charming accounts of the city and the extravagant life of the court and nobility, one of the most recent being Nathaniel Wraxall's *Tour Through Some of the Northern Parts of Europe* in 1775.

Precisely which aspect of Russia – the grandeur, the lack of sneering British tourists, the natural beauty – had most piqued Elizabeth's curiosity is hard to tell, however. Perhaps she had heard other stories, prurient speculation about Catherine the Great, which had given her hope that the Russian court might not be squeamish about a little bigamy. Or maybe she was merely eager to meet the Empress who, with herself and Mrs Rudd, had recently been described as one of 'the three most extraordinary women in Europe'.[46] Whatever her motives, Elizabeth had decided to travel there in splendid style, by sea in her own personal yacht – wealth, though it could be a burden, clearly did have *some* compensations.

The previous year, when the dust had barely settled on her trial, the newspapers had already remarked that a 'fine new ship'[47] for the Duchess of Kingston was nearing completion at Mr Haine's dockyard in Deptford, according to the *Public Advertiser*, though other papers suggested Rotherhithe or Limehouse instead. This vessel, a replacement for the *Minerva* about which the Romans had been so condescending, reportedly contained accommodation for fifty visitors as well as the crew and cost 5,000 guineas to build.[48] By March, John Williams was able to declare 'Her Grace is new Shipe is all most Ready for Sea',[49] to be gradually loaded with its cargo of treasures – the damask chairs, china flower pots and other items from Thoresby, along with copious amounts of wine and beer – over the next two months.

By May, Elizabeth was able to turn her attention to the question of who, rather than merely what, would accompany her on the voyage to St Petersburg, aside from her usual entourage. Her first thought was to take the gardener from Thoresby, for ever since the early 1760s, when the Russian nobles had finally been granted permission to travel abroad and the end of the Seven Years War had made travelling easier, wealthy tourists had been sending back enthusiastic reports of the English way of gardening. Catherine the Great, though she had never seen an English garden for herself, was known to be passionate about the new natural style which made such a contrast to the formality and straight lines of French planting. Accordingly, the Duchess wrote to her steward at Thoresby: 'Pray tell the Gardner to write down orders what is to be done in the Garden till October in case I sho^d send for him at a Minutes Warning to go a Journey with me. and if there are any pine apples I sho^d be glad to have them by the 25th of this Month.'[50]

But while Elizabeth excitedly carried on with her plans, not everything was going so smoothly. The various bits of legal business were rumbling on in London, although both Hervey and Elizabeth had made full use of every lawful ruse to avoid answering the case brought against them by the Meadows family in Chancery, and in early May had delayed matters again.[51] The church court case, however, was causing more problems. From Thoresby, the Duchess's agent Sam Sherring wrote to one of the Duke's trustees:

> You have heard before this of the Jactitation Cause being again opened; the Issue of the dispute appears plainer to me than the consequences that will attend it; tho' till the Muzzle is taken off from the Earls Mouth, I mean the injunction of silence, I hope I may go in safety, in receiving & paying for the Duchess, tho' I cannot avoid telling you some of the Tenants have taken the alarm & have refused payment of their Rents & I dare not Distrain in her name.[52]

Another legal matter, this time in France, was also taking time to be resolved. Because French law decreed that the possessions of foreigners who died in France were automatically forfeit to the Crown, Elizabeth had applied in May for letters patent giving her the right – while retaining English nationality – to buy and own property in France, and to sell it, give it away or bequeath it to whoever she chose by her Last Will and Testament 'whether she lived in the Kingdom or out of it'.[53] This was an important step, for although the income from the Duke's estates was hers for life only and would pass to Charles Meadows on her death, everything else – from the contents of his houses to the money in his bank account – had been left to her without reservation. It belonged to her absolutely, and was hers to bequeath however she pleased. It took several months for the French paperwork to be completed, though, and it was not until the opening days of August that the application was formally granted by the parliament of Paris.[54] Importantly, from Elizabeth's point of view, the letters patent were issued to her in the name of the Duchess of Kingston.

Despite Elizabeth's application to the French authorities, she was obviously keeping her options open over where she would eventually settle down. In June, she had written to the Elector of Bavaria to express a wish of buying an establishment in that place. However, as Morton Eden, the British representative there, explained, 'having already made a vain attempt to be received at his Highnesses Court under the title of Dutchess of Kingston, and being utterly averse to appear under her own, she has applied to his Electoral Highness for letters Patent creating her a Countess in Bavaria'.[55] Fearful of displeasing George III, the Elector agonised for several weeks about his decision, before finally, in late July or early August, conferring upon Elizabeth the title of Countess of Warth. Morton Eden reported that she had 'obtained this grant through the mediation of the Electress Dowager of Saxony, who honours her with the strongest marks of favour and protection'.[56] Evidently, the Elector had decided it was far worse to displease a strong-willed sister than a British monarch. It was, Elizabeth said when she heard the news, 'an Honour for which I stand much obliged'.[57] The Bavarians confidently predicted a visit from the new Countess towards the end of the year, although, 'as she will find here many Countesses not less proud than herself, we shall not probably possess her long time'.[58]

Finally, with business matters in hand for the time being, the last remaining stores could be loaded on to the Duchess's handsome new yacht in readiness for sailing. A few days before its departure for Russia, an English traveller managed to obtain an order to see the yacht,

which was beyond any thing of the kind. 300 Tons, an Organ cost One Thousand Two Hundred Pounds Sterling, the Pannels & ornaments were of cut Looking Glass in a very Costly Taste – the Expence Indeed equaled the Absurdity. There was a suite of Apartments hung with Crimson Damask with Gold Borders, Chairs of the same, the Wood work Gilt, a Stone Kitchen with many

Stoves, and every other Conveniency. There we saw two Sanguines, small Animals of the Monkey kind with two Young ones Litter'd there. The Room for Dining in was 32 Feet by 24. State Room over it of the same Dimensions, a Water Closet, Cold Bath, two Buzagio Stoves so fixed as to warm Four Rooms, Placed in the partition & appearing as a Basso Releivo, & made an agreable piece of Furniture. Venetian Blinds to all the Windows, it is said to have Cost the Owner upwards of Twenty Thousand Pounds.[59]

The Duchess, it seems, was determined to arrive in the Russian capital in as impressive a fashion as possible.

CHAPTER 15

Northern Lights

The greatest object of true curiosity. . . one of the
most magnificent cities of the earth
Nathaniel Wraxall on St Petersburg

E lizabeth set sail from Calais on 7 August 1777 in her magnificent new ship, which she had named *Duchess of Kingston*. From
its mast fluttered the flag of France, for had it carried that of
Britain it would have been an easy and lucrative target for the
American privateers who stalked these waters. For this reason, it also
carried a French crew; Captain John Harden had refused point-blank
to sail under the colours of the enemy – no salary, not even £100 a
year,[1] could make such a thing remotely tolerable – and most of his
men had agreed. The addition of a French crew, of course, meant
that the Reverend John Forster would be ministering to the spiritual
needs of the Duchess alone; for her Catholic sailors she invited an
Abbé Séchand 'to accompany her on her voyage, [and] engaged to
pay him a certain yearly allowance, as Roman Catholic Chaplain to
her ship'.[2] He arrived, so rumour had it, with no luggage at all except
a violin.

Just before her vessel departed, Elizabeth wrote to Lord Barrington
to thank him again for his kindness towards her and also to share her
worries, for even on the brink of her great adventure she could not
entirely shake them off:

> While I saw the British Shore I could not consider myself absent
> from my best of friends, that lessned distance pass'd revives in my
> sorrowing heart the remembrance of all my Sorrows, I bear them
> with Christian fortitude, but tho' I cease to murmur, I do not cease

to feel my agonising situation. I am now my Lord at the mercy of another Element, it cannot be more unkind than what I have before experienc'd on my Native Shore, My Secretary will in half an hour quit my Ship and will have the honor of conveying this, my remembrance of all your friendship to me and the assurance of the everlasting regard and respect I have for you.[3]

Elizabeth's main concern was that she had left her journey too late, and that she would not be able to return in time to defend herself against Hervey at the start of Michaelmas Term in November. In her anxiety, she allowed herself to feel, and show, all the resentment that had built up over more than thirty years against the husband she had never loved, and which had now grown into something perilously close to loathing. As she told Lord Barrington:

Lord Bristol I understand would offer terms of accomodation but you and all mankind can tell how little he is to be trusted and when he desires to converse with my friends on that Subject, it is with a design only to defame me for he has ever with a double Tongue stung me to the Heart . . . if any accident should retard my return for that first Term and he should pursue his point in the Doctors Commons in my absence I never will accomodate with him.

Four days later, the *Duchess of Kingston* sailed into Elsinore* where, Forster later remembered, 'we stayed twenty-four hours, part of which we employed in visiting the castle (Cronenburgh)[†] in which the unfortunate Queen of Denmark was confined'.[4] This was the former Princess Caroline, Augusta and Frederick's youngest daughter, born after the death of her father and married off in 1766 to the unstable King Christian of Denmark. It was not a happy union, and in early 1772, after a coup, the unpopular, too-English Queen was made the excuse to execute her former physician Struensee, who had risen rapidly to power during the King's recent travels abroad. Caroline herself was imprisoned in the turreted Gothic castle, and died in 1775. After they had satisfied this 'melancholy curiosity', the Duchess

---

* Elsinore, or Helsingor, on the north-east coast of Denmark's easternmost island of Zealand.

† Kronborg Castle, also the setting for *Hamlet*.

and her entourage continued with a good wind to St Petersburg for, as Elizabeth boasted to a friend, 'We out sail Everything.'[5]

They reached Cronstadt – a seaport town on the island of Kotlin at the eastern end of the Gulf of Finland, home to the Russian navy – on 20 August, where it was discovered that the yacht was too large to approach any nearer the shallow mouth of the River Neva than Peterhoff. Accordingly, Vice-Admiral Count Ivan Chernyshev went in person with his equipage to meet Elizabeth and escort her in style to St Petersburg. Chernyshev was a flamboyant character who, though involved in politics, was probably better known for his expensive clothes – he was enormously wealthy – and his prominent role in the social life of the Russian capital. He was also 'an Anglophile without knowing why',[6] as one Frenchman remarked, perhaps a little crossly, and had served as Russian Ambassador to London for two years from June 1768. Here he could not have failed to encounter the famous Miss Chudleigh for, as the Duke of Kingston's valet had remarked, she entertained all the foreign diplomats at one time or another.

Two days later, on 22 August,[7] Elizabeth arrived in St Petersburg, where she had her first glimpse of Peter the Great's extraordinary new city at the mouth of the Neva. Here, until 1703, there had been only marshy riverbank and low-lying islands with a scattering of fishing huts, surrounded for miles by birch forest, and swamps infested with mosquitoes and frogs. Now there were broad paved streets (although a few were still finished with wooden planks instead), with smart brick houses decorated with stucco to look like stone. Along the edge of the Neva were most of the finest buildings, including the vast town mansions of the Russian nobles which were 'furnished with great cost',[8] according to one English observer. On one of the islands, visible from some distance, the copper gilt spire of the cathedral of St Peter and St Paul – very different from the Oriental onion domes of Moscow – glinted in even the weakest sunshine. What many first-time foreign visitors found striking about this city of 200,000 people, however, was the way there were 'some streets very magnificent but there are stately palaces & miserable ruins mingled throughout . . . you find a mixture of grandeur & filth; in & out of their houses, in every Street'.[9] More experienced Russia hands merely noted that this mixture of little wooden houses and fine buildings was less prevalent than in Moscow.

Catherine was then secluded at her country palace at Tsarkoe Selo, built by an Italian architect, Bartolomeo Rastrelli, in the 1750s for the Empress Elizabeth. It was a vast place, 'the compleatest triumph of a barbarous taste',[10] one unimpressed Briton called it, its long grey-green façade of columns and porticoes glittering with gold. Everything was gilded, inside and out, even the huge statues of Atlas supporting the columns on the upper storey. Catherine, however, had commissioned a Scottish architect, Charles Cameron, to remodel some of the state rooms in a plainer, neo-classical style, and once this was done Tsarkoe Selo became her favourite retreat. When she was there, she saw almost no one, so it seemed unlikely that Elizabeth would be granted an audience with her for some time. In fact, as soon as the arrival of the English Duchess – 'famed for her beauty, her wit, her luxury, and her licentious adventures',[11] as one resident put it – was announced, Catherine sent her a note to appoint a day in the near future for receiving her.[12]

The British representative, Richard Oakes, informed his superiors in London at once of St Petersburg's newest and most exotic arrival though he obviously did not expect to be troubled by her. 'To conclude from the Sense she shewed of the Disappointment she met with at Vienna with regard to her Title', he wrote, 'and from some preparatory steps she seems to have taken here, she means to be presented at Court as Dutchess of Kingston, through the Canal of Count Ivan Chernichew, and not apply to me on the Occasion.'[13] Elizabeth had indeed taken preparatory steps, for the previous December John Williams had been fretting about 'them 2 Pictures Which you and me took Down in the Blue Room – I tould you that that her grace has given away'.[14] These two paintings from Thoresby were sent as presents to Chernyshev, and they turned out to be very generous gifts indeed. Elizabeth, whose inability to differentiate between good art and 'perfect trash' had been so remarked upon in Rome, had innocently given away a Claude Lorrain and a Raphael.[15]

In the circumstances, Chernyshev's energetic championing of such a generous English visitor was hardly surprising. As Oakes predicted, he was not called upon to present 'Lady Bristol' to the Empress; there would be no repeat of the embarrassing events at Munich and Vienna. Instead, it was 'through Count Ivan Czernichew's good offices'[16] that she was invited by Catherine to Tsarkoe Selo just five days after her arrival, where she was received as Duchess of Kingston. 'Her being introduced by that Gentleman, in a less ceremonious Manner than is usual, – was probably the Salvo thought of for The Empress passing over her Pretensions with regard to Title.' This first meeting was apparently a great success. Elizabeth was 'treated with a great Deal of Distinction' by the Empress, with whom she had a long conversation before joining the Imperial family in watching a comedy that had been staged especially for the occasion. It was noted that the Empress gave the Duchess the seat to her right, which was the highest honour for a visitor, and that the Grand Duke and Duchess, Catherine's son and daughter-in-law, 'shewed the utmost attention and politeness to our heroine'.[17]

Elizabeth was thrilled by such a flattering welcome – and as the Duchess of Kingston, too – and was soon happily writing to Lord Barrington that 'Her Imperial Majesty is gracious as she is great to me she was all gentleness courtesay & affection, gave me the same honours appartments attendants as to the King of Sweden – gave me preceedence after the Grand Duke & Duchess, her feeling and sympathysing Heart loves me because I am unfortunate'.[18] In fact, Catherine's attitude to the new arrival was one of amused curiosity as much as anything. Privately, she confided to one correspondent, 'Speaking of follies: the Duchess of Kingston has come here in her own yacht with French colours . . . she is certainly not lacking in spirit, of course: she likes me a great deal, but as she is a little deaf and I am unable to raise my voice, she will derive very little benefit from it.'[19] If Elizabeth hoped that this was the start of a friendship as close as the one she shared with the Electress of Saxony, it seemed her wish was unlikely to come true.

As the ever-observant Forster noted, the Duchess now exerted herself to return the compliment by hosting a magnificent dinner aboard her ship. Chernyshev and his party arrived in a large gondola, shaded from the sun by an awning of crimson velvet embroidered with gold. The Admiralty yacht and another twenty gondolas carried the rest of the guests to their destination. As soon as the food was served, 'a band of music, composed of fifes, drums, clarinettes, and French-horns, played some English marches, and other pieces suitable to the occasion. After dinner there were some concertos on the organ, which is placed in the anti-chamber.'[20] All this was too much for one of St Petersburg's resident English Reverends, William Tooke, who complained bitterly that the Duchess, 'instead of exhibiting that dignity of behaviour and elegance of manners which might have been expected from a person of such exalted rank, seemed at times, by ostentatious displays of her wealth, to rival the entertainments of the palace'.[21] This was slightly harsh; thanks partly to the availability of cheap domestic labour, lavish parties were hardly a rare occurrence in Russian high society. Forster mentions, in the space of one week, splendid dinners given by the ambassadors of France and Spain and one in honour of the Duchess by Chernyshev, whom she later described as 'un excelant Bon homme'.*[22]

In any case, it would have been difficult to even approach the scale and opulence of Catherine's court and its entertainments. Even on normal court days, 'the riches and splendour . . . united the profusion of asiatic pomp with the ingenious invention of european luxury',[23] as one resident Briton later wrote. What made such a striking impression was the way that the clothing of both the men and women was covered with 'a prodigality of precious stones' and 'loaded with diamonds'. With their passion for jewellery, these were clearly people after Elizabeth's own heart. Besides these regular court days, there were endless festivals, banquets and masked balls for victories in war or in honour of various orders of chivalry, and for royal birthdays and anniversaries. Moreover, during the winter when the snow lay thick on the ground, there were vast masquerades at the palace, sometimes 8,000 people spread through twenty magnificent rooms.

In this whirl of dinners and dancing – so enjoyable that she had extended her stay to four weeks, instead of the fortnight she had talked about when she first arrived[24] – Elizabeth recovered much of her former energy and enthusiasm for life, even if Hervey's quest for a divorce still preyed on her mind. On 19 September, she wrote to the eternally patient Lord Barrington:

> You will not be surprised my good friend that my troubled spirit has sought repose even on the wat'ry element, the Baltick sea, nor the more colder northern clime has not treated me so Unkindly as have the cruel Lords my countrymen my relations my companions and many that call themselves my friends – I quit this place unwillingly tomorrow was I to bend my steps towards the place where you & a very few of my friends Inhabbit I might be

* 'An excellent gentleman'.

comforted but I return, for what?; to be again persecuted in the November term, by Lord Bristol – I have not deserved it of him I will not allow myself to be bitter and if I speak of him I must be sorrowful . . . I would he was in Heaven for he bears hard on my breaking Heart.[25]

Elizabeth was expecting to set sail 'if the wind is favourable on tuesday the 23 of Sept the Equanoxial winds does not fright me'. However, a mere two days after her letter to Lord Barrington, during the early hours of 21 September, St Petersburg was hit by a violent storm. This 'Hurricane of Wind',[26] the British Ambassador called it, raised the height of the Neva in a few short hours to between ten and fourteen feet above its usual level, before it dropped away again just as quickly. The damage caused by the sudden inundation was enormous, especially in the low-lying areas around St Petersburg; hundreds of people were drowned, houses destroyed and stores of food and wine utterly spoiled.[27]

There was another casualty of the storm, the Duchess's famous yacht, whose four anchors were unable to prevent it being flung on to a sandbank, losing its rudder and two of its masts in the process: 'there she now lies', she told a friend sadly, 'all the little pleasure I proposed in my life, was to be in her'.[28] The captain was blamed by some for the disaster, while others merely commented that 'the truth is that he lost his head for a moment'.[29] Besides, his English second-in-command had proved no better qualified to deal with such an unexpected situation. As a disconsolate Elizabeth told Lord Barrington:

> On friday the 19th Instant I had the honour to write to your Lordship that my ship lay'd ready for sailing with my baggage on board, waiting only for a fair wind, Eleven days brought me here, from Calais, and I might easily expect to arrive there, before term begins in November, which is upwards of two months – the ship laying four miles from St Petersburg – A Hurricane arose on the 20th such as are only known in the West Indias – she lost all her Anchors Cables rudder all her riging, masts, long boat &c – she is strain'd every where, and is little better than a   blessed be God the crew & company are safe, but how to get home with upward of fifty persons in this Season, God will I trust in his mercy

direct – Lord Bristol will not pursue me this term, Your Lordship will I hope interpose with him on that subject, and I will return to settle affairs as soon as possible.'[30]

Elizabeth wrote, too, to the Electress, who was exceedingly distressed by her friend's unhappy news and wasted no time in dashing off an emotional note in her own dreadful hand. 'Ah my dear friend how your last letter grieved me that at the very moment when going by the letter I received from you from Petersburg I believed you near to Calais, happily returned from a voyage of which you had every reason to be pleased you had suffered new sorrows you had been on the verge of being killed!'[31] This last was not, in fact, true; in her worry, the Electress had perhaps misunderstood Elizabeth's letter, or maybe Elizabeth had overdramatised the report of the shipwreck. However, the sorry episode had clearly troubled the Electress, who begged her friend to give up the thought of returning by sea at such a dangerous time of year, trembled at the idea that she might even now be on some stormy ocean, and assured her she would not have a moment's peace until she knew her 'dear, unfortunate friend' was safe.

The next task was to salvage and repair the magnificent yacht, Elizabeth's pride and joy, which was now resting on a sandbar in two feet of water.[32] Removing it from this position would be extremely difficult and take a great deal of time, effort and expense. To Elizabeth's relief, however, she was informed that the laws of hospitality required that all this work be done by her hosts. The British Ambassador explained, 'The Empress has undertaken the Expence of getting off and refitting Her yatch, (which cannot however be compleated before next Spring,) and the Vice Chancellor has been ordered to dispatch a messenger to England to prevent Her [the Duchess] suffering in Her Law Suits from Her unforeseen Detention here, by the Loss of Her Ship.'[33] To that end, the ship's stores and furniture were brought on shore to be kept safely in the offices of the Admiralty. Not until winter had set in, however, and its owner was long gone was the yacht eventually lifted on to the ice – 'with the labour of some hundreds of people, and by means of levers and engines constructed for the purpose'[34] – where the necessary work could be done.

The Duchess could hardly fail to appreciate such a flattering attention to her yacht by the Empress, whom she could not praise highly enough; Catherine was 'gracious, compassionate and generous, she has not an equal in the world for nobility of mind',[35] and 'so deserving of all the praise one can bestow upon her'.[36] It was not long before Elizabeth was expressing a desire of returning the following year. Richard Oakes shrewdly observed in one of his dispatches: 'Her Friend Ct Ivan Czernichew encourages a Design she pretends to have of spending the remainder of her Days in this Country; and I cannot help suspecting it of some parasitical View upon her Wealth.'[37] This was a problem she was to face many times in the years to come, although it was hardly surprising in this instance if Chernyshev came to the conclusion that a woman who could casually give away Raphaels as if they were mere baubles must be rich beyond imagination. Such a generous friend was definitely to be encouraged to spend more time in Russia.

For now, however, Elizabeth was under pressure to make her way back to France as soon as possible, in order to deal with her lawsuits. She had hoped that the Empress would lend her a frigate to take her back to Calais, but the offer was not forthcoming[38] and by early October she was making plans to sail a few days later on board a merchant ship instead. However, this must have fallen through, for on 21 October Richard Oakes was writing that Elizabeth was still there and 'is determined to depart by Land',[39] although she had not yet decided either her route back to Calais or the date she would be leaving. Her loyal butler at Kingston House, when he heard the news, said, 'I am glad of it – for this time of the year is very Dangerous to come by Sea.'[40]

Busy as she was making the necessary arrangements for transporting herself and her entourage back to France, Elizabeth was unable to ignore her impending lawsuit with Hervey, which continued to distress her. Even before the storm that had stranded her frigate, she had asked Lord Barrington to speak to Hervey on her behalf, and once she knew that her return to France would be delayed she confided in Lord Barrington that she was 'as serene as you have ever seen me under great afflictions, waiting and trusting in the Allmighty to deliver me from this world of sorrow – but why Lord Bristol should add affliction to the afflicted, without cause of resentment is beyond my penetration'.[41] Though she might put a brave face on it, the outcome of her trial had affected her badly, and in her more anxious moods she blamed her unwanted husband for it all and saw plots in his every action. At least she was fair enough to admit, however, that his desire to prove their marriage was not motivated by greed for she 'never heard he was covetous when he had less than he has at present'.

Hervey, for his part, was becoming increasingly frustrated by the delays in bringing the ecclesiastical court case to a conclusion, though he had long since ceased to be surprised by them. As he explained that October to Lord Barrington, who had written to request an interview, although he had begun his quest for a divorce soon after Elizabeth's trial, he had made every effort to regain his liberty without giving her any more trouble than necessary; 'as to her Fortune, as she knew, I never had received a Guinea from her on any Occasion whatever, nor any thing but an old Gold Snuff Box, given her by Ld Stair – so I did assure her I never would touch any thing of hers, which she must be convinced of, from my having refused absolutely when she married her Duke, even the repayment of the many very Considerable Sums I had formerly paid her Creditors for her'.[42] Since then, however, he had met with 'nothing but Chicane, delays, & expence from the Ladies <u>Proctors, Attorney & Agent</u>'. Clearly Elizabeth, fearing that as a spurned wife she would be more vulnerable, was making every effort to have the suit delayed until *after* she had settled with the Meadowses. The exasperated Lord could only say, plaintively, 'that all I wanted was my Liberty, that as to her Fortune, were she worth the Indies I w^d never have a farthing'.

As to that fortune, by November Elizabeth was still in St Petersburg cheerfully spending some of it. Early that month, she wrote to James Cox, her favourite jeweller in London, to let him know that she had arranged for the Empress to see some diamonds that Cox had prepared specially, in the hope that she would buy some of them. As a footnote, she added that she was well and would be leaving as soon as she had sorted out the small matter of her French crew, who had mutinied and deserted the ship on which she had arranged their passage back to France. It was a nuisance, she admitted, but at least she had the consolation of finding in Her Imperial Majesty 'a perfect friend'.[43] These pieces of news, she concluded, were for Miss Chudleigh, her shy cousin Isabella. In Elizabeth's absence, Isabella – Bell, her family called her – was now the chatelaine of Kingston House, and it was for her use that hampers 'with two couple of Rabett & two Pair of Ducks and 4 fine fowls – & pork all good and fine'[44] trundled down weekly by wagon to London from Thoresby.

In St Petersburg, a more famous Chudleigh had, in a flurry of activity, put the finishing touches to her travel arrangements. On 13 November, she wrote again to Lord Barrington to tell him the news:

the day before yesterday - 33 of my ships company saild out of this harbour, with their Captain – I have only taken these two days, to endeavour to settle my affairs here, leaving all my Cloaths baggage &c with every thing belonging to the unfortunate wreck – the Post Horses are now in the Court, and at the first Hour after Midnight, I set out on the most horrible journey that, can be Immagined – the Roads ever bad through Courland are as they are here, made Infinitely worse by the Inundations I dare believe Lord Bristol will soon be sattisfied – for my strength cannot hold out this journey, my Constitution is weak'ned by sickness & sorrow, I have at this present the St Antonys fire allmost all over me, but Ill fortune has not yet Conquerd my resolution – I still walk forward bearing & forgiving nor have I ever Injured or ever will even my greatest persecutor – I recommend myself, my good friend to your protection your friendship is a comfort to me in all my sorrows And be assured that I will forever Persevere in that resolution I have long since made, to endeavour to conquer fortune by daily study how to bear it.[45]

The conscious innocence that had been Elizabeth's great support during her trial by the Lords at Westminster Hall was clearly still as strong as ever. Whatever the Lord High Steward had said at the conclusion of those proceedings regarding the punishment her own conscience would surely supply, even though the Lords could inflict none, Elizabeth continued to regard herself as the injured party. Her misfortunes were not of her own making; they were the fault of Hervey, for having married her in such mysterious circumstances, and the Meadowses, who refused to accept that the Duke had preferred not to leave them his money. They chose to persecute her, as she saw it, for their own advantage, and all she could do was return as soon as possible to deal with them all.

CHAPTER 16

A Terrible Journey

I am I think a wanderer upon the
face of the Earth.
Duchess of Kingston,
25 November 1777

Elizabeth's gloomy predictions on the awfulness of her impending journey were soon proved all too correct. The weather was so dreadful that it took eleven days instead of the usual three to reach Riga from St Petersburg, and would have taken longer if Her Imperial Majesty had not provided Elizabeth with a gentleman escort called Mikhail Garnovsky, 'in whom she had, justly, great confidence',[1] who had been given full powers to order whatever was necessary to make the Duchess's road a little smoother. As she told Lord Barrington in a letter dated 25 November:

the floods & snow have destroyed the roads entirely and I have been four Hours going one Mile – My servants have had beds but one night not being able to arrive at those posts where they would have been better provided – Her Majesty has commanded the Governor of this fortress to assist me in Every thing in his power and to do me all the Honours of service possible – he has Implicitly Obeyed her or I must have remained here notwithstanding my Inclinations to go forward, the Rivers are froze in many places, but he has kepd the ferrey open by passing large boats backward & forward for thirty six Hours untill my coach arrived that it might be got over with safety but how I shall perform the rest of my journey I am at a loss to tell for I cannot expect to find another Empress of Russia in any other part of the world nor can I tell why she has taken your unfortunate friend so much under her protection & friendship but she is so good as to say that she will be my advocate my council & friend forever.

She was still bewailing her fate and the twin-pronged attacks of Lord Bristol and Evelyn Meadows, who 'persecutes me because he would not deserve his Uncles friendship'. As if these lawsuits and the dire state of the roads, which meant that her carriage had to be serviced at every stop, were not enough to make her anxious, she was also miserably ill. In a flood of self-pity, accompanied by a classic example of self-delusion, she assured Lord Barrington that in two days' time:

> I shall again set forward on my journey with this only fear that my health & strength will not suffer me to proceed – last night I had a fever from Nine Oclock till five in the morning and as sorrow does not assist my slumbers my weary spirit tires of saying who have I injured who have I offended if it is my fortune that they want, I think my Lord I had better give it, but to Evelyn it is Impossible, because it would frustrate the Good Dukes Intention, a very little would content me but I believe they aim at all. I flatter myself that notwithstanding the many Imperfections I do possess I shall ever deserve your friendship for the high value I set up it.

By mid December Elizabeth had struggled, at great cost to her physical and mental strength, as far as Königsberg,* where she confided in Lord Barrington that 'if my mind was made to despair I should think it Impossible that I should arrive in any wishd for Port, Evelyn Meadows declared on the day of tryal I should have no rest while on the face of the Earth, and minds guided by superstition, might be led to beleive that he could Influence my Desteny'.[2] Much like her previous letter to Lord Barrington, this was a catalogue of woe and disaster. In some places the rains had been so severe that it had taken twenty horses to pull her carriage through the axle-deep quagmire, making the journey painfully slow; in others, the bad roads

---

* The German name for Kaliningrad, then part of Prussia and now the main town of the tiny piece of the Russian Federation wedged between Lithuania and Poland.

had repeatedly obliged her to get out of her coach and shiver in the snow and hail, which had resulted in 'a violent rheumatism' in her back and four days of fever. She was so tired and so depressed that on their approach to Prussia, where they were stuck in quicksand for three hours with nothing to do but look at the melancholy view of ships wrecked by the September storm, she was reminded of her own fate, 'toss'd by a troubled sea, each wave divides me from my friends & my fortune my fortitude alone stands unmoved & providence in whom alone I trust gives me strength to bear those evils that cannot be avoided'.

Elizabeth left Königsberg in the direction of Berlin on 16 December, a journey she assumed would take ten days, even 'in the bad state of health I am in'.[3] Thanks to the weather, unfortunately, it took considerably longer than that to reach the Prussian capital. On Christmas Day, Elizabeth wrote to Lord Barrington from the middle of nowhere, 'the most melancholy place I ever saw, it is near Marienburg* a new acquisition of the King of Prussias from Poland'.[4] She had been severely delayed again on the road, which had done no favours to her fragile health. As she informed Barrington:

I am at this Instant made a prisoner by the frost this is the 8th day I have been obligd to stay at an ale house by the side of the river nogat, which is not sufficiently froze to suffer any Carriage to pass, but is closed so firm as not to be able to pass in any ferrey; the post is obligd to leave his Carriage and to pass on foot; a Courrier from St Petersburg, going to Berlin offer'd a Hundred Crowns to go over and they would not attempt it, they flatter me with the hopes, that, this nights frost if it should continue to morrow might make it sufficiently strong to pass the river the day after, the Carriage must be taken to pieces, and at three miles from this place I must pass the River Vestule† twice.

Elizabeth eventually arrived in Berlin on 8 or 9 January 1778, despite problems with her coach,[5] for the awful roads had been as hard on it as they had been on its occupant's physical and mental health. Although the Duchess assured Lord Barrington that the

---

* The German name for Malbork, now part of Poland again.
† Vistula.

Prussian king Frederick the Great had been kindness itself, had offered 'any part of his dominion to reside in, with everything he can do to make me happy',[6] there is some evidence to suggest that her welcome in his capital might have been less than enthusiastic had she had time to test it. In an undated letter to his wife, whom Elizabeth had seemingly asked to present her at court, he wrote: 'If "la Chudleigh" wishes to be presented, she must apply to the English minister,* so that we can know in which name to receive her; but the best thing would be not to see her at all.'[7] The question of what to call his English acquaintance was certainly on Frederick's mind; a few months before, during a meeting with several foreign ministers, he interrupted his conversation with the Russian Prince Dolgorucki to ask Elliot, 'What is the Duchess of Kingston's family name?'[8]

Not long after her arrival, on the evening of 9 January, Elizabeth waited on Elliot, for she had learnt that he had some letters 'which she Imagines are of Consequence, beeing directed to his Care, without her knowledge'.[9] Having seen him, however, she suddenly remembered what a terrible hurry she was in to reach Calais. She would, therefore, be setting off again the following day if her coach had been mended in time. As a result, she informed him sadly, she had written to Frederick 'to make Excuse for not paying her Duty and respects before her departure but will have that Honor in the spring as she goes by Venice to Rome'.[10]

This was neither the first nor the last time that Elizabeth would suddenly remember an urgent reason to be elsewhere immediately after an interview with the resident British minister. It came to be a convenient face-saving fiction in countries where her welcome at court turned out to be rather less flattering than she had hoped, and created an indelible image of her scurrying restlessly and relentlessly across Europe. It was an impression she was also aware of, for in one letter to a friend she commented sadly, 'I am I think a wanderer upon the face of the Earth but it will please the Allmighty God some day to give me my place of rest.'[11]

In this particular instance, the polite excuse was lent considerable support by the undeniable fact that she really *was* in a hurry to reach Calais, for the letter she had just received informed her that if she did not meet her legal advisers there on 19 February she risked losing the

* Hugh Elliot.

suit that Hervey had brought against her. She took her leave of Berlin at once, stopping only to ask Hugh Elliot's opinion on the best route to her destination, for she thought Westphalia was 'a terrible country'[12] and wondered if she should not go via Frankfurt am Main instead. She asked, too, if he could kindly alert the appropriate people that, because of the bad roads and weather, it was impossible for her to reach Calais before the end of the month at the earliest.[13]

Whatever Elliot's travel advice, Elizabeth carried on in the direction of Dresden, where she arrived on the evening of 13 January, despite further problems with her coach. At once she went to see the Electress Dowager, with whom she shared a quiet supper.[14] It was a bittersweet reunion for the two friends, for ten days earlier the news had reached Dresden of the sudden death of the Elector of Bavaria on 30 December.[15] The demise of her brother had been a complete shock to the Dowager Electress, as it had been to her son the Saxon Elector. This was not the only surprise in store for him, however. Two years before, his mother had made over to him her rights of inheritance to several large family estates in Bavaria, on condition he paid her considerable debts – 'around 700,000 dollars',*[16] the British representative thought. Now, it was discovered, these estates had been bequeathed instead to another relation, the Elector Palatin: an arrangement of which, it seemed certain, the Electress Dowager must have been aware. Not surprisingly, her son was furious with her apparent deception, and she was obliged to stay away from court for some time.

Elizabeth, despite her hurry to move on towards Calais, remained quietly in Saxony with the disgraced Electress Dowager for four days while her coach was made roadworthy again.[17] The pause provided her with an opportunity to answer a letter from Prince Radziwill, who had persuaded the Austrians to return his estates in their new Polish territories and was hoping to persuade the Russians to do the same. Elizabeth was full of encouraging words, advising him to make his peace with the King of Poland, and to trust in the favours of Catherine the Great. 'She has already returned everything to Prince Czartorichsky',[18] Elizabeth pointed out, 'why may she not do the same for you.' Elizabeth was anxious to provide more practical assistance, however; she assured Radziwill she would do all she could to enlist her friends in St Petersburg to his cause. They had, after all,

---

* Presumably he meant the Saxon 'thaler'.

promised each other that they would be friends, and as such she took an interest in everything that concerned him, and was grateful for the interest he showed in return.

Unable to do any more for now to help her friends, Elizabeth set off once again on her exhausting journey to Calais, 'and if my strength will permit I shall travel night & day',[19] she told a friend in England. She would, however, be continuing without the much-trusted Mikhail Garnovsky,[20] who had accompanied her on the Empress of Russia's orders all the way from St Petersburg. The weather, unfortunately, was still against her. On the road between Eisenach and Bercka – if there was one – the snow was so deep that eleven people had to help support the carriage to prevent it overturning. Eventually, it stuck so firmly in the snow that part of the coach broke and it had to be left there all night while the Duchess was taken in a cart to a grubby little inn which compared unfavourably with the worst parts of her own stables at home. Only her philosophy sustained her, she solemnly told Lord Barrington.[21]

By the end of February or beginning of March, she had reached Brussels, where she heard terrible news. On 24 February, while she was still battling her way to the French coast, the ecclesiastical court had heard Hervey's cause and confirmed the verdict of the House of Peers; 'and . . . accordingly gave it as their opinion, that the marriage was strictly legal'.[22] Elizabeth was now the Countess of Bristol in the church courts as well, and her Earl could set in motion his plans for a divorce on the grounds of adultery. If he succeeded, she believed she would be more vulnerable to the Meadowses' attacks. 'I have as I dare say you are well acquainted, appealed to another court I suppose it will avail me little more than time to remove my effects or to settle with Lord Bristol which I believe will be difficult',[23] she wrote to Lord Barrington when she eventually reached Calais in early March. 'I fear he has me now at a great disadvantage . . . patience is my only support and blessed be God I have a Double Portion.'

Her spirits weakened by the arduous journey she had just completed, Elizabeth was sufficiently disturbed by the decision of the 'Pious Dr Bettesworths' to make an extraordinary suggestion to Lord Barrington. She asked her friend to talk to Lord Hillsborough, who had been her champion in the House of Peers prior to the Westminster Hall trial, to see 'if the Lords could not be moved, to reverse their sentence . . . and if it was well managed with some leading Peers to Acquiese it is highly probable that the Ecclesiastical Court to whom I have now appealed would follow the Judgment of the Lords and reject Lord Bˢ cause in their courts and he would be as much at libberty as by a Divorce'. If that happened, of course, Elizabeth – with her reputation restored – would no longer have anything to fear from the Meadowses. It was a powerful motive for proposing it, and she had nothing to lose by doing so, though it is hard to believe she really thought it possible. She finished her note with a postscript, half weary, half boastful : 'PS The Chancellor said in his Court that my case was the Hardest, that ever appeard before the Lords.'

It was a relief to have Prince Radziwill to write to, for his own problems made hers seem less significant, and she had the added pleasure of feeling that she could be useful to him. Advising him, that March, to go to St Petersburg and apply in person to Catherine the Great for the return of his 'belles terres', it was obvious Elizabeth had the happiest memories of the Russian Empress: 'Towards me she has behaved like an angel – a true friend and I wish for nothing more than to see her again which I will surely do.'[24] Eager to help Radziwill, she proposed writing on his behalf to Count Chernyshev and, more importantly, Prince Potemkin. This, Elizabeth said, was the key to Radziwill's success, for Catherine had total confidence in Potemkin. 'I am sure you will be pleased with him', Elizabeth wrote, 'he is not a proud man but full of fine and great qualities he has a compassionate, generous and unselfish heart, he is a man of letters.'

Agreeable though it was to think about Russia, Elizabeth could not ignore her current situation. For the next few months, letters about Hervey's plans for a divorce flew backwards and forwards across the Channel as fast as the King's Packet could take them, with Lord Barrington the unfortunate go-between. In her frenzy of scribbling – sometimes from six in the morning until far into the night, by which time she was so tired that the servants had to keep waking her up – it was clear that as far as Elizabeth was concerned there were two main obstacles to her compliance. The first was that, in law, unless there had been a proper agreement before the wedding, all a wife's property actually belonged to her husband; the Married Women's Property Act was more than a hundred years in the future. Hervey might be sincere in his protestations that he gave 'his word of honour, that he will not give the Lady, any trouble with regard to her possessions and fortune; that as he has never been benefited one shilling by her, he desires to remain so; nor will he avail himself by any means of what the Law even in this moment authorises'.[25] However, as Elizabeth pointed out, given what the law allowed, Hervey's honour alone did not provide her with enough protection. She continued to protest that riches themselves were of no interest to her – really believed it was true – and even told Lord Barrington that 'if the fortune he [Hervey] obtains by establishing a Marriage give him as little sattisfaction as it has done me the sooner he has it the better'.[26]

Hervey, who took great pride in his performance of the part of a gentleman, grew increasingly frustrated and irritated by Elizabeth's unwillingness to accept his word that he had no designs on her worldly goods.[27] He failed utterly to understand how vulnerable she already felt, and how much more vulnerable she believed she would become if matters were not arranged with great care. He should perhaps have been less surprised, therefore, that she had received his proposals 'with the highest indignation',[28] particularly as he had threatened to cause all kinds of difficulties for her if she did not comply with them. As Elizabeth pointed out, 'as a gallant and gay Lothario he ought to know, that a woman of spirit can only be conquer'd by soft perswasion, and soothing eloquence'.

Another cause for concern was the fact that Hervey had the same counsel as the hated Meadowses, which Elizabeth felt was deeply unwise, even though their Chancery suit was apparently stalled. She did not share Hervey's opinion of that family's motives or principles, nor his feeling that 'they despair of success'.[29] She believed, not without cause, that 'they lay still to see what turn affairs take between Lord Bristol & me'. In the circumstances, it would be better for her unwanted husband to choose another lawyer to defend him against her appeal. The Meadows family were not the only people with a personal interest in Hervey and Elizabeth's affairs. Hervey's younger brother, the Bishop of Derry, to whom the Bristol title and riches would pass if Augustus died without a legitimate heir, had been doing some snooping in Rome and had tried to find out from her steward and her secretary if Elizabeth would, or would not, oppose the divorce. Elizabeth's insistence that Hervey must keep their business dealings 'a profound secret',[30] so easy to dismiss as paranoia, is more understandable given how many people had a vested interest in the proceedings.

Still, there is no doubt that the whole prospect of a divorce, even from a man she loathed, made Elizabeth deeply unhappy. Her letters

to Lord Barrington – who had 'shewn so noble & steady a friendship'[31] towards her, so Hervey said – are scattered with comments
on her state of mind and health. In late March, she confided 'my
Enemys have treated me so Ill that I am contented to remain in a
Voluntary Banishment';[32] by early April she commented, 'if Lord
Bristol should take my all, I am not in a worse condition than when
I enter'd on this painfull journey from this life to a better';[33] at the
start of May, she had 'had an attack which she thought would termi-
nate in a fit of the Palsy',[34] and was going to Monsieur de Cocove's
country house at Recques-sur-Hem for a few days.

All the same, Elizabeth was not so preoccupied with her legal affairs
that she could think of nothing else for these few months. In April,
she corresponded with her London jeweller James Cox, enclosing
four pearls to be set round with diamonds and a rough sketch of the
intended design; precious stones, it seems, were a wonderful panacea.
So, clearly, was food, for later in the month the Duchess ordered two
hundredweight of cheese from Thoresby. At the same time she asked
for some chintz furniture 'with the chair covers etc';[35] there was no
point in leaving it in England when she had already resigned herself
to the fact she would never set foot in the country again.[36] It is
extremely unlikely, however, that she also requested a copy of Samuel
Foote's *A Trip to Calais*, finally published in book form, in which she
was apparently 'depicted to the life'.[37]

By the end of May, with encouraging signs from London that
Hervey was making a serious effort to satisfy his wife's demand for
some more legally binding security for her money than his honour,
Elizabeth could turn her thoughts to that other unfortunate, Prince
Radziwill. She had finally received a reply to her last letter – the post
had been extremely slow – and was thrilled to hear that he was making
plans to visit St Petersburg. All the same, she could not resist prof-
fering some advice, advice that revealed she had appreciated one
aspect of Catherine the Great's world: that he should go alone or
with only a small entourage, for if he took any of his family they
might make different contacts 'and the slightest thing creates jeal-
ousies at Court'.[38] For the Empress herself, though, the Duchess had
the highest praise, and admitted: 'I love her more than I could express.'
A week later, on 4 June, she wrote again to urge him more strongly
to waste no time in heading to St Petersburg, and enclosing letters
of recommendation to Potemkin and Chernyshev for him.

By mid June, and with Hervey for now not giving her 'any apprehensions for my fortune, having appointed an emminent Council to treat with mine',[39] Elizabeth began to feel more hopeful that she might be able to deal with another problem that had been worrying her since her arrival back in Calais that spring. As she had explained to Lord Barrington at the time:

> it is absolutely necessary I should be at Rome – my steward has plundered my pallace my library where of well choosen Books considerably Large, which are now dispatched over Rome I had a fine collection of Pictures, my whole wardrobe, the common service of Plate which was in use till the day I left Rome and many valluable trinkets which was left in a Commode most of them are Pawnd and if I do not get there soon to redeem them, they may be sold for a trifle the first theft was Pawnd for five hundred pounds & I cannot tell what else may have been since disposed of in short my good Lord I am plundered every where.[40]

By June, the rescue was more urgent than ever. Despite her apprehensions about travelling in the heat of summer, Elizabeth arranged to leave at the end of the month 'to salvage what little is left'.[41] There were fresh difficulties about the legal agreement to safeguard Elizabeth's fortune, with Hervey protesting on one side that he had 'ever been, & is ready to give the Lady any proper Security for her Possessions to be deliver'd her',[42] and Elizabeth replying indignantly that she thought it 'the most unreasonable request on Earth, that I should not be made secure for all I possess on earth but by words'.[43] With Hervey muttering darkly that he 'must now proceed, or loose another year again; & therefore whatever disagreable Consequences may Ensue to her, from any further delay to Lord Bristol must be the Ladies own seeking',[44] Elizabeth decided Rome could wait no longer. Pausing only to tell Lord Barrington that she was aware Hervey could 'be very inconvenient to me if he pleases but he allso knows, that his business cannot be done without my approbation and consent',[45] she put the finishing touches to her plans to set out with all speed to rescue her goods from the city where she had once been welcomed so graciously.

CHAPTER 17

Trouble in the Eternal City

Contentment lost, each other treasure
To ease the mind essays in vain,
Riches and pomp take place of pleasure,
And misery leads the splendid train.
The London Chronicle, 4–6 August 1778

Elizabeth set out for her third visit to Rome on around 2 July, and by the middle of the month was at Lyons 'in perfect health'[1] and sending instructions home to the housekeeper at Thoresby 'that she need not trouble herself to pickle or preserve any thing, as . . . no such articles will be wanted'. Two weeks later[2] she had reached Leghorn* by felucca from Marseilles,[3] while at Kingston House her gardener Henry Mowat prepared to head for St Petersburg with a present from his mistress for the Empress: 'Twenty brace of Gold pheasants, and such a collection of other divils as I beleive was never got together in one place'.[4]

The Duchess was in Rome by 15 August,[5] a day earlier than the Italian newspapers had confidently predicted.[6] This was in spite of the fact that, unlike at Lyons, she was now in a 'very bad state of health'.[7] She had been in too much of a hurry to stop at Florence to reminisce with Horace Mann, which led him to speculate whether 'the rebuff that she met with at Vienna will induce her to shun this Court hereafter'.[8] But her haste was in vain. On her arrival in the Eternal City, she learnt that the distressing reports about her property were only too true; as she later told a friend, she had 'been robbed at Rome of many thousands'.[9] Her first action was to remove

* Livorno, on the north-west coast of Italy.

the valuables she had wisely left for safekeeping in the Monte di Pietà. Some were shipped to Leghorn to be taken by Russian warship to Calais; the rest – 'the richest part of it'[10] – were dispatched to the Italian port in wagons. Unfortunately, by the time its precious cargo arrived, the Russian fleet had already sailed and Elizabeth was forced to return to Rome with her treasures.[11]

As if this was not enervating enough, the weather was unbearably hot. Since June, Rome had been a well-fed brazier, as one drained visitor described it, 'in which we are alternately broiled, stewed and baked'.[12] To add to Elizabeth's woes, it was also made abundantly clear that her travelling countrymen, who made up such a large part of the society in Rome, were determined to make life in that city as disagreeable for her as they could. With smug satisfaction, one female tourist noted that 'no persons of fashion noticed her; however she pushed herself into the public conversazioni, but the reception she met with did not admit of her going twice'.[13] There turned out to be little benefit to Elizabeth in having, as another British observer noted, 'worked her way into the great houses'[14] and made friends among the Roman nobility. The fine welcome given to the hordes of wealthy British visitors, once such a benefit to Elizabeth, now became a handicap to her. Everywhere she went in the city – from Piranesi's famous print shop near the Spanish Steps to the ruins of the Coliseum – she was bound to encounter someone from the land of her birth. The only place she was sure to escape them was in her first-floor apartment in the Palazzo Guarnieri, which her agent had rented for her after she had been asked to quit her former accommodation the previous year, for most shared the view of one British visitor that 'we cannot visit the Scarlet Woman stigmatised & burnt in the hand by metaphor'.[15] There were even rumours that the Pope had ordered the bigamous Duchess-Countess to quit the city.

Whether there was any truth in this, Elizabeth had probably taken her leave of Rome by the beginning of October at the latest, for she had never intended it to be a long stay. Several boxes of the more valuable possessions were apparently moved to the Convent of the Ursulines under the care of an English nun called Mary Wortley Montagu,[16] a relation of the Duke of Kingston, and would be sent for later. Only the most basic furnishings were left in the Palazzo Guarnieri, which Elizabeth continued to rent.[17]

In any case, by early November Elizabeth was back in Calais, after an exhausting journey made infinitely worse by the elements. As she told one correspondent, 'allmost every disaster by land and sea made my voyage tedious as it was dangerous'.[18] Somewhere, presumably between Leghorn and Marseilles, they had been 'on the point of ship-wreck',[19] though as Elizabeth explained to the Duke of Newcastle with quiet pride, 'I was the first that leaped into the boat to save myself from the Perils of the sea.' Propped up in bed in Calais at last, safe though far from well, she could catch up on her more urgent correspondence.

The most important letter was one of condolence to that kind Duke who had found her guilty 'unintentionally'. Newcastle's son Lord Lincoln, on his way to Rome for the recovery of his health, had died on the journey through France. Elizabeth rushed to offer some philosophical crumbs of comfort:

> I pray you in the name of all your friends none more sincerely attachd than myself to be comforted beleive me my Lord that good Souls who depart this life are in a far happyer state than we poor mortals left on Earth and never beleive that we are separated for ever for your faithfull wife, dear son. my ever loved and honourd husband are only gone before and we shall once again see them and share with them that place of rest & peace not to be found on this side of Eternity.[20]

If she showed real sympathy and concern for the Duke's problems, she was not less eloquent about her own sorrows. Her spirits lowered by ill health, she was clearly finding it difficult to live up to her own favourite 'excellent maxim . . . of Sir Francis Bacons that Fortitude would Conquer Fortune', as she poured out her feelings to Newcastle, and urged him:

> do not forget the persecuted Dutchess of Kingston who was wretched, askd the consent of the laws of her country to be happyly united to the man she loved, lived five years in perfect happyness, now deprived of him she adored, unfatherd, unmotherd, no child to comfort me, and bereft of brother, sister and all of kindred obligd to seek for peace & quiet in a foreign land all united at home to deprive me of my fortune and for w^h fortune . . . I only

contend to support the Will for the sake of the adopted of the late
Dear Duke of Kingston, I am weary of my pilgrimage, and now
safely in my bed I think myself willing to pay the debt to nature.

Accompanying this letter was another brief, businesslike one asking
Newcastle for his support for the Duke of Kingston's nephew Charles
Meadows, who a few days before had arrived in Nottingham to offer
himself as a candidate for the parliamentary seat left vacant by Lord
Lincoln's death. However, it was to another Meadows that she wrote
next, for she had evidently received a business proposition of some
kind from Charles's increasingly debt-ridden older brother Evelyn.
It was one, though, that she was obliged to turn down for, she
explained, 'as putting you in possession of his Estate was absolutely
Contrary to the purport of his [the Duke's] Will that Consideration
. . . lays me under a necessity of refusing the Compromise offerd'.[21]
More in sorrow than in anger, she reminded Evelyn of his own
part in creating his current misfortunes. After all, on several occasions since the reading of the will she had offered to settle money
on him, because she felt sorry for the fact that he had been cut out
entirely from the Duke's succession. Even after the trial, she had prof-
fered an annual income of £2,000 'as a Gift'. Yet all he had done in
return was attack her and, given that 'Self preservation is the first
law in nature', she had been forced to defend herself. Now it seemed
that the validity of the will would finally be tried in the Court of
King's Bench in the coming term, although Evelyn was trying to have
it put off in the hope, so the Duchess thought, that some of the
witnesses in her favour would die in the meantime.[22] She, however,
had no objection to the cause being heard soon; the prospect held
no fear for her, she told her adversary. All the same, she urged him
to 'give up this bad proceeding and trust to my generosity to Assist
to make You happy'.[23]
A few days later, Elizabeth was writing to her jeweller James Cox,
who had some troubles of his own, to assure him that she hoped he
would 'soon get the better of your misfortunes'.[24] Unfortunately, he
would have to do it without financial assistance from her, for not only
had she been robbed in Rome but in Calais, too. Peter Dessein, the
wily owner of the Channel town's main hotel, through whose hands
more than £1,700 of the Duchess's money had passed in the first half
of the year, had cheated her: as she complained to Cox, 'Mr Dessin

has given me bills of Exchange on Bankers who had none of his money, and I beleive I shall loose Eight Hundred pounds.' However, this loss did not prevent her asking Cox to do more scraps of work for her, such as repairing a pair of garnet earrings. He was also engaged on a larger commission for Elizabeth, who was planning a return visit to Russia: a book to be presented to Prince Potemkin, finely decorated with his coat of arms. There was some practical business advice in the letter, too, for jewellery was something that Elizabeth took a real interest in and about which she was also knowledgeable: 'if you wish to have anything done for you at St Petersburg, I shall go to the Empress soon – but that you must not mention, I think the things you send there are too rich no person but the Empress can buy them, they like diamonds of a carrot or half a carrot each, strung to wear in any shape – pearl bracelets they like much'.

The news of the Duchess's intention to return had already reached Russia, along with her head gardener Henry Mowat and his collection of birds for Catherine the Great. One person looking forward to her return with mixed feelings was her chaplain the Reverend John Forster, whom the Duchess had been forced to leave behind in St Petersburg as he had 'a fit of ye Gout'.[25] Enraged though she might have been at his decision, it was a wise one on his part; he was an old man, and the rigours of the journey would surely have finished him off.

It was some time, however, before the anticipated reunion could take place, for by early February 1779 – with Charles Meadows safely elected in Nottinghamshire, and Bell Chudleigh back in Kingston House after a visit to Bath – Elizabeth was still in Calais, waiting for a shipment of Lisbon wine and rum from Thoresby[26] and unburdening herself to her jeweller.

I Received your Letter by last Post, I have a great deal of business to transact by this Mail, and should have had more if I could have got a Passport for John Williams to have returned to England. I have been obliged to send an Express to Versailles, for it is not possible to get even one blank Passport, I am very much indisposed; I was obliged to write all yesterday, until five this morning. I was up again at half an hour after eight, and am as fresh for writing as if nothing had happened, My disorders are all Nervous, and proceed from sorrow. I have annexed such dark and terrible Ideas to a Divorce that it shatters my whole Frame. I can bear a great deal, but when I look back on what I have born, I wonder at my strength.[27]

Summoning up all her fortitude, however, Elizabeth returned to the matter in hand, which was chasing up a few little commissions, settling any outstanding payments and asking Cox to find out how much it would cost to have 'two Mottos made in Brilliants for two Bracelets, which are to be put upon black velvet Ribbands'. The words were from Virgil, although Elizabeth was modest enough on this occasion to admit that as she was 'not positive or conceited about my Latin, you may shew it to a Good Latinest, and if I am not right, let me know'. Unfortunately, once this business had been dealt with, Elizabeth's fortitude seemed suddenly to evaporate. Clearly drained from the hours and hours of writing the day before and from lack of sleep, she allowed herself to become overwhelmed by her fears; so much so that with appalling indiscretion she chose to pour out her concerns in writing to her jeweller, just because he seemed 'so truely anxious for my happiness' and she was desperate for any sort of a friend in whom to confide.

Her main worry was that Hervey would eventually succeed in obtaining a divorce, in spite of all the obstacles she and her lawyers had put in his path. Her feelings of vulnerability all too clear, she confessed that 'I still think as I did from the beginning that I run a greater risk from Mr Meadows as soon as the Divorce takes Place. I feel my Danger, by that means I have no claim to anything that is his, and I risk my own.' Why, she asked Cox, could Hervey not understand that her resistance was not through any desire to be Countess of Bristol? As she pointed out, she had other titles, including that of Countess of Warth of Bavaria, and in her youth 'not one, but two Dukedoms, was at my option; but I have no regret on that Subject for neither of the two would have made me happy'.

She clung still to the idea that the Lords might be persuaded to reverse their 1776 verdict, particularly if 'a great Friend <u>not in England</u>' – meaning the Russian Empress – could lend her support. But here even Elizabeth in her agitated state realised she had been indiscreet, though not enough to tear up the pages and start again; so she issued strict instructions to Cox that he should burn the letter (which were obviously ignored). Secrecy was paramount for this plan to succeed, as Elizabeth stressed in another scribbled note to Cox, possibly added as an afterthought to this already long letter: 'You must be sensible this is a dangerous Letter to leave with any Person . . . I am under Fears lest a certain Great Personage Abroad should think I mention too much of her Friendship and make myself too sure of her extending her Favors to the length I have reason to imagine she will.'[28]

Again, she had been eager to reiterate that her happiness was 'not fixed on Riches'.[29] This oft-repeated assertion, along with her claim to both Newcastle and Evelyn Meadows that she was resisting the attempts to overturn her dear Duke's will only to uphold his dying wishes, seems at first glance to be so much humbug. Perhaps, though, what Elizabeth had begun to realise was that money for its own sake no longer held any interest for her, not since the death of the Duke, which she lamented 'more and more each hour that I live'. All the same, that did not mean she was willing to go into a lonely old age in abject poverty. The Welfare State was a long way in the future, and she could hardly rely on the Meadowses for financial support. In such circumstances, self-preservation was indeed the first law in nature.[30]

As February passed, though, Elizabeth was forced to come to terms with the fact that, barring intervention at the highest level, she could not put off the divorce for ever. By the latest set of papers that Lord Barrington had sent across, it was clear that the Earl of Bristol was willing to give her every security she could desire for her property. She had one small demurrer, regarding the two small estates in Devon she had not received from the Duke of Kingston – the one she had inherited from her father and another she had been given by Mr Pulteney – 'yet as I see the intentions are fair, and well intended on all parts', she told Lord Barrington, she was returning the papers signed. If these other estates were not covered by the agreement, she was sure it would be sorted out.

With all the toing and froing between London and Calais, it was almost inevitable that some word of Elizabeth's plans should slip out. On 3 March, the Duchess wrote to James Cox to reassure him that she had 'not the shadow of a suspicion that you had had the least hand or concern in propagating what required the most profound Secretcy, I thought only the Actors* knew anything of it'.[31] All the same, she asked him to return all her papers – although 'only in case of Death' she explained.

* Presumably herself, Hervey and Lord Barrington.

The rest of March and April passed in a flurry of preparations for the Duchess's next Russian visit. There were mundane business matters to deal with in England, despite a high fever, such as appointing someone – a Mr Penrose, presumably some relation of the Miss Penrose who had been her companion for several years – to one of the church livings on her estates.[32] Elizabeth also needed James Cox's 'very honest woman'[33] to string some pearls for her 'in the best taste you can' to decorate a petticoat. One worry was that Prince Potemkin's book was not finished; the sample of his coat of arms had obviously never arrived, and Elizabeth would be unable to remedy the omission until she reached Russia 'and my object was to have it there before'.

Book or no book, the following month the Duchess was on her way to St Petersburg aboard one of the Empress's own frigates. On 12 May she wrote to Prince Radziwill that she was 'at this very moment on board the Russian flagship twenty leagues* from Elsenau'†[34] on her way to lay herself at the feet of 'Her Majesty whom I love with all my heart'. Six days later, she had arrived, to the wry amusement of that same Majesty, who had been trying to arrange for a collection of books to be brought to Russia from France, with less success: 'It never even occured to me that these vessels could make a left turn in the Channel and collect this library from Calais.'[35] The Duchess's influence with Vice-Admiral Chernyshev was evident, though it was unclear how long it would last. Elizabeth had obviously already begun to demand the return of the two paintings, the Raphael and the Claude Lorrain, that she had so blithely sent Chernyshev more than two years earlier, claiming she had only asked him to look after them for her. As Catherine wisely remarked: 'My Vice-President has shipped his Duchess here in vain, she will deceive him like many others, and all he will ever have are the paintings she entrusted to his care and the lawsuits concerning these paintings.'

The warm breeze that had wafted Elizabeth from France to Russia also reunited her with her famous yacht, which having been repaired at the Empress's expense was at Cronstadt, where it made a pretty attraction for visitors.[36] It also brought her to a city where she felt

* Approximately sixty miles.
† Elsinore, or Helsingor, on the north-east coast of Denmark's easternmost island of Zealand.

valued – a rare enough situation in recent times – and whose people she consequently found delightful: the Empress herself, the 'honourable and gallant'[37] Prince Potemkin, the Countess Chernyshev, who was 'a charming woman a true friend'. Only the new British ambassador, Sir James Harris, stood aside, never once mentioning her in his official dispatches to London and refusing even to acknowledge her existence. Privately, however, he boasted that 'she fears me more than she loves me, & I believe no one ever went such lengths as I have ventured with her, without being exposed to her invective & dirt'.[38]

For Elizabeth, St Petersburg was one of the very few places apart from France where she was known by her former title, where as Duchess of Kingston she could enjoy the pleasures of a St Petersburg summer, with its endless days and white nights. Apart from such simple diversions as boat trips up the Neva to picnic and fish and listen to music, there might be breakfast parties such as one at the Summer Gardens for the Duchess of Courland and her friends on her birthday where 'they were all dressed men & women in a uniform – dancing on the hot sand in the sun shine, fountains playing and a fete like those ones has heard ones G Grandmother speak of in other countrys',[39] as Sir James Harris's sister Gertrude put it. Later that June there was a series of masquerades at Peterhoff, another of Catherine's palaces just outside the city, on the shore of the Gulf of Finland. The British traveller Nathaniel Wraxall had attended one of these only five years before and had been impressed by the grandeur and scale of the event, for there were at least 4,000 people there, although hardly any in fancy dress. The illuminations were better than anything he had ever seen before, for everything was lit up – the ornamental canal, the fountains and cascades, the grotto and long arched walks – and even in the woods beyond 'hung festoons of lamps differently coloured'.[40] Quite overcome with the magnificence of it all, Wraxall noted, too, the 'summer-houses, pyramids and temples of flame; and beyond all appeared the imperial yachts on the water, in the same brilliant and dazzling ornaments. Nothing could be better calculated to produce that giddy and tumultuous feeling of mingled wonder and delight.'

Elizabeth had quieter moments, as well: there were always house calls, including one from Gertrude Harris,[41] then on an extended visit to her brother; and in August she was in Cronstadt, dining with

Admiral Grieg,* where she came across Miss Harris again.[42] Then there was the more serious matter of how she could help Prince Radziwill regain his estates, using the influence she believed she possessed at the Russian court. Radziwill had been delighted to receive her letter of 12 May, and had written back to assure her how much she had been in his heart and how worried he had been in the absence of any news from her. 'How joyful I am to be honoured with your gracious remembrance! I can never grow tired of reading this letter in which you assure me of it, as well as by your backing of me with Her Highness the Grand Duchess of all the Russias.'[43] Without a personal visit by Radziwill to Russia, however, there was little of real importance that could be done, and by October Elizabeth was occupied with her own more mundane business matters.

The housekeeper of her property in Bath had died, and Bell Chudleigh had made sure that no one had been able to take advantage of this to make off with any of the contents. 'Shering writes me that many people solicit her place, who cannot well expect it',[44] Elizabeth wrote to her cousin. 'Mrs Speake, I do not think it is safe to give it to her, as her husband drinks very hard & one drunken fit may set fire to the whole town of Bath.' The Duchess was having a few financial problems, for the Duke's will was still not settled, and having fought against it for so long she was now urging Bell to 'for god sake press Mr Field to have the Trial at Kings Bench in November Term – it wo'd be a dreadfull thing if the Duke of Newcastle was to dye before the decision'. But before the case could be heard, in the last days of December, one of Elizabeth's greatest fears was banished for ever. Three days before Christmas, Augustus Hervey, third Earl of Bristol, worn out with 'gout of the stomach', finally died at the age of fifty-five. There would be no divorce for Elizabeth after all, and although hers might not be a respectable widowhood, it was better than being a shamefully discarded wife.

As 1780 opened, the relieved Countess-Duchess flung herself into the life of a St Petersburg winter with enthusiasm, for the city was a gloriously romantic sight when the Neva froze solid enough to take the weight of the beau monde's richly decorated sleighs, their fur-muffled occupants gliding swiftly through the snow and ice, pulled

---

* Sir Samuel Greig (1735–1788), born in Scotland, but served in the Russian navy from 1763 to his death.

by pairs of small and nimble Russian horses. Some of the sleighs and carriages were very fine indeed; one traveller noted, 'They are quite open, and the most elegant I have seen have the appearance of shells, painted with showy colours; so that the ladies and gentlemen who drive in them resemble Divinities of the sea.'[45] It was wonderful, too, to see people at the end of a journey stepping into a noble mansion, its rooms as warm as toast thanks to huge brick stoves as tall as the ceiling, and shedding their furs 'like so many gaudy butterflies bursting suddenly from their winter incrustation'.[46]

On the last day of February, happy but so tired she miswrote the date, Elizabeth sent a glowing picture to her cousin Bell of the way she was spending her time in the Russian capital:

> I flatter myself that every Day draws nigher to the moment that I shall have the happiness of seeing you Her Majesty goes a Tour of Six Weeks to visitt her new aquisitions in Poland, and then I sett out I am so tireed with the pleasures of this Week* that I can hardly hold my Head up to Day, We have had four Balls running, where there was Her Majesty, the one more Magnificent than the other, I think that all the Jewels I ever saw in all the Courts of Europe, are not more in number than them here, I suped last Night with Her Majesty in a Green-House that was three Hundred foot long, the Walls was not only cover'd with Orange and Lemmon Trees but there was Walks of the same – as likewise Naturel Flowers, in the Month of February the same as in summer. The supper was Magnificent . . . I am going to spend the Evening with the Grand Dutchess they have just brought me word that I shall be too late I have not Dined nor Dress'd at 3 oclock & at 5 I am to be there.[47]

The way of life in St Petersburg clearly appealed to Elizabeth, and the climate agreed with her. By early April she was able to assure her cousin Bell: 'I am perfectly well – have lost the shortness of breath & sleep all night.'[48] Her former gardener at Thoresby, Henry Mowat, was also able to send back to England a heartening report on the Duchess whom, he said, had 'good spirits and better health, by much, then at any time since the Dukes death, go's to bed about ten, & gets

* Carnival.

up most mornings ab^t five, seldom later then six, works hard all day, and can get up stairs & down nearly as well as I can, Her Lungs are strong & good, and gives her cheers as often and as loud as ever!'[49] Although Mowat was now working for the Russian Empress, his former mistress did not neglect him; he saw her every day, 'she is my great friend, and more to me than a mother'. Mowat was particularly impressed with the Duchess's living quarters in St Petersburg near the Obukhov bridge over the Fontanka river, and not far from the Summer Garden, which she had rented from the Vorontsov family.[50] For, in typical style, 'Her Grace' had 'fitted up a very large House here, in the most Elegant manner possible, (the Furniture intended for the great gallery at Thoresby) Crimson Damask hangings, D^o Window Curtains, most splendid fine Musical Lustres! Grand Organ, plate, paintings: and other ornaments display'd to the greatest advantage.'

The contesting of the Duke's will was still in Elizabeth's thoughts, though she had grown increasingly confident about the outcome. That early April she was sufficiently buoyant to tell her cousin Bell to expect to see her in England 'the latter end of July or the middle of August . . . if the law business is finish'd before Ld Mansfield It will be the greatest satisfaction in the World to see you again I love you more and more each surviving day & never shall forget the thousand actions you have done for me'.[51] Once in England – the thought of which filled her with joy – she would be able to sort out several matters regarding the running of her various estates, in consultation with Charles Meadows who would, after all, inherit them one day.

Thrilled at the prospect of setting foot on her home soil again, Elizabeth began making arrangements for the journey. On 11 April, she told Prince Radziwill of her intention to set out on 12 May, and perhaps hoped to meet him on the way – although she did not say so – as her route would take her through his native territory. 'I will travel very slowly', she informed him, 'and I have to go by Reval* where I am obliged to stop for five days.'[52] Radziwill's problems continued to be of concern to her but, although she reiterated her willingness to do everything possible to help him, she sounded less sure of her own influence in the Russian capital than in the past. This was not just false modesty. Elizabeth – no fool, for all her talent for

* Now Tallinn, in Estonia.

self-delusion – had noticed a change: that in Catherine's court, with its ever-shifting alliances, her star no longer shone so brightly. She complained to her chaplain the Reverend Forster that she was going to Dresden soon, 'because people don't respect her enough here. She keeps open house but can't prevail upon any but Russian officers, who want a dinner to come to see her. The Empress is polite to her in public but she has no private conferences which is what she expected and what she herself had put into the English Papers.'[53] Sir James Harris, though hardly an objective observer, seemed to confirm this alteration when he wrote to a friend later that month that the Duchess had 'neither interest nor esteem & supports herself solely by impudence & an enormous expence'.[54]

Miles away in London, however, events were turning very much in the Duchess's favour. On 14 April, the Court of King's Bench at last heard the arguments from both sides in the case of the Duke of Kingston's disputed will. Nearly ten years had passed since the Duke's death, during which the Meadows family had done everything they possibly could to win their titled relative's riches for themselves and Elizabeth had done her utmost to prevent them. Now, in the space of just one hour, the will of the late Duke was finally and fully established in her favour,[55] thanks to the testimonies of the Duke's apothecary and his attorney. 'The latter', reported the *Morning Chronicle*, 'gave it in evidence, that when the Will was drawn, his Grace directed, that a blank should be left for the name in whose favour the greatest bequest in it was made, not chusing that the drawer of the Will should know, who that person was; and it appeared, that the Duke himself, filled up the blank, with the name of the Dutchess.'[56] To Elizabeth's overwhelming relief, her tireless persecutors were defeated at last. Her reputation might be lost for ever, but her fortune, at least, was entirely safe.

CHAPTER 18

The Queen of Poland

Bid him wake to new delight—
Crown the magick of the night.
The Gentleman's Magazine,
April 1780

If there was good news from London for the relieved Duchess, the reports from Dresden that spring of 1780 had been much less comforting. The Electress Dowager of Saxony's health had been declining since the previous December, when she had been laid low with what her anxious physicians had described as 'a flying gouty disorder'.[1] She remained ill throughout January and February, and several times her doctors feared the worst. By mid March, she appeared to be rallying. However, she had not appeared in public and, the British representative there feared, 'never will again, I had the honor of being admitted into her apartment two days ago and found her so low & so altered that I think she cannot hold it out much longer.'[2] He was right; Maria Antonia, Electress Dowager of Saxony, unable to fight her 'severe and tedious illness'[3] any longer, died on the afternoon of Sunday 23 April at the age of fifty-five. She was buried six days later, with great solemnity, by the members of her own court and household, who promptly embarked on six months of the deepest mourning.

Elizabeth, far away in St Petersburg, was suddenly deprived of one of her closest and most important friends. The Electress Dowager had been a valuable support in her darkest moments and a truly generous ally, with whom she shared a love of music, jewellery – and spending money. Here, Elizabeth proved to be no match for the gloriously extravagant Electress Dowager. According to the British representative in

Dresden, she died with debts of 400,000 'dollars',* although a mere
five years earlier her son the Saxon Elector had paid out on her behalf
somewhere between 500,000 and 700,000 thalers, much of the money
being used to redeem jewels – including some of the Elector's – that
she had pawned in Rome without his knowledge.[4]

In Russia, Elizabeth reacted to the mixed news with typical spirit.
That May, she gave a 'great Bal Masqué'[5] to which all the world was
invited, presumably including those who had laughed at her a few
weeks before at a concert at some Russian nobleman's house where
she 'fell asleep every time the music play'd piano, and awaked with
the forte'.[6] Even a humble Englishman called Samuel Bentham,
brother of the political philosopher Jeremy Bentham, whom Elizabeth
had previously refused to introduce to Russian society on the grounds
he was a mere architect,[7] was welcomed – though, sadly, he did not
condescend to give an account of the occasion, and there was no
Russian Walpole there to supply the deficit. It was a brief flash –
almost the last, though she did not know it then – of her old style,
when she had been such a famous London hostess.

On 21 May, Catherine the Great and a vast entourage, including
Chernyshev and an entire Italian opera company, set out on a six-
week tour of Russia's new Polish provinces, acquired by the 1772
Partition of that rapidly shrinking country. Elizabeth was also
expecting to depart soon after to rendezvous with Prince Radziwill
in Birz,† a village in lands that he still owned. On the way, she was
also planning to look at an estate in Estonia‡ which she had a mind
to purchase, even though the Empress had already given her a piece
of land outside St Petersburg on the banks of the Neva. As Samuel
Bentham commented, not entirely kindly,

> there are about 7000 slaves to this Estate, she is so full of the
> Thoughts of having so many subjects to lord over, that the poor
> woman is almost out of her sences. Sambouski . . . go's with her
> . . . to take a view of the Premises. – Before she can purchase an
> Estate she must have rank in the Country, that is, a Military Rank:

* Presumably he meant 'thalers'.
† Now Birzai, Berg in German, a village on the borders of Lithuania and
Russia.
‡ Then a province of Russia.

This the Prince* can give her or rather get for her, as high a one as she pleases. She will then be wanting Orders. She spends five or six hours at her Toillette now; when she has a Ribband and Star, to adjust, she will have no time left for Eating & Sleeping; – as to the latter indeed she spends very little time that way, a nap or two while she is in company seems to serve her.[8]

In mid June, in daily expectation of the Duchess's imminent arrival in Birz, Radziwill wrote to tell her – 'his best friend and protector'[9] – that he had put all his business dealings and other duties on hold. Unfortunately, he was to have a considerable wait. Elizabeth's departure from St Petersburg had been delayed by her 'fragile health which always seems to put obstacles in the way of my pleasures'[10] and which had forced her to travel even more slowly than she had envisaged. She had succumbed to fever passing through Potemkin's estates, had been bled at Narva, and had had to spend three days in bed with a high temperature further along her route. After 'all the difficulties in the world', she finally made it to Reval on 24 June. From there, her ill health making her a little irritated, she wrote to Radziwill to express her surprise at not hearing from him about her proposals for helping him which she had entrusted to the Polish courier by whom she had sent her last letter.

She was fretful, wondering if the trip had been such a good idea, for the Empress would be back from her tour of her Polish provinces by now, preparing to welcome the German Emperor Joseph II to St Petersburg. Elizabeth was concerned that she would be unable to return to Russia in time to pay her compliments to him, to be presented to him there as Duchess of Kingston, and thereby make up for the humiliation of four years before when the British ambassador at Vienna had refused to introduce her to him by that name. She was also worried that she might be obliged to return instead to England or France to consult her lawyers on various business matters. However, upon calmer reflection, she told Radziwill she would be leaving Reval on 30 June, and expected to arrive in four or five days in Riga.[11] From Riga it was only forty miles to Birz, where Radziwill kicked his heels for eight weeks while his limited funds ran so low that, as he told his brother, 'it is barely enough to escort the Duchess

* Potemkin.

to Niesweiz. That expenditure neither could nor should be spared since much of our family's fortune on which I am currently working may rest upon the assistance of that Lady.'[12] Not everyone shared that opinion, however, cautioning him against managing his business in St Petersburg through her for 'she does not seem to have a particularly substantial credit there'.[13]

At last, in early July – having had the good fortune to cross paths with the Emperor himself on his way back from Russia – Elizabeth reached Birz to a magnificent welcome, only the first of many entertainments that Radziwill would lay on for his guest, which Elizabeth later described as 'of an unequalled Beauty and Magnificence'.[14] If an account of these, provided by 'a foreign gentleman, who was of the party',[15] that appeared in print eight years later can be trusted, this was no exaggeration on the part of the Duchess. The celebrations, it seems, began the morning after Elizabeth's arrival, when Radziwill turned up in great state in a carriage pulled by six horses. Behind him, a line of thirty-nine similar coaches carried members of his family and entourage. 'In addition to these, there were six hundred horses led in train, a thousand dogs, and several boars; a guard of Hussars completed the suite.'

From here, Radziwill escorted his guest to a pretty village in the woods, which had been built specially for the occasion and decorated in the finest 'rustic' taste with leaves and branches. At the heart of the cluster of timber houses were three rooms laid out for a feast. First, however, the company was regaled with 'splendid fireworks', set off over the adjoining lake so that their reflections would increase the impact of the display. To add to the drama, there was also a mock naval battle between two small ships. Next came the magnificent meal, served on silver dishes, which was a great success. Afterwards Radziwill conducted Elizabeth back to the sleeping village where, on cue, the shutters of the houses were thrown open to reveal little stalls within, brilliantly decorated and full of 'the richest commodities of different kinds'. The Duchess was presented with 'a magnificent topaz, rings, boxes of all descriptions', before returning to the dining rooms to open the ball with the Prince. The evening ended with a huge and very extravagant bonfire, for no sooner had everyone left the ballroom than it was set alight, and rustic locals were seen dancing round the flames.

Pausing at every opportunity along the way for more lavish celebrations, Radziwill escorted his English friend to his estate near

Neisweiz. Here he held another feast, followed the same night by a boar hunt, which was attended by many of the Polish nobility. It was an extraordinary sight, for the woods were lit up by the flickering torches of an entire regiment of Hussars as well as those of the huntsmen. At some point, Elizabeth was also taken to spend a few days with the cultured Count Oginski, a political ally of Radziwill, who had his own theatre and orchestra at his estate at Slonim. Radziwill then continued with his guest to Warsaw, where he discovered that all these weeks of 'Finest Fetes'[16] and 'Most Magnificent Illuminations' had given rise to an interesting rumour. For in early August it was being whispered in the Polish capital that Radziwill was about to marry the Duchess although, his correspondent told him, 'the King himself and other leading officials do not lend credit to it'.[17]

The rumour took several months to filter back to England from the wilds of central Europe – for there was no British representative in Warsaw at the time and Poland was far from the well-trodden paths of the tourist trail – but when it did it caused a sensation. Forgetting in their excitement that the Duke of Kingston had left his money to Elizabeth with the proviso that she remain a widow, and that Radziwill was already married, they eagerly recounted the news that 'Mademoiselle Chudleigh, Hervey, Kingston, Bristol, Wartz; is now Princesse de Radzivil, and may be Queen of Poland, really married to him. The Prince of Radzivil is a grandee of Poland, and has it in contemplation to be King there at the next general election, which will make a curious finishing to the edifice of her extraordinary fortune.'[18] One correspondent thought he knew the reason for it, for he had heard from a very good authority that the Radziwills were considerably in debt, and had been negotiating for a loan in Amsterdam – that much *is* true, for Elizabeth had already suggested it would be cheaper to borrow money in England[19] – 'when Fortunately the Duchess of Kingston passed through Poland & offered a much easier Mode (In their opinion) of discharging their incumbrances'.[20]

But, even before the ridiculous stories had made their way to England, by September Elizabeth was travelling back to St Petersburg to settle her affairs, more than content with her fabulous reception in Poland and the 'beautiful decorations for the lavish entertainments'.[21] Glowing from the warmth of her welcome, she repeated to Radziwill her assurances that she would use 'all the little credit' she had at the Russian court to help him. She was probably back in the Russian capital as early as October, and definitely by 21 November, when – as it was being gossiped at home that she had now jilted Radziwill[22] – she wrote to her cousin Bell:

> I am under the greatest concern imaginable at not hearing from you – had you not been so very ill I might have been more patient, Till yesterday I quariled with the wind for their was three packets due, but yesterday the mail arrived & I was disapointed of a letter from you – & some times I hear from John Williams how you do but yesterday I had no letter from him & the frost has been set in 13 or 14 days & the Rivers was frose sufficiently to go 40 miles upon it We was all in expectation that in a week or ten days it would be hard enough for coaches to pass but a thaw & [rain] is come & I believe it will be a great while before the passage will be safe for coaches I am thank God very well this climat agree with me so well that if it was not to see you I had rather give half my income than come away. My nerves and numness in my limbs is quite gone – I wish you was as well.[23]

It had been a year of varying fortunes for Elizabeth. The death of the Electress had deprived her of a dear friend, whose faithful support would be greatly missed. On the other hand, the trip to Poland had been fascinating and the attention paid her there enormously flattering. More importantly, the threat from the Meadows family seemed to have been lifted for good, though the poverty-stricken Evelyn was spotted in Bonn in late November, 'in search of the Duchess of Kingston, to compromise matters with her'.[24] Elizabeth could now begin to put her finances in order in expectation of the Duke's will at last being settled, an event which his late Grace's unfortunate creditors were also looking forward to with relief.[25] Now, too, Elizabeth could complete the purchase of the estate in Estonia she had seen several months before. In March 1781, the *Revalsche Woechenliche Nachrichten** carried the announcement that a contract of sale had been concluded between Baron Johann von Rosen and the Duchess of Kingston for the properties of Fockenhoff, Toila and Orro, at a cost of 85,000 roubles.[26] As she told her cousin Bell with great delight:

* A Reval (i.e. Tallinn) newspaper.

I have got a mannificent estate Her Imperial Majesty has given it the name of Chudleigh & at the next revisian of Russia it is to be inserted in all the maps of Russia . . . I have one lawn of near 30 miles round 19 miles to the sea the rest bounded by woods with timbers fit for large shiping, the lenght of the woods I cannot yet tell, but in depth 16 miles in general part the lands are all good & two very profitable manufacturys* on them.[27]

Elizabeth could now embark on her ambitious project to turn this corner of the Russian Empire into a little piece of England. Maybe the pleasures of city life in St Petersburg were no longer as sweet now that the capricious Catherine appeared to have grown bored with her; or perhaps Elizabeth was homesick despite her strenuous efforts to always make the best of the hand that Fate had dealt her. Here at least, at Chudleigh, she would be able to keep herself busy, and show the Russians what a proper English garden looked like into the bargain, though it would be a challenge given the poor soil. She would also be able to grow fruit, as she had at her house in London, for the Russians produced nothing but strawberries, raspberries and currants; everything else – melons, pomegranates and pineapples – had to be imported from Astrakhan, which took three weeks.[28] They did, however, one traveller noted, 'have an Apple, which is called a Transparent Apple; and, when it is ripe, is so clear, that you may see the Kernels through it: The Taste is superior to any Apple I ever met with in England'.[29] As for vegetables, the Russians grew plenty of asparagus, french beans, spinach, lettuce, cabbages, turnips and carrots, but the cauliflowers were dreadful, assuming you could even get them.

Wasting no time, Elizabeth sent at once to Thoresby with her orders, and in the middle of April the delightfully named *Happy Meeting* – captain, William Posgate – set sail from Hull to carry its curiously mixed cargo to Narva.[30] There were five cases of bound books; an organ with all its pipes and barrels; ten casks of sea shells, to decorate a grotto, perhaps; a tent large enough to require eleven packages to

* There was much amused talk by Elizabeth's contemporary biographers about her becoming a distiller of brandy, and according to a 1792 survey of the Russian Empire, it was one of the main businesses of the region. However, it is unclear what the 'two very profitable manufacturys' actually produced.

hold it all; shrubs, flower roots and several ploughs, including one 'that goes without holding';[31] furniture and household china; and a 'Box of Pine Apples'.[32] For drinking, there were six casks of 'British Brewed Beer', '44 Dozen Bottles of Red & White Portugal Wine Quant^y 120 Gallons' and twenty gallons of white Spanish wine.

The rest of the consignment was rather livelier, including as it did an assortment of birds such as turkeys, ducks and turtle doves, along with six heifers and one bull 'with provision for the same', including hay. Also bound for Narva were four pointers – brown-eared Pero and Moll, the lemon-and-white Ponto and 'much spotted' Juno – along with an equal number of spaniels, the pedigree of each carefully noted on the inventory.[33] This small menagerie would be tended on the voyage by a young Lincolnshire man, Richard Maw, 'very honest, sober, industrious and well skill'd in all farming business',[34] who was heading to Chudleigh to work as the Duchess's farmer for a year 'for the sum of Fifty pounds . . . and to have his freight bore there, and to be found a House to live in his Table, and Firing, and if he does not like his place after one years service, to be allowed his freight back to England'.[35]

From Russia, shortly before the *Happy Meeting* set sail from Hull, Elizabeth wrote to her cousin Bell. She was still toying with the idea of a visit to England, although her agent at Holme Pierrepont, William Sanday, thought it unlikely given how many things she had ordered to Narva.[36] However, on 10 April she was still at St Petersburg, as she told Bell, 'waiting for the Roads being passable the great snows & frosts now breaking up is a time that lays two Neighbouring Countrys under water Courland & Prussia, as our coaches drove over the Ice the Bridges where taken a way the ice is almost gone & the passage not safe for a hevey carriage the Bridges will soon be replaced & in a week or two I shall set forward'.[37]

Elizabeth was 'thank God very well', although the same could not be said for Bell Chudleigh, who was clearly extremely fragile and desperate to see her cousin once more. Elizabeth urged her to travel slowly to Spa, to take the healing waters, and offered to meet her at Ostend, despite the risks: 'I shall be near you & if you want me I will come tho' it was at the consequence of my life, but my liberty if I was taken by the Dutsh* would be lost for ever.' If the journey proved

---

* Britain had declared war on the United Provinces in November 1780.

impossible, Bell would certainly see her in England the next spring when 'the peace will be concluded'. Anyway, by the end of June she would be in Calais 'by the sea side wishing for my dear friend'.

June and July came and went, and there was still no sign of Elizabeth in Calais. In fact, it was not until early August that she was spotted at a posthouse west of Chudleigh by an English couple, Baron and Baroness Dimsdale, who were heading to St Petersburg to inoculate the Empress's grandchildren against smallpox. The Duchess told the Baroness 'she was going to France, expressed great joy at seeing the Baron, and said I must go into her Room and breakfast with her, as she had very fine Tea, and Butter from her Country House which she had lately purchased and it was a very fine Situation'.[38] Indeed, the travellers soon had an opportunity to see Chudleigh for themselves, for the Duchess offered them her bed for the night and wrote at once to her steward Mr Wilkinson to warn him to expect them. Baroness Dimsdale noted in her journal:

The House stands delightfully pleasant, having a fine View of the Baltic which looked smooth and calm, but when I recollected how dreadfull it appeared the morning after travelling from the Haff, I should be very sorry to live so near it. We went about the Grounds the Steward said when the Dutchess returns next Summer there is to be very great Alterations, a new House built and the Grounds laid out. She gave sixteen thousand Pounds for it, and has only eighty Slaves. The Steward said she ought at least to have as many more. The Baron and I lay very comfortably in her Ladyship's Bed, every part of the Bedstead was Iron, and the Furniture white Dimity.* We were very well entertained, a good Supper and Breakfast.[39]

Wherever else she paused on her journey, however, Elizabeth was in Calais by early October and writing to her cousin about her plans and her problems:

My dear Bell, it is a real satisfaction to know my self so near you

---

* That is, the bed hangings were made of a plain, hard-wearing cotton; the house had obviously not yet been decorated to the Duchess's more luxurious taste.

by reason <u>if you cannot be easy without my coming to you I shall run all risks to make my dear friend happy</u>. I came here for that purpose 2500 miles I was rejoyced to find by a letter from your hand that you was better had moved onto a better air & that you was so reasonable about my coming to England; I shall now settle all the affaires, have the debts pay'd that are due by the Trustees of the late Dukes will, get some of my best things home by my own ship next summer, without any persons in Foreign Countrys suspecting of it; I must have livery & things fitt for my recerption, & not after so long an absence make a worse figuire than formerly; it would be shocking to have a mob at my heals for other peoples debts or faults, for certainly Mr Heron might have fulfill'd the Dukes will long ago.[40]

Elizabeth was full of pleasure at the thought of returning to England and seeing her cousin Susanna Haines's children again, especially the oldest boy Chudleigh, but most of all she longed to see shy, kind, quiet Bell, who had always been so close to her. Sadly, it was not to be. On 18 October, while Elizabeth fussed about debts and liveries, Bell Chudleigh died at Chalmington, her family home in Dorset, at the age of fifty-eight and was buried at nearby Cattistock five days later. The cousins had been close friends, had lived in the same house for many years and corresponded when apart, and now Bell, like the Electress, was gone for ever. The Duchess's circle of true friends was slowly, inexorably shrinking.

Life, however, went on and, by Christmas, Elizabeth – with no reason now to head for England – had abandoned dreary Calais and was in Paris in poor health. An attack of fever had left her energy levels depleted and she was forced to cancel her social engagements. She was sixty, no longer young, and despite all her efforts to increase her stamina by taking a walk every morning, she feared she would have too little strength for a visit to Versailles on 30 December. As she told her unidentified male correspondent:* 'You who have travelled, well know how important it is not to be the object of ridicule, to be in Paris for the great celebrations, and to see nothing; would be the same as going to Rome without seeing the church of St Peter.'[41] However, she hoped she would be better by the following week, and

* The letter is addressed to 'Monsieur'.

was looking forward to gossiping with him about their friends in his 'pays de délices'.*

Poor health was not Elizabeth's only problem as 1782 opened. Despite the Court of King's Bench's decision in her favour in April 1780, her financial affairs were still unsettled and she was still owed a considerable amount of money that she had paid out in funeral expenses and the like after the Duke's death. On 2 February, she wrote from Paris to one of the trustees, Sir Richard Heron, to complain about the continued delays:

> The loss and Expense that I have been at, is beyond all any Body can Imagine, The Anxiety, care, and sorrow, is what your humane heart can easily conceive, I am encline'd Sir, to think that with your assistance these tiresome affairs can soon be finished, and I do not doubt your Friendship and good Nature in that particular, and I entreat you Sir, to send to Mr Feild and beg him to forward every thing that regards those afairs. I have made a purchase of a pretty and profittable Estate in Estonia, it is a perfect Paradise; I depended upon the money I was to receive from the Trust to pay for it. it has been a great Mortification to me, and I have with great dificulty paid it, and that by takeing it from my Revenue, for the Law exhausted all my ready money.[42]

Elizabeth was impatient to sort out her finances for she had already found yet another property that she wished to buy, this time a house in Paris. It was an indication, perhaps, that Russia had lost some of its charm, and that she was contemplating settling permanently in France, the only other country to recognise her title of Duchess of Kingston. The sale of No. 16, rue Rochechouart in the parish of St Pierre de Montmartre was finalised on 14 February, with Elizabeth agreeing to pay Monsieur le Chevalier de la Crosse the sum of 78,000 livres for the property, and a further 12,000 livres the following July for the furniture, which included a large marble statue of Bacchus. However, she would not be moving in immediately for, the building inspectors reported, 'as the mansion appeared to the Duchess to be inadequate for her to live there comfortably, she suggested to Sʳ Chevalier de la Crosse that he have built . . . an extension to the building determined by a plan

* Literally, 'land of delights'.

which was attached to the sales contract'.[43] The additions were vast, more than doubling the size of the original structure, and would cost a further 60,000 livres. Leaving La Crosse – eager for a sale, as well he might be given that he had apparently paid only 24,000 livres for the house[44] – to organise the work, Elizabeth returned to Calais as soon as her health permitted to make arrangements for her next trip to Russia, for she had not yet given up on the place.

Before she could head once more to St Petersburg, Elizabeth had a few financial matters to take care of. She had been spending heavily, to the limit of her income, and in May there was the real danger that her bankers, Messrs Drummonds, would refuse to honour one of her drafts because there was not enough money in her account. There was a frantic scramble in England to collect the next round of rents from her various estates in time to avert the disaster, a process that was to be repeated several times more that year. As if all this were not enough to worry her, Elizabeth had also taken it upon herself to help the most unlikely candidate: Evelyn Meadows. That May, she answered a letter from Evelyn's wife with uncommon charity, given how much the family had subjected her to in their quest to relieve her of the Duke's money:

My Dear Madam

You will not measure my friendship by the length of my letter – nor by the swiftness of my return to yours – for in every thing that may be to your or yours of consequence I shall add feathers to my wings and give that speed to friendship that was deny'd to ceremony . . .

PS I pray to God to bless your babes – and send my kind love to Mr Medows – all shall be done that on me depends for your satisfaction.[45]

In fact, Elizabeth had already taken practical steps to ease the young Meadowses' largely self-inflicted financial problems, for one of her most striking characteristics in her later years was her capacity to not merely talk of forgiveness but to act on the words. Even when the memory of her trial was fresh in her mind, she had told Lord Barrington with real conviction, 'I still walk forward bearing & forgiving nor have I ever Injured or ever will even my greatest persecutor.'[46] More recently, to another correspondent, she had reiterated her belief that 'Revenge is not the part of a Christian.'[47] Willing not only to forgive but to help her penniless former persecutor, she had already paid out in March the sum of £200 from her account at Drummonds to 'E. P. Medows half of years allow^e to 25th Decr 1781',[48] and she continued the half-yearly payments for the rest of her life. Perhaps in the hope of a lucky windfall to boost her *own* cash reserves, Elizabeth was also indulging her old love of lottery tickets again, for she spent £48. 9s. on five of them that year.

The Duchess was soon on the move again; setting out not long after her letter to Mrs Meadows, she was at her estate near Narva by mid September. She had travelled overland this time, for at Hanau in Hesse she had stopped to write to several friends in Rome, including 'L'abbe Finatery'. Safely at her destination, Elizabeth now wrote to him again with a gentle rebuke for his failure to reply:

> I no longer call you my friend, because you have forgotten me; I had the honour of writing to you from Hanau, not a word of reply: I wrote by the same post to the Cardinal Prince, and was truly delighted to see by his response that he was in good health. I would like to be able to think that you are well also: Sometimes I think you must be ill, and sometimes that you must be dead, I do not know if I should weep for you because you are no more, or if I should be angry with you for your neglect; rescue me from this anxiety by sending me a few lines in St Petersburg . . . You must tell me by letter and not by the Gazettes everything that is happening in Rome. What has happened to my relation Princess Justiani, and my friends at Rome? Is it true that the Emperor has converted the Pope, and that he is to marry? If he has not already made a commitment, give me a letter of recommendation, he is the only husband I would accept. While awaiting the ambassadors of the Sacred College, I will remain your faithful friend for as long as you will allow me to be.[49]

For the next few months Elizabeth remained at Chudleigh, from where she complained frequently to the rent collectors of her various estates about the 'scarcity of money',[50] for she had told John Williams 'that she had drawn for a good deal, and was afraid there was but little in Drummonds hands'.[51] Not only was it a potentially embarrassing situation, it was also frustrating, for Elizabeth had a plan that she was eager to put into action. Without money, it would be impossible.

CHAPTER 19

Mansions and Mountebanks

The ill-natur'd world has on me frown'd,
And malice plays the wanton,
Old time may all their schemes confound
And help the Duchess of Kingston
Ballad

More than a year earlier, Elizabeth's steward at Chudleigh had said that when Her Grace returned to her Estonian estate there were to be 'very great Alterations, a new House built and the Grounds laid out'.[1] However, she had left France later than she intended and travelled slowly, dogged by ill health. It was perhaps a measure of how important it was to be addressed as Duchess of Kingston that she was still prepared to make the long and difficult journey at all, especially as she had fallen out of favour at the Empress's Court. Instead of setting the work at Chudleigh in motion that summer of 1782, as she had hoped, Elizabeth would be forced to wait until the thaw the following spring. In the meantime, as Russia shivered through an unusually early and severe winter, she became embroiled with someone who demonstrated all too clearly how her generosity was sometimes lavished on those who had done little to deserve it.

Major James Semple had come within the orbit of the Duchess by marrying one of her goddaughters, a Miss Grant from a Devonshire family of that name, in around 1780. He was apparently a charming and lively man, 'a most engaging companion',[2] but without the means to support himself in the style to which he aspired. As a result, he had spent the two years after his marriage in a debtors' prison in Calais. On his release, sometime in 1782, the gaolbird had approached his wife's wealthy godmother for help, for, as his contemporary biographer commented, 'To conceive that JG Semple would let slip so favourable an opportunity of improving his fortunes, would be but paying a very bad compliment to his penetration.'³ Presumably with her unfortunate goddaughter in mind, and thinking that Semple might find employment in Russia, Elizabeth was receptive to his approaches. 'Mr. Semple was a fine man, the lady had been a fine woman, and is still a great wit; she received him with hospitality, and promised to introduce him to the Empress.' Semple set out for Russia not long after Elizabeth, and passed through Chudleigh – where Elizabeth was spending Christmas – on his way to St Petersburg.

Here Elizabeth furnished him with a letter of recommendation to Sir James Harris, the British representative in St Petersburg. It was, though she did not know it, full of lies and half truths:

As Captain Semple is come to this Country upon business for me he is solicitous of having the honor of paying his respects to you, and as he was not certain if he should not overtake me at Dantzig he is not provided with any letters for you, I cannot denny him the justice of accquainting you that he is son to a Gentleman of family & fortune in Scotland & Grandson to Lord Semple, he claims the title of Lord Lyle & the attorney General has acknowledged his claim to be Just. He has served in America four Campaigns & was obliged to return on account of his wounds, he is now in a Corps of Royal Volontiers. He flatters himself that you will do him the honor to present him to her Imperiale Majesty, his stay in St Petersbourg will be but a few days.⁴

Semple had reached St Petersburg by 11 January 1783, for that day he dined at Sir James Harris's house,⁵ and soon he 'was introduced, and promised promotion'.⁶ Potemkin apparently took to him at once – at least according to Semple's own memoirs – and offered him a commission as captain in the Russian army. Armed with this happy news, Semple returned to Chudleigh, where he found the household in turmoil. Elizabeth had argued so badly with her companions – Mme Porquet, sister to Monsieur Cocove in Calais, and a male secretary – that the Frenchwoman had refused to leave her room. Elizabeth, in irritation, had locked her in, and it was only with a great deal of persuasion that she could be prevailed upon to release her and pay her passage back to France.

Semple's next trip was to Danzig, to collect his wife and take her to a house on the Chudleigh estate. He was late returning to St Petersburg to collect his orders, and the night he left to rendezvous with Potemkin he managed to gamble away all his money, including some entrusted to him by the Empress, and was forced to borrow 500 roubles from Sir James Harris. Despite this, he seems to have served Potemkin for eighteen months, before falling out of favour – perhaps because of his reluctance to pay his bills. As for the Duchess, they had quarrelled long before. He left for Stockholm some time in late 1784, leaving a trail of unpaid debts across Europe on his slow progress back to England. Here his past finally caught up with him and he was tried in September 1786 after hiring a coach which he did not return.[7]

In the opening months of 1783, while St Petersburg society exclaimed at the dubious character of the Duchess's latest worthless protégé, Elizabeth was impatiently waiting for spring when she could embark on her proposed changes at Chudleigh. As soon as the season allowed, the first ships left Hull bound for Narva, carrying bundles of trees and other plants suitable for a thoroughly English garden:

No 1	4 sorts of sage southernwood Lavender Roses
No 2	Polianthus, 3 plants of greenhouse jasamine, violets, camomile varigated periwinkle
No 3	Blue periwinkle Ribon grass white periwinkle
No 4	primroses peppermint Daisies of sorts, artichokes
No 5	Daffodils, Narcissus, Crocus, Snowdrops, Hyacinths, 3 parsels of Tulip Roots jerusalem artichoke
No 6	Orange & Lemon trees 6 Lignum Vita 4 Arbutus & yellow jasmine Some turnop seed and a small box within the large one with 6 pine apples and 50 sorts of flower seeds[8]

Elizabeth's mind seemed to be full of property matters, for sometime that year she wrote to Catherine to ask her permission to 'purchase some village or other'.⁹ With the arrival of summer, however, she was forced to turn her attention away from Russia to Paris, from where there was unwelcome news about the house in Montmartre that she had bought the previous February. An official inspection on 7 August confirmed that there had been several problems with the alterations and additions that Elizabeth had requested, which had ostensibly been completed. The first master mason that La Crosse had employed had had to be fired, and his successor – clearly not supervised properly – had misread the plans,¹⁰ so that nothing was the right size or the right material. In his defence, the builder was claiming that the plans were at fault, for they had been done in a hurry with the Duchess impatient to leave for Russia and La Crosse anxious to complete a lucrative sale. Furious, Elizabeth had been forced to go to St Petersburg to deliver her side of the story at the consulate-general of France, and was withholding the rest of the money due on completion of the work.

From the Russian capital in early August, the strain perhaps telling on her health, Elizabeth wrote to the Empress to ask 'that she be sent off, without delay, to the waters of Carlsbad, swears that she has no debts and will not take any fugitive serfs, and says that she has erysipelas* on her legs and is anxious to travel back in the middle of October'.¹¹ Permission was readily granted; from Tsarkoe Selo the Empress ordered the Vice-Chancellor, Count Osterman, to 'show this letter to the Petersburg town governor so that she is not delayed. Let her travel where she wishes.' Elizabeth was a great advocate of 'the waters of Carlsbath in Bohemia'¹² which, she later assured a friend, 'only fail for a Dropsey',† nor was she less taken with the place itself, 'two days Journey this side of Vienna in a charming Country'. The setting was, and is, glorious, for the town was squeezed into a narrow, steep-sided gorge cut by the twists and turns of the river Tepla. All around were woods, and the air was clean and fresh. The buildings were less distinguished, for two-thirds of Carlsbad had been destroyed by fire in 1759 and it was only in the nineteenth century that it acquired its ornate wedding-cake appearance.

---

* An acute bacterial infection, characterised by large raised red skin patches, especially on the legs and face, with fever; it could be recurrent.
† An old word for oedema, in which the body stores excess water.

Whatever use she made of her free passage, Elizabeth had returned to St Petersburg by 4 October to grapple with the ever-increasing annoyance of her finances. Incredibly, despite the Court of King's Bench ruling in her favour more than three years before, there were matters related to the Duke's last will and testament that were not yet settled. The Duke's Trust Estates – the income from which had been earmarked for paying his legacies, debts and funeral expenses – had not yet delivered up their funds. Elizabeth was still owed the £1,092.15s. 5d. she had spent for coffins, mourning clothes and all the other paraphernalia of her dear Duke's interment; the £3,447.8s. for 'what her Grace paid to sev[era]l cred[ito]rs';[13] and the balance of £9,727.17s. 1d. left over from the accumulated rents after all the legacies, lawyers and the rest had been paid. To make up the short-fall, the trustees had negotiated a £10,000 mortgage with 'Mr Medows', presumably Charles.

Elizabeth, though impatient for the money, bombarded the Duke's trustees in England with questions, for she was less than ecstatic about the manner in which the business had been conducted. In early October, she wrote to Sir Richard Heron – the other trustee, William Feild, having recently died – to express her concerns and complaints. Beginning with a barbed comment aimed at Sir James Harris, now the former ambassador to Russia, she explained:

> I am disappointed to find that the News was premature of your being appointed to this Court, it is Time that we had a Minister here, that would dignify our Country . . . I am now Sir to enter on the Point of Business, Mr Field wrote me in his last Letters that the money in question should be lent upon Mortgage, that I should have good Security & proper Interest; I returnd for answer that I desir'd the Particulars of those Affairs, & the Questions I ask'd you shall find at the End of this Letter, not one of which has been answer'd nor have I yet seen the Copy of the Account deliver'd to Chancery of what was due to me, & by the Letter that I have had the Honor of receiving from you the money disburs'd by me to Creditors amounts only to £3447 – By my Calculation it amounts to more than double the sum.[14]

She was annoyed that she had not been shown the calculations before they were laid before Chancery, and suggested that she be allowed to petition for the larger sum, along with the interest on the total amount due to her. There were other grievances, too: for a start, she was not being paid enough interest on her money, and was frustrated at not being able to invest it where she chose. In Russia, a country where she was 'dispos'd to spend great part of my Time . . . being tempted by the Friendship of the Soveraine & the Excellency of the Climate, which for weak nerves is a soveraine Remedy', she explained that she could obtain three times the return on her money.

As a result of all these delays and difficulties, Elizabeth's finances were in chaos. She had 'a Sum to pay in January next & I depended on this Money to answer that Demand; I have purchased a large Estate & paid it'. Faced with the prospect of being unable to fulfil her financial commitments, Elizabeth was wretched; it affected both her health – which, now that she was nearly sixty-three, was increasingly fragile – and her composure, so that she allowed herself in this business letter to be overwhelmed with bitterness about her trial, 'that Star Chamber proceeding' she called it, that had put her in such a position. Her financial problems, however, needed nothing to magnify them. By the end of that October, Elizabeth, 'recovered from her late illness'.[15] was overdrawn at Drummonds to the tune of nearly £2,000.

Heron was quick to remind Elizabeth that she was not the only one to be suffering from this delay in settling the Duke's affairs. It was indeed, he pointed out somewhat tartly, 'unfortunate that so large a sum as the Rents of the Trust Estate amount to should have remained without Interest; but under the Circumstances which occur'd the Delay was unavoidable'.[16] Moreover, if Elizabeth had taken out a loan at the time of the Duke's death to pay his debts and so on, she would have been out of pocket by considerably more. The Duke's creditors, 'several of them needy Tradesmen', were the ones who had truly suffered, for they had been 'Ten Years without their Money and without Interest, a Loss extremely distressful to many of them'. Stung by the reproach, Elizabeth had signed the necessary papers by the beginning of December and was impatiently awaiting the first instalment of money.

She amused herself in St Petersburg as well as she could in the meanwhile, but it was a sign of how low her fame had sunk there that among the dinner invitations she issued in the first week of 1784 were two to humble Samuel Bentham, whose company had once been so beneath her.[17] She was in no mood for extravagant socialising, however, for not only was her health poor but as the year progressed it became clear that there would be a further delay in paying her the money she was owed. This left a hole in her finances that not even a £500 prize from the previous year's lottery could plug, a hole which would cost her almost £140 in interest on her overdraft at Drummonds by the end of the year,[18] in spite of the strenuous efforts of her various agents in England to collect the rents on her estates as promptly as possible.

Notwithstanding the financial constraints, the alterations at Elizabeth's estate in Estonia continued through 1784. The garden was gradually taking shape, helped that spring by the arrival of a parcel of thoroughly English garden and grass seeds from a nursery in Pontefract, brought by the *Watson* through the Baltic waves from Hull to Narva.[19] By late summer, much of the work was finished. A young traveller from Kent passed 'thro a woody morassy Country to Chudleigh' at the end of August, where he found 'a plaister house whitened, stands upon the summit of a Cliff, with a boundless view of the Sea, towards Petrg & Sweden; in a fine climate it would be sweet, but here the sea looked black & dismal, & in such an unin-habited country, that a man can never be very cheerful'.[20]

If that was so, it was perhaps not surprising that as early as June, the Duchess's English staff were being told to expect her arrival at her house in Calais by the end of August,[21] and in August that she would be there 'before the next term commences'.[22] Perhaps Elizabeth had been alarmed by the recent disturbances over taxes in the area, which had left a bad atmosphere.[23] The company in St Petersburg that autumn would probably have been surprised to learn that she was *not*, at that moment, on her way to France, for she made so little noise in the Russian capital that one English visitor was moved to comment, 'the Duchess of Kingston is sunk into neglect. nobody thinks of her.'[24] In fact, Elizabeth was still in Russia, writing from St Petersburg at the end of October to Sir Richard Heron about the appalling state of her finances.

For some reason, the money she had been expecting in January – in anticipation of which she had spent freely – had still not made its way out of the labyrinthine paths of the Court of Chancery. The situation, in particular with regard to her bankers, was making her very anxious.[25] Nor was she destined to find relief for many months, for the saga continued to drag on throughout the whole of 1785 as well. That March, matters reached such a pitch that her bank refused to honour three of Elizabeth's drafts for a total of £700, leading her to comment bitterly on 'all the disasters that M^{srs} Drummonds have caus'd me'.[26] Her staff in England – the conscientious Mr Pickin at Thoresby and Mr Sanday at Holme Pierrepont in particular – were forced to 'strain every nerve'[27] to collect the rents at once and remit the money to Drummonds as soon as possible, in order 'to prevent the ill consequences of her Bills being returnd'. It was a far from happy situation, whose effects reached beyond the Duchess's immediate circle, for, as Sanday commented anxiously, 'how I am to get the parsons paid I cannot at present tell'.[28]

Despite these terrible scrambles for money, which were to punctuate the year at regular intervals like a Greek chorus, Elizabeth had not quite abandoned her project of moulding her thin-soiled lands in Estonia into her vision of English perfection. Not that they needed much embellishment to accord with the newest fashion for landscapes; as she told one correspondent whom she was trying to persuade to pay her a visit at Chudleigh, 'you would see upon my estate some of the finest Romantick Prospects in the World, and fifteen miles of the finest coast and a bold sea, Every ship that passes from any part of Europe to St Petersburg passes before my windows, it will be a pleasing sail that brings you to an anchor on my small coast.'[29]

All the same, the ships continued to arrive at Narva bringing their miscellaneous booty from Hull. First came the *Vigilant* with two bundles of trees, a box of flower roots and shrubs, and a hamper of pigeons with the remains of the 'couple of strike of pease'[30] that had been their food on the voyage. That was followed closely by another mixed consignment on board the *Young William*: '25 Baskets of Pine Plants, 2 poynters, & 2 Spaniels'.[31] These were accompanied by a quantity of oatmeal and 'Tallow Craps',*[32] used to make a slimy concoction known as 'sea stock' for feeding the dogs.

Even as the garden blossomed, however, Elizabeth was making plans to be elsewhere. As early as 25 March, she had half decided to 'be at Calais in the month of June'.[33] Perhaps she was homesick, longing for even a glimpse of the cliffs of Dover; or maybe there was

---

* The residue from rendering fat.

a limit to the enjoyment to be derived from 'Romantick Prospects', no matter how fine they might be, and the Duchess was eager for a change of scene and, hopefully, a more welcoming society than Russia's had become. In any case, from France she would be better placed to settle her financial problems once and for all. In early August, William Pickin was reporting from Thoresby that the Duchess would be setting out from St Petersburg sometime in the next ten days.[34] However, it was only on 22 September that she finally departed,[35] leaving Sanday and Pickin to deal – without too much difficulty this time[36] – with Drummonds over another of her drafts, this time for £1,000, due on 5 October.[37]

By 8 December she was in France, 'tired from a journey of three months',[38] though her health was at least a little better than it had been. Her arrival was less happy than it might have been, however, had the house in Montmartre that she had acquired in 1782 not turned out to be such a disaster. The planned alterations, which would have created a handsome townhouse, had been so badly botched in every way possible that Elizabeth had refused to pay the vendor the balance of the sale price, which had been deposited with her bankers in Paris. He had taken her to court at Châtelet* and lost, but while Elizabeth had been in Russia he had taken his appeal to Parliament, which had overturned the Châtelet decision. The whole business had been a expensive nightmare, had given her nothing but worries and yet more lawsuits, and she was still without a suitable place to live in Paris.

In her exhaustion, Elizabeth poured out the sorry saga to a friend, concluding: 'they found in his favour, he took my money† and I have to pay him six thousand louis which I will have to borrow, for I do not have it on me, and I will have a shoddy building on my hands, which puts me in a bad mood'.

The recipient of this letter was a curious and colourful figure, whose connection with Elizabeth was to excite the more fanciful of her contemporary biographers into wild and unlikely assertions. She had, according to one, met him during her first visit to Italy, in 1774, 'when she ruled almost like a sovereign at Rome',[39] for one day she

* One of the courts in Paris, which dealt with both criminal and civil cases.
† The money originally left on deposit for when the work had been completed satisfactorily.

had 'received a visit from an Albanian prince named Warta,* who was certainly the handsomest man that nature ever produced. He was magnificently dressed, absolutely glittering with jewels . . .' Another claimed she had encountered him when he was disguised as a humble pilgrim, who only reluctantly revealed his noble birth. Both were agreed on one point, however: that Warta – Worta as it was more commonly spelled – had flattered her, and that the susceptible Elizabeth, 'whose fancy was easily fascinated by what was courageous and brilliant',[40] fell deeply in love with the bold gallant, and would even have married him if she could.

The *true* story of John Worta was quite extraordinary enough not to require embellishment.[41] His real name – for he built up quite a collection of aliases over the years – was Stefano Zannowich, and he had been born on the shores of the Adriatic in Venetian Albania. He came from a family of chancers; his father, a merchant, had made his fortune in Venice by gambling, and his older brother Premislas had been the player who had relieved Lord Lincoln of 12,000 guineas in 1771, and had then tried to sell a counterfeit of one of the promissory notes in Amsterdam. Bright, but often short of money, Stefano had travelled widely throughout Europe, dabbling in politics and sometimes supporting himself by writing dramas and, more recently, pamphlets in support of the American cause, and often having to flee to escape his creditors. With his brother he also defrauded an Amsterdam trading house, Chomel & Jordan, of a substantial sum and nearly provoked a war between that country and Venice into the bargain. He had spent time in Dresden, Warsaw and at Count Oginski's estate at Slonim; had been received by Frederick the Great; had been introduced to the French King's brother the Comte d'Artois and the Prince de Ligne. As one of Elizabeth's chroniclers put it, 'He had certainly strong feelings, and a very superior understanding . . . He was, altogether, a most extraordinary character.'[42]

Exactly where and when Elizabeth had encountered this dashing adventurer thirty years her junior is not clear, though she would have heard of him from their mutual acquaintances. That it was not on any of her visits to Rome we can be fairly sure, for Stefano was elsewhere each time; otherwise, the only certainty is that the introduction was

---

* More usually spelt 'Worta'.

sometime before Elizabeth's return from Russia. As for the nature of their connection, the letter she wrote to him that December 1785 was, even allowing for the formality of the times, hardly that of a woman passionately in love. She wished him friendship, expressed her concern at his political activities, and assured him, 'You are an Excellent friend and well deserve to have them yourself.'[43] Unfortunately, she could not give him any money to pay his debts, which was evidently what he had asked, as 'at the moment there are so many things wrong with my affairs, three and a half years of illness, have reduced me to such a state that you would think I was eighty'. She had once pitied his financial problems enough to give him her small estates in Devon,[44] but could not help him now. She was 'a true friend' who admired his wit and spirit, but nothing more.

CHAPTER 20

Decline and Fall

The once celebrated Duchess of Kingston
seems doomed to involve herself
in eternal lawsuits.
The Times, 4 September 1786

Preoccupied with the prosaic matter of sorting out her own money problems, Elizabeth wrote to Sir Richard Heron from Calais on 21 December 1785 to ask for a copy of the papers 'the accountant General requires me to sign, to receive the money now in his office. If it is possible to get me this money', she finished, a sigh almost audible in the words, 'you will oblige your friend.'[1] Nearly six years had passed since the establishing of the Duke's will in her favour, and still the money had not been released to her. Now a new stumbling block had been put in Elizabeth's path, for in order to claw back the sum she had paid out in funeral expenses and to some of the Duke's creditors she was expected to sign the latest bundle of legal papers not as the Duchess of Kingston but as the Countess of Bristol, at which she baulked.

It was more than three weeks into 1786 before she was honoured with a reply from Heron, full of insincere protestations of friendship and pompous excuses for not answering sooner. It contained unwelcome news for Elizabeth. Although Heron was of the opinion that 'the Direction which requires the Signature was improper Your Grace being in Law as much Duchess of Kingston as the wife of any Duke in his kingdom is his Duchess',[2] he had to advise her that now the court had taken the decision she would never extract her money from the Accountant General without giving in and being the Countess of Bristol for the purpose. All he could suggest was preparing another legal document to the effect that 'submitting to the Order of the Court would not be prejudicial to your Grace in any other Respect'. No doubt to Elizabeth's disbelief and irritation he added, 'If on the other Hand you have no Occasion for the Money it is very safely deposited and whenever you may chance to want such a sum will know how to have it.'

This was not the only matter for concern, for there was also nearly £10,000 in back rents from the Trust Estates that for some complicated reason had not yet been released to the Duchess. To speed up payment, it had been suggested that Charles Meadows and his younger brother, 'the General', would advance her the money instead, in return for a mortgage on the Trust Estates for the same amount. It was a sensible suggestion, apart from the fact that the General could only provide his share – £5,000 – once he had settled his own law business.[3] As Elizabeth, who had decamped to Paris for a three-week stay in mid January,[4] commented by return of post, 'the Money is absolutely needfull to me, it has been upwards of twelve years in their Hands with a totall loss of the Interest . . . I never heard that he [the General] was engaged with Law, and when that will end I leave to your well founded experience in these matters . . . If the Generals Law affairs are as tedious as mine it will be at least thirteen years.'[5] However, she added, she was resolved not to show her anger to the two Meadowses for what she saw as their thoughtless and impractical plan. Protesting, with some justification, that she had always tried to do her utmost to help the nephews of her 'faithfull and tender Friend the dear Duke', she continued:

Revenge is not the part of a Christian and I have forgiven and I hope have made happy my two greatest Adversarys, I might say Persecutors, I feel it in my constitution, I feel it in my Heart and in my injured Fame. These Wounds can never be cured: I never meant, thought or beleived that I desearved the Vehements and Rancour with which I have been treated and can only say with Mr Addison in his Cato 'the best may Err but God is Just and mercifull.'

By late March, Elizabeth was still in the French capital, plainly in no hurry to leave its pleasant society. As the house in rue Rochechouart was uninhabitable, she had taken a lease on another, the Hôtel du

Parlement d'Angleterre in rue Coq-Héron, the same street in which the discredited Franz Mesmer* had briefly lived. The Parisians were intrigued by this English curiosity in their midst, 'about whom public report had invented a thousand stories',[6] though there were conflicting tales about how much Elizabeth made it her business to mingle with them. On the one hand, the English press such as the *Daily Universal Register* opined that she made 'little or no noise'[7] in Paris; on the other, the Baroness d'Oberkirch claimed that her new residence 'became the rendezvous of everyone distinguished by either talent or rank'.[8] Perhaps the Baroness, though not always a trustworthy witness, was a little nearer the truth. Elizabeth might not, of course, be part of the social milieu of resident and visiting Britons and her health and age meant she could not be as active as she once was, but even as Miss Chudleigh she had enjoyed entertaining people of other nationalities, especially the more colourful and talented ones. This continued in Paris; she was, for instance, apparently a popular member of the Polish and Italian Exiles' Club.[9]

As for the French, Elizabeth certainly encountered the Duchess of Bourbon, accompanied by the diary-writing Baroness d'Oberkirch, several times that March. On one occasion, the Baroness stayed to eat with her, later noting, 'Her suppers are celebrated for their refinement and luxury. She is somewhat of a gourmand, and patronises the gastronomic art.'[10] Nor was it only the food that the Baroness found remarkable. Of her hostess, she wrote: 'She is really a most extraordinary woman . . . Her great knowledge of society, her wit, and brilliant imagination, which reflected as a mirror all that passed before it, give a brilliancy to her conversation that I have seldom seen equalled. She is proud and self-willed, opposed to almost all received maxims, and yet variable and inconstant both in her fancies and opinions.' There were still traces, too, of the 'more than ordinary beauty'[11] that had once captivated Dukes and of the grace that had made it worth noting that 'Miss Chudleigh danced minuets'; she evidently retained her less appealing characteristics as well, for the Baroness was also moved to conclude that 'it may be that persons gifted with some superiority in one way, sink below the ordinary standard in others'. Perhaps, then, she had not abandoned such habits as rising

* The Swabian-born physician had claimed to be able to channel a healing force he called 'animal magnetism'.

from the dinner table on hot days and fanning herself 'by taking hold of her petticoats, and well shaking them', as the Duke of Kingston's valet had remembered, and then blaming the resulting smell on the dogs.[12]

That March evening, after a pleasant supper, the Baroness and the other guests were shown the Duchess's jewels, including the 'two pearls of considerable value'[13] that the *Daily Universal Register* was moved to mention to its British readers. What impressed the nosy Frenchwoman most, apart from the number and value of them, was the way they were so carefully arranged and numbered. Elizabeth pointed out several that she intended to leave to particular friends, for as early as three years previously she had asked Sir Richard Heron for his advice in drawing up a will. She had now begun considering the matter in earnest, although the final document would not be signed until October. The pleasant contemplation of her valuables, and how to dispose of them on her death, however, could not alter the fact that Elizabeth was extremely short of ready cash. On 18 April, she wrote again to Stefano Zannowich – 'Monsieur le Prince' as she called him – to explain with regret that she could not offer him any financial assistance:

It is with great sorrow that I learn of the losses you have suffered and the distressing position into which you are plunged. Your sufferings are all the more real to me, as I find myself on this occasion able neither to reduce them, nor put a stop to them. I am short of money myself at the moment, as the payment of the sum I am owed is delayed, and an expensive court case, and other unexpected expenses absorb my income.[14]

Zannowich would never receive another penny from her, nor from his other former patrons. Since his civil arrest in Holland by disgruntled creditors at the beginning of April, the tangled web of aliases he had woven over the years had been slowly picked apart. Chomel & Jordan recognised him as one of the men who had defrauded them so handsomely more than ten years earlier, and other demands for repayment of debts soon came rolling in. In mid May, he was moved for interrogation to a criminal prison in Amsterdam, where he killed himself ten days later.[15] The story sprang up, and the Baroness d'Oberkirch repeated it, that he had left a long, passionate and florid letter for Elizabeth in which he bade her 'farewell, farewell beloved' among much else.[16] The likelihood of this can be judged by the assertion that he also admitted in the same note to being the son of an ass-driver from Trebizond,* when his father was neither. Elizabeth may have been saddened by his premature end, but she was unlikely to have been heartbroken.

By early August, escaping the heat of the city, Elizabeth was once more in Calais 'but Mr Williams was not gone to her, the beginning of the week, but expected to go soon'.[17] Here she would have received the welcome news, shipped from England in the hamper that brought the venison every week from Thoresby, that the money she had been expecting for so long would soon be hers. On 7 August, her bank balance was swelled by a payment of nearly £5,000 from the Accountant General, and a week later it grew again by another £9,795.7s.[18] It was a huge relief, but Elizabeth was not to be allowed to enjoy the feeling for long. In early September, the newspapers reported that the 'wandering Duchess'[19] was about to become embroiled in yet another lawsuit, this time being brought by the Catholic priest who had sailed with her on her first voyage to St Petersburg. Abbé Séchand, who was seeking arrears of pay, claimed that 'when they arrived at Petersburgh, that she lurched him, leaving him to grope his way to France, and to provide himself with necessaries during the journey'. The case does not seem to have ever come to trial. Perhaps Séchand was merely trying to embarrass the Duchess into paying him money to go away, for had his grievance been genuine it is difficult to understand why it had taken nine years for him to mention it.

Elizabeth spent the remainder of 1786 flitting between Paris and Calais. In mid September, she was in the French capital dining with the Cosways,[20] talented portraitists both, who had been friends for many years. In late October her faithful servant John Williams, just returned to Kingston House after nine weeks in France, 'Left her grace Well at Paris',[21] but by the end of the month she was back in Calais, where she received a visit from Richard Cosway who was on his way to London.[22] It was probably at this time that Elizabeth sat for him for a portrait, of which a preparatory drawing still exists.[23] Only the face was coloured in – the rest was an energetic pencil

* On the north coast of Turkey, now called Trabzon.

scribble of drapery, furniture and a faint coronet – but it was a strong face, the mouth still pouting, and those famous eyes were as full of wry humour as ever. A trace of former beauty remained in the sixty-five-year-old woman, though her youthful figure was long gone. It was clearly the portrait of someone who had lived a full and eventful life.

Soon after there were rumours in the newspapers that the Duchess would shortly be following in Richard Cosway's steps, 'in order to close the evening of life in this her native country',[24] and that her town house was already being made ready to receive her. Judging by the flattering manner in which Elizabeth was described in the report, it is plausible that it had in fact been placed there at the behest of its subject to test people's reactions, and that at present the return home was more a wish than a certainty. A fortnight later, Elizabeth was still in Calais, replying to a letter from the tender-hearted Maria Cosway:

> I thank you for all the trouble you take over me . . . tell Mr Cosway I will send him the dimensions of the frame that he asks for soon; Forgive me if I do not say any more today, I am writing to you in haste, I am so overburdened with business affairs that it is five o'clock, and I have not yet dined. I will write to Mr Cosway to send him the measurements of the portrait. I wish you were here sometimes – I would have liked to spend my last week here with you.[25]

But Elizabeth's next journey was not to London but to Paris, and she was still there in early March 1787.[26] She had been contemplating the idea of buying another house, for she could not live in the semi-ruin in rue Rochechouart, and had finally found one she considered suitable. On 21 June, the Paris correspondent of the *Times* sent home the news that 'The Duchess of Kingston has purchased the chateau and small estate of St Assize from the Duke of Orleans, for 120,000 livres* . . . It lies about a league from Fontainbleau.'[27] The report was right about what Elizabeth had bought, but not about the price she had paid; the elegant house with its graceful porticoed porch had actually cost her ten times more than was thought, the colossal sum

* Around £5,000.

in those days of around £50,000,* to be paid in instalments.

This was a stretch even for someone with a handsome income, and Elizabeth found herself obliged to pawn some of her jewellery at the Mont-de-Piété† to raise the money for part of the first payment.[28] There were unconfirmed stories – probably no more than idle gossip – that she had recouped some of her outlay almost at once, for the estate was apparently swarming with rabbits which she had had shot and managed to sell for 3,000 guineas.[29] There is no doubt, however, that one of her first actions was to apply to the King for permission to change her new estate's name from St Assise, as it was spelt in French, to 'Chudleigh', which was duly granted at the end of June.[30]

Such extravagant purchases, though they seemed whimsical, at least provided the Duchess with something to occupy her thoughts and time, for she had fewer and fewer close friends to whom she could write or pay visits. The Cosways, of course, kept in touch from London, although that July Maria had to ask Thomas Jefferson – who eventually became the third President of the new United States of America – to deliver some letters and a parcel for her as she did not know where to send them.[31] Elizabeth had not quite slipped from public view in her native land, and the newspapers continued to carry occasional stories about her. That summer, *The Times* printed an anecdote that, although the events described may never have happened, at least gave an idea of how she was viewed in some quarters in Britain:

> This Lady was always remarkable for having a very high sense of her own dignity; being one day detained in her carriage by a cart of coals that was unloading in a very narrow street, she leaned with both her arms upon the door, and asked the fellow, 'How dare you, Sirrah, to stop a woman of quality in the street?' 'Woman of quality!' (replied the man) – 'Yes, fellow,' (rejoined her Grace) 'don't you see *my arms upon my carriage*?' 'Yes, I do indeed' (he answered) 'and a pair of d——d coarse arms they are.'[32]

---

* Something like £3,000,000 in modern terms.
† Situated in Rue des Blancs-Manteaux, here anyone could borrow money against portable goods at a fixed rate of interest; all profits went to support the city's hospices.

By the time the tale was printed, the Lady had been back in Calais for around a month where, following a fall at Paris by which 'she was Hurted very much',[33] her health had been giving several members of her household cause for concern. By mid August, her Thoresby steward William Pickin wrote from Calais to his counterpart at Holme Pierrepont that she had 'had a slight Fever since her arrival here, but is now got pretty well again'.[34] John Williams confirmed at the start of September that he 'Left her grace at Calais much Better in Health then She Was Some time before When I Went over about 2 months ago she Was but very indifferent indeed – but now much Better.'[35] She was at least well enough to remember to order some venison to be sent to Sir Richard Heron, whom she had recently obliged by appointing his nephew to a vacant living in her possession.

One project, however, would now have to be given up. Although fifteen parcels of shrubs and pine plants for the Estonian estate had been shipped to Narva the previous year on the *Benjamin*,[36] Elizabeth would not be following them as she had hoped. In August, though she had just written to Mikhail Garnovsky[37] to express her regret that she would not see his employer Potemkin until the winter, she was forced to give up 'the Russian Voyage'[38] entirely. As John Williams commented, 'her grace does not go to Russia this Winter and I hope never Will again for I think the Journey will be to much – Her grace is health is not so Well as I Wish'.[39]

Though her few friends and acquaintances in England might be concerned about the Duchess's increasing frailty, others were more fascinated by Elizabeth's reconciliation with her former persecutor Evelyn Meadows, which had only recently come to light. Earlier in the summer, the newspapers had noted with surprise that the man who 'brought the Duchess of Kingston to a trial, and would have had her hanged, if it had been in his power, and the laws would have suffered it'[40] and the woman who 'triumphed in the expensive and ruinous consequences of the prosecution to her antagonist' had, after 'ten years violent abuse of each other', become the best of friends. They could hardly bring themselves to believe, let alone understand, how someone who had fallen below the level of acceptable behaviour in one area could rise above it in another. Even Walpole, who had not written a word about his former playmate since her trial, was moved to ask a friend if she had heard 'that the Duchess of Kingston has adopted the eldest Meadows, paid his debts, given him £600 a year, and intends to make him her heir? Methinks this is robbing Peter to pay *Peter*.'[41] In fact, Walpole was considerably behind the times. Elizabeth had acted long before this to help Evelyn, for she had begun paying him an allowance of £400 per annum in spring 1782, which she had recently increased to £600.[42]

Elizabeth was now, by the standards of her times, a very old woman, with all the limitations and frustrations that came with it. The ill health that dogged her had plainly lowered her spirits, so that she felt her mortality; according to John Williams, his mistress planned to remain at Calais until Christmas 'if Please god she lives – this What her Grace tells me'.[43] That October she even told Garnovsky how unhappy she was because she was insulted by all the world.[44] Despite her lowered morale, she retained the characteristic generosity that even the most critical of her contemporaries praised. That November a small English boat, the *Sunderland*, foundered on the north coast of France not far from Calais. Elizabeth, who had experienced the sea's treacherous moods at first hand, without hesitation donated five guineas to help the survivors.[45]

The ailing Duchess had not yet given up on life, however. Early in the new year, she decided to head to Paris for a five-week visit. From there, on 11 February, she wrote another letter to Maria Cosway, who had been such a kind friend to her. After a rambling and rather sad story about someone who had done her a great injury – who and what are not clear – she concluded:

> Goodbye, my dear little one, I wish that the moments that you spent in Paris in the winter had been for me; I envy greatly the Princess and I am very angry with your husband that you and he did not come to see me; I am in Paris for 5 weeks, and after that I intend to return to Calais, where I flatter myself that I will have the pleasure of seeing you and your dear husband . . . PS. I am living in the Hotel du Parlement d'Angleterre Rue Cocqueron.[46]

She must have been living very quietly in Paris, though, for in April a rumour sprang up that she had died. Elizabeth rushed to contradict the story, telling a friend that 'thanks be to God, I am very well; and will you please tell this to my Bankers and my family'.[47] She might not be dead but, according to the Duke's former valet Thomas Whitehead, who was acquainted with one of Elizabeth's female attendants in Paris, she was increasingly unhappy and finally 'brought so low, that she was obliged to call in one of the faculty'.[48] The doctor, 'finding that her disorder originated from uneasiness, thought it necessary to desire she would keep to her Madeira; but in small quantities, and always mixed with water'.

Early on the morning of 26 August 1788, Elizabeth asked her attendant to help her out of bed and into an armchair, with a stool for her feet. Once she was comfortably seated, the Duchess requested a glass of Madeira, which was at first refused unless it was mixed with water. Elizabeth insisted, however, and the servant 'being . . . obliged to comply, gave her one: she drank it, and insisted upon having another, which being given, she desired the attendant to sit down beside her. This was complied with, and the attendant having seated herself, the Duchess took hold of her hand, and without a struggle, immediately died.' In the cool of a summer early morning, the sixty-seven-year life of a remarkable woman had come, at last, to its peaceful conclusion.[49]

CHAPTER 21

A Slow Unravelling

The late Duchess of Kingston, though by no
means distinguished among the train of Diana,
was not destitute of good qualities.
The Times, 5 September 1788

It was faithful John Williams who broke the news four days later to Sir Richard Heron and the Duchess's other executors that Elizabeth had 'Dy^d the 26 at seven oclock.' Truly grief stricken, he added, 'I am in great Trouble . . . and the Body What is to be done – and Where is it to be Buried.'[1] Elsewhere, however, there was rather less in the way of sorrow at the Duchess's passing. Barely had she breathed her last before 'a great consequent confusion instantly arose'[2] in the house in rue Coq-Héron, with 'every one striving to get what they could, before the broad seal was put on'. The chief plunderer was Evelyn Meadows, who hastily spirited away most of the silverware, jewellery[3] and other valuable effects before the superintendent, Monsieur Guyot, arrived to put the official seals on the doors and windows. Meadows later claimed that the goods had been brought to his apartment by 'a Person unknown during the absence of him the said Meadows and that the person was accompanied only by Doctor Gem, who declares that the Effects were sent to the said Meadows by the Dutchess of Kingston'.[4] As for her Grace's clothes, they were divided among her attendants, who joined in the plundering with enthusiasm.

With this pressing business completed, the servants quickly realised that they had another, more disagreeable matter with which to contend. As the Duchess's embalmer later related, she had 'died in the most sultry days of summer and in a habit of body so prone to putrefaction, that in less than twelve hours her domesticks and neigh-bours began to be alarmed'.[5] Another twenty-four hours passed before Doctor Fergus MacDonnell could proceed to his gruesome task, by which point, 'the remains of the Dutchess, having been more than usually unpleasant, dangerous and embarrassing', he was obliged to listen to his assistant's protests and call in three other people to help complete the job with all possible speed.

Not until 3 September did the news of the Duchess's death finally reach the pages of the British newspapers, where it stirred renewed interest in her past. Walpole might have been 'weary of her folly and vanity long ago',[6] but evidently this was not a view shared by everyone. The anonymous chronicler who commented that 'the demise of so extraordinary a character as the late Duchess of Kingston will, there is no doubt, give rise to a variety of details respecting her life and conduct'[7] was far nearer the mark. Over the next few weeks, many column inches would be dedicated to not particularly accurate accounts of her adventures, and slim biographies came racing off the presses at several London printers.

Public interest in the 'wicked' Duchess was sustained by the dawning realisation that the events following her death promised to be quite as fascinating as those of her life. For, as the executors had quickly discovered, untangling Elizabeth's estate was not going to be a straight-forward task. Elizabeth had lodged her will in France in October 1786, but a fuller version of it had been in preparation in England for a while. This, unfortunately, had not reached the Duchess in time for her to sign it before she died. This left only the 1786 will, a curious document which, though it appeared meticulous, turned out to be nothing of the kind.

Elizabeth had aimed at generosity, with a great list of specific lega-cies; to servants such as 'Mr Angel my Interpreter' who was to receive an annuity of £50 a year for life; to friends in several countries, such as the unmarried sister of Mr Caffieri of Calais, who had been so kind to her; and to the surviving members of her own family, who were to sparkle in her precious jewels:

To Sir Harry Oxenden* as Heir Looms my set of Brilliants and

---

* Who had married her cousin Margaret Chudleigh, daughter of the fourth Baronet, in 1755.

Topaz's presented me by the Electoress of Saxony a pearl Drop in the Shape of a pear a pearl Ring a pair of Brilliant Embroideries for Ladies Shoes and also eight Brilliant Roses which were the trimming of a Gown with 4 Brilliant Leaves belonging to the same to make a pair of Buckles and £320 to purchase 32 Brilliants to make the large part of the Buckles.

To Mr Chichester Son of my Cousin Sir John Chichester Bart by Mary Chudleigh his Wife one of the Daughters of Sir Geo: Chudleigh as an Heir Loom the 23 Diamond Tassels to my Gown.

To my Couzin Mr Prideaux who married Miss Maria Chudleigh my large Diamond Necklace which I commonly wear in my Hat

To Miss Elizabeth Chudleigh Sister to the late Sir John Chudleigh £300 and direct my Executors to lay out £2000 in the purchase of an Annuity for her life

To Miss Diana Chudleigh 100^l for a Ring

To Mrs Strong my Cousin £500 and all my Rubies set with Brilliants & Brilliant Buttons Pearl Necklace consisting of 6 rows my Sapphires and yellow Diamonds consist^g of a pair of Earrings two single Sapphires for Buttons 3 small flowers like Daizys one Butterfly a Sapphire Ring set with white Brilliants and a Sapphire Drop set with Brilliants to hang to the neck one single Stone yellow Diamond Ring and a Diamond hoop ring the Diamonds and precious Stones as Heir Looms

To my Cousin Miss Elizabeth Chudleigh third Daughter of the said Sir George Chudleigh the Brilliant loops I wear in my Gown Sleeves and a Brilliant Knot with which I fasten my Morning Gowns and my large Cluster Brilliant Ring.[8]

There was a substantial legacy to Charles Meadows, including gold cutlery and salt cellars, and an array of silverware. There were also more philanthropic bequests. Elizabeth's 'musical slaves' at her estate in Estonia were to be given their freedom in six years, and in the meantime were to receive an annual salary. The unsatisfactory house in rue Rochechouart was to be sold, and some of the proceeds used to buy a perpetual annuity to fund both the boys' and girls' schools in Calais, to build a prison for debtors and prisoners of war to keep them separate from the common criminals, and to build a water mill to grind corn for the poor three days a week 'as at certain periods when the wind fails the poor are distressed for bread'.[9]

Unfortunately, Elizabeth's good intentions were undermined by several important problems. For a start, there were gaps in the will: sometimes it was the nature of the bequest that was missing, and sometimes the name of the legatee. Of the St Assise estate there was of course no mention at all, though thanks to its recent purchase much of the Duchess's jewellery was in the Mont-de-Piété and would have to be redeemed. Moreover, Elizabeth had died with substantial debts in France: £34,000 remaining to pay on St Assise, a £9,000 mortgage, £5,000 in interest on the loan from the Mont-de-Piété and £8,000 still owing to La Crosse.[10] Added to that, there was some question as to whether the will was even valid in France, as it had not been executed according to that country's law; if that were the case, the next of kin would share equally, but also be responsible for any debts. Sorting out the Duchess's tangled business affairs would be a thankless task for her unfortunate executors, George Payne, Sir George Shuckburgh and Sir Richard Heron, particularly in France where, Heron commented, 'the Business is a perfect Hydra, and requires a Hercules to combat it'.[11]

A more immediate concern was that of burying the Duchess, 'in England according to her Directions; or, if that cannot be done now, the depositing the Body properly in France'.[12] Elizabeth had given instructions in her will that if she died near England, her body was to be conveyed 'without Pomp and buried in the Church Chudleigh* and directs a handsome Monument at 500ll'.[13] Charles Meadows, who had now taken the name of Pierrepont, declared himself 'very willing, that her Grace should be buried in the Family Vault of the Duke of Kingston'.[14] However, despite his and Sir Henry Oxenden's repeated protestations that they were perfectly prepared to advance the money necessary, it was some time before this particular problem could be resolved.

In the meanwhile, a Doctor Freeman had arrived in Paris to see if he could restore the Duchess to life with the power of what Mesmer had called 'animal magnetism'. Unsurprisingly, Freeman's strenuous efforts met with no success which, the newspapers said, 'was owing to the surgeons who embowelled her grace, having cut the right ventricle of the heart'.[15] There was some consolation for the doctor at Calais, where he revived seven drowned kittens and was given a

---

* Presumably the church in the Devon village of Ashton.

medal for his efforts; the Duchess, however, remained dead and unburied. It was not until 1 November that her corpse was finally 'deposited . . . in a vault in the Protestant Burial Ground' where it was to remain until the executors sent for it.[16]

In the interim, little progress had been made towards vanquishing the 'perfect hydra' of the business in France. George Payne's initial reports from France, in the week from 12 September,[17] were not encouraging. It seemed almost certain the will was invalid, and that everything would therefore go to the next of kin, once they had paid off any debts. Fearing these might be considerable, the Chudleigh cousins were understandably cautious about pressing their claim. No doubt hoping for a fat commission, 'an Avanturier of the name of Cocove'[18] came to England to offer his services to Elizabeth's immediate family, but they refused. He had more luck, though, with a second cousin called Colonel Phillips Glover, formerly one of Elizabeth's orchestra. Glover was completely taken in by Cocove's plausible manner and allowed himself to be persuaded into setting off for France at once to press his own claim, although he was only a second cousin.

The immediate problem in Paris was Evelyn Meadows, who, not content with carrying off the Duchess's valuables, was now claiming the property of St Assise and 'all the Diamonds and Jewels not deposited in the Mont de Pieté under a Gift from the Dutchess previous to her Death'.[19] This claim was based, so he said, 'on the Testimony of several of the first Personages in France, who were ready to declare, that the Duchess of Kingston had repeatedly told them, she had bought St Assize for Mr E. Meadows'.[20] In November, he was indicted and ordered to appear before the criminal court of Châtelet in Paris at the end of the year to answer charges of depredation on the Duchess's estate.[21] In the interim, the next of kin were granted 'Lettres de Benefice', with priority to Glover.[22] In December Evelyn Meadows was forced to deposit everything he had removed from the Duchess's house – including the silver from which he had already erased the arms of his uncle and substituted his own[23] – by order of the courts.

During the following year, while France simmered and then boiled into revolution, Glover succeeded in establishing his position as the Duchess's sole heir at law, largely by virtue of being there and not working through agents, and by paying off the other, wiser cousins.

Far from making him his fortune, however, it eventually left him £18,000 in debt,[24] for he had also made himself responsible for the massive sums the Duchess owed. Not surprisingly, given the political situation, Glover had great difficulty selling the main assets, such as the several houses, at anything like the price that had been paid for them. As for the fabulous jewels in the Mont-de-Piété, the best Glover could manage was an offer from Christie's in London for £5,500.[25] Moreover, Cocove quickly showed how little he deserved Glover's initial assessment of him as 'a man respected and beloved in his own country, and of a character exalted greatly above that of any country Esquire'[26] by purloining several sums of money he had been given to pay the interest at the Mont-de-Piété[27] and more besides. Even after Glover's death in 1796, Cocove and others such as Evelyn Meadows continued to plague his widow with spurious claims against the estate.

In Italy, too, there were rival claimants even for the few possessions the Duchess's steward had not already pawned. According to Father John Thorpe in Rome, it was being said that they were 'devised by her to an Italian Abbé Filateri who went from hence with the Nuncio [Panefili] to Paris, afterwards got about Cardl Rohan, & also insinuated himself into the Dutchess's favour'.[28] In her will, however, despite what Filateri pretended, Elizabeth had left everything to a physician, Doctor Agostino Frey, 'a man of good character and in strained circumstances'[29] to whom any legacy – even one he had to go to law to receive – would be welcome. This was perhaps fortunate for, in the opinion of the young man who went to Rome early in 1789 to handle the business, 'if her effects in other parts of the world fall as much short of the description in the Testament, as the specimen of her effects left at Rome does, I am afraid her Succession and Legacys will not in reality be so splendid as they appear to be'. This was certainly true of her gift to the Pope of a miniature by Raphael of the Holy Family in a gold snuffbox, which was nothing of the sort: 'If Her Grace really meant to say that the miniature picture was done by Raphael, it must be accounted for by supposing that her Grace was imposed upon in that respect.'

There were more frustrations for the executors in Russia, once they finally turned their attentions that way. It was not until towards the end of 1789 that George Payne set off for St Petersburg, where he arrived at the start of the new year to find Anthony Seymour, the Duchess's steward there, firmly entrenched in her house, enjoying her cellar of fine wines, and refusing to allow him access. 'I have been obstructed by that Rascal Seymour from proceeding in the Business',[30] Payne wrote in the first of a series of increasingly irritated letters to his fellow executors, although there was some consolation in that 'nothing material has been embezled as Cramp and Seymour have been checks upon each other'.

Once Seymour had been forcibly ejected by government officials, and an inventory taken, Payne plainly hoped that matters would soon be cleared up. However, he had reckoned without the tenacity of Seymour, who had taken full advantage of his employer's fine cellar to win himself influential friends in the city. After a prolonged legal battle, Seymour succeeded in having the French translation of the Duchess's will – by which he was left 100,000 livres – confirmed as the true one, rather than Payne's attested English version, by which he would have received a tenth of that sum, only £1,000. The court also decreed that Payne should sell all the effects, the 'voluminous Inventory of Nothings', by auction. Accordingly, everything that Elizabeth had detailed so carefully in her will – musical instruments, globes, telescopes, books, furs and mirrors – went under the hammer. The properties, too, were to be sold: the estate in Estonia, the house at St Petersburg and the one called 'Casterkabac', on the road to Tsarkoe Selo, that the Duchess had acquired in 1785.

By late May, heartily sick of Russia, Payne was desperate to return home. As he told Sir Richard Heron, 'If I could have foreseen that I should have met with so much trouble and vexation as I have experienced here, and have suffer'd so long an absence from my family I should not have been induced for double my Legacy to have undertaken the business.'[31] Just before his departure for England he appointed Colonel Garnovsky, who was to receive 50,000 roubles by the will, to complete the sales and pay off the debts, in return for the surplus 'if any',[32] a disbelieving Payne reported. For him, as for Glover in Paris, it turned out to be a poisoned chalice, though for different reasons. Garnovsky made sure of a surplus by failing to pay all the debts and legacies, and eventually ended up in a debtors' prison.

At least in the Duchess's native land, the business of sorting out her debts and legacies ran more smoothly, though it took until 1793 to tie up every loose end. Here, too, the props of Elizabeth's life were gradually auctioned off to strangers. First to go were the contents of Kingston House, sold on the premises by Mr Christie during four days in May 1789. The rooms where Elizabeth had given dinners, card parties and concerts to fashionable London society were stripped bare of their paintings, elegant cabinets, Smyrna carpets, double-headed couches and bedsteads, all the way down to smaller items such as guitars, candles and a collection of fossils. Nothing was left out, not even the 'large yard dog, with kennel, and chain',[33] lot 95, which fetched 15s.

It was the same story at Thoresby in June, where it took Mr Christie eleven days to disperse 'all the Rich and Elegant Furniture, Pier Glasses of Distinguished magnitude, suits of tapestry in fine preservation, capital pictures, collection of fine Dresden, old Japan & Enamel'd Porcelane, curious and valuable firearms, plate, linen, wines, mathematical instruments, several thorough-bred Pointers and Spaniels, And a great variety of Curious and Valuable effects'.[34] Nothing was left in the green damask bedchamber, the blue paper bedroom or the ground floor drawing room; and Jenny, Bonny, Wagg and the ten other dogs would hereafter bark in different kennels.

The final sale, in February 1791, and the one that would have upset Elizabeth the most, was of the 'superb jewels, pearls, &c' that Christie had bought from Colonel Glover. Among the lots was 'a pair of capital single drop brilliant ear-rings, of matchless beauty and perfection'[35] that fetched 920 guineas; 'Twenty two brilliant buttons and tassels, a complete set for a dress suit of clothes', which sold for 850 guineas; and a 'capital single stone brilliant ring' that made 400 guineas. Among the more prosaic items was an eight-day clock mounted in ormolu by a Parisian maker, and several gold filigree objects such as patch boxes and rosewater bottles.

Nearly all of Elizabeth's possessions were now scattered throughout Europe. Only one thing still lay where it had been deposited so perfunctorily in November 1788. In Paris, while Revolution and the bloody Reign of Terror raged overhead, the mortal remains of the Duchess of Kingston lay undisturbed in a vault in a Protestant burial ground waiting for a funeral that never happened. Elizabeth would not lie beside her dear Duke at Holme Pierrepont nor with the bones of her Chudleigh ancestors under a monument, handsome or other-wise, in the ancient church at Ashton.

If Elizabeth's death was sad, however, the same could not be said for her life. It was true that there was no one to mourn over her grave, but that can happen to even the most virtuous who outlive their friends. Sir Richard Heron might talk of 'dropping the Curtain decently over this sad Tragedy',[36] but Elizabeth herself would not have seen it that way, although her life had had its share of tragic moments. Yes, she had made a foolish decision to marry a man she did not care for, but she had eventually found love with the Duke of Kingston and had been loved in return. She had travelled widely in Europe, far more than many men of her generation, let alone the women; met many of its most important, most talented, most flamboyant characters and claimed some of them, with justice, as her friends. Her conversation sparkled with wit, and a wide experience of life made her a fascinating raconteur. Striving to live up to Sir Francis Bacon's saying that 'Fortitude will conquer fortune', she had also shown enormous courage and resilience in dealing with difficult situations, even if the difficulties were frequently of her own making.

There were flaws, of course. No human character is without them. Her personal habits could be coarse, her behaviour vulgar. Her chaplain Reverend Forster thought her vain and obstinate. Once she became a duchess, and even more after she was publicly 'unduchessed', she was often insufferably proud and haughty, complaining when others did not show her enough respect. She was wilful yet restless, so that having exerted every ounce of strength to get what she wanted she would often lose interest in it. Nor was she free from the self-delusion that often afflicts people.

Yet, for all that, she was a faithful friend to those closest to her, always willing to put herself out for their benefit. People liked her despite themselves; ambassadors who found themselves unable to introduce her as Duchess of Kingston at some foreign court or other frequently betrayed in their reports home more admiration for her than they would have been prepared to confess. Even her fiercest, most relentless critics were forced to admit that she possessed some shining qualities. As *The Gentleman's Magazine* put it, 'Whatever might have been her faults and singularities . . . few will deny that she possessed a noble munificence of spirit that would have transferred new lustre to the proudest title. She was splendidly generous, and unostentatiously charitable. She remembered favours with gratitude;

and was not only capable of forgiving, but even of assisting, a fallen foe.'[37] It had not always been a strictly virtuous life, but it had always been a full one.

Notes

ABBREVIATIONS USED IN NOTES

Bedford Archives = Bedfordshire and Luton Archives and Records Service

Beinecke, Osborn MSS = James Marshall and Marie-Louise Osborn Collection, Beinecke Rare Book and Manuscripts Library, Yale University

BL = British Library

Dresden = Sächsisches Haupstaatsarchiv Dresden

HMC = Historical Manuscripts Commission

LMA = London Metropolitan Archives

NHA Belarus = National Historical Archive of Belarus

NLS = National Library of Scotland

NLW = National Library of Wales

University of Nottingham = Department of Manuscripts and Special Collections, University of Nottingham

PRO = Public Record Office, Kew

Suffolk Record Office = Suffolk Record Office, Bury St Edmunds

WSRO = Wiltshire and Swindon Record Office

INTRODUCTION

1 *The London Chronicle*, 16–19 December 1775, p.588.
2 A brief account of the former, and considerably more on the latter, is found in Andrew/McGowen, *The Perreaus and Mrs Rudd*.
3 Turner, *Amazing Grace*, p.157.
4 *The Weekly Magazine; or Edinburgh Amusement*, Thursday 23 March 1775, p.389.
5 *Town and Country Magazine*, 1775, p.10.
6 *The Times*, 21 June 1788, p.3.

CHAPTER 1

1   Family histories and pedigrees of varying degrees of accuracy
    can be found in *Chudleigh Memorials* (privately printed 1916);
    Burke's Extinct and Dormant Baronetage (London 1841), *Thomas
    Westcote's View of Devonshire in 1630* (Exeter 1845), *The Worthies
    of Devon*, by John Prince (London 1701, new ed. 1810), and *The
    Visitation of the County of Devon, in the Year 1620*, ed. Frederic
    Thomas Colby (London 1872).

2   Prince, *The Worthies of Devon*, op. cit., p.216.

3   Edward Earl of Clarendon, *The History of the Rebellion and Civil
    Wars in England, Begun in the Year 1641* (Oxford 1702), Vol. 2,
    p.305.

4   *A Declaration Published in the County of Devon by that Grand Ambo-
    Dexter Sir George Chudleigh Baronet* (London 1644).

5   Chudleigh, *Poems and Prose*, p.83.

6   Wharton, *Poetical Works*, Vol. 2, p.113.

7   Ibid., p.114.

8   Chudleigh, *Poems and Prose*, p.136.

9   BL, Stowe 224, f.1.

10 For Thomas Chudleigh's army career, see Charles Dalton's two
    books, *English Army Lists and Commission Registers 1661–1714* (6
    vols, London 1892–1904), Vol. V, pp.144–145, 186, and Vol. VI,
    pp.135, 197, 230, 371; and *George the First's Army* (2 vols, London
    1910), Vol. II, p.412.

11 Westminster Archives, St Martin-in-the-Fields parish register,
    9 and 10 October 1713.

12 PRO, WO 247/30, f.5; E 351/1783.

13 PRO, RG 4/4330.

14 Plymouth and West Devon Record Office, Harford parish:
    Churchwarden's accounts. 'Col Thomas Chudleigh for Hall' first
    appears as rate payer in 1720.

15 *Army List* (London 1740), p.42.

16 House of Lords Record Office, South Sea Company, B63:
    Subscription books, 3rd Subscription for Sale of South Sea Stock,
    17 June 1720, f.42.

17 *Weekly Journal or Saturday's-Post*, Saturday 1 October 1720,
    p.573.

CHAPTER 2

1 Elizabeth Chudleigh's year of birth is usually given as 1720, which would have been true at the time when the new year began on 25 March; so that December 1720 was followed by January 1720. From 1752, the new year began on 1 January. For the sake of clarity, dates in the text have been given in the New Style, e.g. 1721; dates in the notes in both Old Style and New Style, e.g. 1720/1.

2 Defoe, *A Tour Through the Whole Island of Great Britain*, p.345.

3 The most recent edition of Horace Walpole's letters is *Horace Walpole's Correspondence*, ed. W.S. Lewis. See his letter to Horace Mann, Vol. 24, p.198, for references to their childhoods in Chelsea.

4 *The British Journal*, 11 May 1723, No. XXXIV, p.5.

5 Walpole, *Correspondence*, Vol. 24, p.198.

6 Dalton, *George the First's Army*, Vol. II, p.412.

7 Plymouth and West Devon Record Office, 1403/28: Harford parish, churchwarden's accounts.

8 PRO, WO 246/93, unfol.

9 Defoe, *A Tour Through the Whole Island of Great Britain*, p.286.

10 Kearsley, *An Authentic Detail*, p.3.

11 Westminster Archives, Conduit Street Rate Book.

12 *Old England*, 2 July 1748, p.1.

13 Oberkirch, *Memoirs*, Vol. 3, pp.220–221.

14 Plymouth and West Devon Record Office, Acc. 733, Box 3358, unfol.

15 *The Gentleman's Magazine*, Vol. IX (1739), p.496.

16 Melville, *Trial of the Duchess*, p.271.

17 Devon Record Office, Ashton 2016 add. 2A/PB1.

18 *Histoire de la Vie et les Aventures de la Duchesse de Kingston*, p.12.

19 BL, Add. 73563, f.39, Calais 10 February 1779.

20 *Pylades and Corinna*, Vol. 2, p.267.

21 *Memoir of the Duchess of Kingston*, extracted from the *British Magazine & Review*, August 1782 (London 1782), p.92.

22 Royal Academy, 397/NOR/21, 18 April 1776: 'Sir Joshua [Reynolds] has a head of her done by him more than thirty years since at Saltram before he went to Italy . . .'

23 Melville, *The Society at Tunbridge Wells*, pp.185–190 (also in

Samuel Richardson, *Correspondence*), Tunbridge Wells 2 August 1748.

24 Oberkirch, *Memoirs*, Vol. 3, p.244.

25 BL, Add. 73563, f.39, Calais 10 February 1779.

26 BL, Add. 24397, Prince of Wales's Establishment Book, 17 February 1728/9 to 8 October 1744, f.109v. *The Gentleman's Magazine*, Vol. XIV (1744), p.53.

27 For a beautifully illustrated and clear account of 18th-century fashions, see Ashelford, *The Art of Dress*, Chapter 4, pp.121–167.

CHAPTER 3

1 There are several accounts of the life of Frederick, Prince of Wales, and his wife Augusta: these include Young, *Poor Fred*; Edwards, *Frederick Louis*; and Walters, *The Royal Griffin*.

2 HMC Carlisle, p.170, 26 April 1736.

3 This is often quoted in books about the period, though its source is never given: see, for instance, Walters, *Royal Griffin*, p.9.

4 HMC Egmont, Vol. 1, pp.2207–2208, 13 August 1731.

5 'court, clair et saisissant': Oberkirch, *Memoirs*, p.450.

6 Lady Mary Coke, *Letters*, Vol. II, p.403.

7 Smollett, *Humphrey Clinker*, p.92.

8 Kielmansegge, *Diary of a Journey to England*, p.22.

9 LMA, DL/C/555/050/8, Consistory Court of London: Cause Papers.

10 *The London Evening-Post*, 15–17 May 1744, p.2.

11 *Baily's Racing Register* (3 vols, London 1845), Vol. 1 (1709–1800), p.71.

12 Augustus Hervey, *Journal*, Introduction, pp.xxx-xxxi.

13 LMA, DL/C/277, ff.103–104, Consistory Court of London: Deposition Book.

14 BL, Add. 73563, ff.27–28, Calais 8 April 1778.

15 LMA, DL/C/280, ff.343–344, Consistory Court of London: Deposition Book 1776–1780, Vol. 93.

16 Murray of Broughton, *Memorials*, p.120, 1745: 'the then situation of his affairs would not admit of his being so liberal as he inclined; his father having left very large debts, which he was resolved to pay.'

17   National Register of Archives for Scotland, Hamilton archive, C 3/275, 21 February 1744.

18   BL, Add. 73563, ff.29–30, Calais 15 April 1778.

19   'To the Ladies', by Lady Mary Chudleigh, published in 1703; quoted in Chudleigh, *Poems and Prose*, p.83.

20   Quoted in Vickery, *The Gentleman's Daughter*, p.73.

21   Turberville, *The House of Lords*, p.7.

22   LMA, DL/C/280, f.344, Consistory Court of London: Deposition Book 1776–1780, Vol. 93.

23   BL, Add. 73563, ff.27–28, Calais 8 April 1778: 'as a gallant and gay Lothario he [Hervey] ought to know, that a woman of spirit can only be conquer'd by soft perswasion, and soothing eloquence; and that I was not made to receive harsh commands'.

24   Account taken from Ann Craddock's statements, LMA, DL/C/280, ff.342–346, Consistory Court of London: Deposition Books 1776–1780, Vol. 93.

25   Melville, *Trial of the Duchess*, p.251.

26   LMA, DL/C/280, f.342, Consistory Court of London: Deposition Books 1776–1780, Vol. 93.

27   Quoted in Picard, *Dr Johnson's London*, p.69.

28   Walpole, *Correspondence*, Vol. 19, p.161, 15 March 1745.

29   Ibid., pp.174–175, 29 November 1745.

30   Burney, *Memoirs*, p.57, London 1746.

31   *Daily Advertiser*, 23 April 1746.

32   'The Beauties: An epistle to Mr Eckardt, the Painter' (M Cooper, London 1746). The bashful author turned out to be Horace Walpole; quoted with variations in Walpole, *Correspondence*, Vol. 30, pp.324–328.

33   Suffolk Record Office, 941/50/3: Hon. Augustus John Hervey, Diary 1746–1759, ff.6–7, 20 August 1746.

34   Ibid., f.7, 22 August 1746.

35   Ibid., ff.11–12, September-October 1746.

36   Ibid., ff.12–13, 16 October 1746.

37   Ibid., f.14, early December 1746.

38   Beinecke, Osborn MSS 17935, Calais 6 February 1779: 'Lord Bristol well knows it was not one, but two Dukedoms, was at my option; but I have no regret on that Subject for neither of the two would have made me happy.'

39   National Register of Archives for Scotland, Hamilton archive, C 3/1732, 4 December 1746.

40   *The General Advertiser*, Saturday 20 December 1746, p.1: 'This day his Grace Duke Hamilton will set out for his seat in Hampshire.'

41   *The Penny London Post, or The Morning Advertiser*, Friday 9–Monday 12 January 1747, p.3.

42   HMC Townshend, p.370, n.d. [January 1747].

43   Walpole, *Correspondence*, Vol. 24, p.152, 17 December 1775: 'Laudanum she had recourse to formerly on an emergency.'

44   Suffolk Record Office, 941/50/3 (Hervey, Diary 1746–1759), f.17, January 1747.

45   Kearsley, *An Authentic Detail*, p.7.

46   Melville, *Trial of the Duchess*, p.233.

47   Westminster Archives, parish register of St Luke's, Chelsea.

48   A version of the story, told about a Miss A___h, appears in *Lord Chesterfield's Witticisms*, published c. 1773. In *Wit A-La-Mode; or, Lord Chesterfield's Witticisms*, which came out in 1778, the tale appears with Miss Chudleigh as the target.

49   Suffolk Record Office, 941/50/3 (Hervey Diary 1746–1759), f.27, 20 September 1747.

50   Melville, *Trial of the Duchess*, p.233.

CHAPTER 4

1   HMC Townshend, p.369, 8 May 1748 'Augustus Hervey to Lady Townsend. Dated on board the "Phoenix in Vado-bay" and unaddressed'.

2   Suffolk Record Office, 941/50/3 (Hervey Diary 1746–1759), f.44, 10 May 1748.

3   Boscawen, *Admiral's Wife*, p.87, 23 June 1748.

4   Melville, *Society at Tunbridge Wells*, pp.185–190, (also in Richardson, *Correspondence*), Tunbridge Wells 2 August 1748.

5   Victoria & Albert Museum, Dept. of Prints and Drawings, E652–1965/ Z.9.a, 'The remarkable characters who were at Tunbridge Wells with [Samuel] Richardson in 1748 from a drawing in his possession with references in his own writing'.

6   *George Selwyn and His Contemporaries*, Vol. 1, pp.129–130, 22 July 1748.

7   Melville, *Society at Tunbridge Wells*, pp.185–190 (also in

Richardson, *Correspondence*), Tunbridge Wells 2 August 1748.

8   Suffolk Record Office, 941/50/3 (Hervey Diary 1746–1759), f.56, late December 1748.

9   Ibid., f.57, early/25 January 1749.

10 Walpole, *Last Journals*, pp.246–248.

11 *The Daily Advertiser*, 18 April 1749.

12 Ibid., 22 April 1749.

13 *The Gentleman's Magazine*, Vol. XIX (1749), p.185.

14 *The London Evening-Post*, Thursday 20–Saturday 22 April 1749, p.1.

15 *The Daily Advertiser*, 24 April 1749.

16 Quoted in Meara, *Chelsea in the Eighteenth Century*.

17 Walpole, *Correspondence*, Vol. 20, pp.46–49, 3 May 1749.

18 *The Daily Advertiser*, 24 April 1749.

19 Walpole, *Correspondence*, Vol. 20, pp.46–49, 3 May 1749.

20 *The Daily Advertiser*, 29 April 1749.

21 *The Gentleman's Magazine*, Vol. XIX (1749), pp.186–187.

22 Walpole, *Correspondence*, Vol. 20, pp.46–49, 3 May 1749.

23 *The Daily Advertiser*, 3 May 1749.

24 Walpole, *Correspondence*, Vol. 20, pp.46–49, 3 May 1749.

25 Houghton Library, University of Harvard, *58M-110, Mrs Elizabeth Montagu to her sister, 8 May [1749].

26 Wright, *England Under the House of Hanover*, Vol. 1, p.343n.

27 Walpole, *Correspondence*, Vol. 20, pp.56–57, 17 May 1749.

28 'A Poetical Epistle to Miss C—h—y: Occasioned by her Appearing in the Character of Iphigenia At the Late Jubilee Ball at Ranelagh, 1749' (London June 1749).

29 Walpole, *Correspondence*, Vol. 20, pp.56–57, 17 May 1749.

30 Suffolk Record Office, 941/50/3 (Hervey Diary 1746–1759), f.60, 2 June 1749.

31 Walpole, *Correspondence*, Vol. 20, p.122, 25 February 1750.

32 *The Gentleman's Magazine*, Vol. XX (1750), p.7.

33 *The London Evening-Post*, Thursday 8–Saturday 10 February 1750, p.4.

34 *The Gentleman's Magazine*, Vol. XX (1750), p.137.

35 Ibid., p.87.

36 Walpole, *Correspondence*, Vol. 20, p.133

37 BL, Add. 70432, misc 14d (Countess of Oxford, draft letters to Lady Mary Wortley Montagu), unfol., 7 April 1750.

38   *The London Evening-Post*, Thursday 5–Saturday 7 April 1750, p.1.

39   Walpole, *Correspondence*, Vol. 20, p.137, 4 April 1750.

40   *The Daily Advertiser*, April 5, 1750, p.4.

41   *The Gentleman's Magazine*, Vol. XX (1750), p.184.

42   Ibid., p.391.

43   *London Magazine*, Vol XIX (1750), P.572, 4 December 1750.

44   PRO, LC5/23, f.221, 1 January 1750/1.

45   *The Court & City Register*, 1752, p.79.

46   Walpole, *Correspondence*, Vol. 20, p.212, 22 December 1750.

CHAPTER 5

1   *The Penny London Post*, Friday 22–Monday 25 March 1751, p.2.

2   *The London Advertiser, and Literary Gazette*, Saturday 23 March 1751, p.2.

3   *The Penny London Post*, Wednesday 20–Friday 22 March 1751, p.2.

4   *The Gentleman's Magazine*, Vol. XXI (1751), p.522.

5   *Britannia in Tears: An Elegiac Pastoral on the Death of the Prince of Wales* (London 1751).

6   *The London Evening-Post*, Saturday 13–Friday 16 April 1751, p.1.

7   LMA, DL/C/555/050, f.2.

8   BL, Add. 70432, misc 14e (Countess of Oxford, draft letters to Lady Mary Wortley Montagu), unfol., 6 April 1751.

9   *The Daily Advertiser*, 18 January 1752, p.1.

10   Walpole, *Correspondence*, Vol. 20, p.155, 19 May 1750.

11   *The Daily Advertiser*, 15 February 1752, p.1.

12   Whitehead, *Original Anecdotes*, pp.136–140.

13   University of Nottingham, M4416.

14   Hervey, *Lord Hervey and His Friends*, p.256, London 26 November 1736.

15   Ibid., p.255, London 4 December 1736.

16   HMC Dartmouth, Vol III, p.158, [July] 1739.

17   BL, Add. 70432, misc 14b, unfol., 12 June 1745.

18   BL, Eg. 3539, f.198, 1745.

19   Wortley Montagu , *Complete Letters*, Vol. 2, p.347, 20 August 1749.

20   *The Penny London Post*, Friday 8–Monday 11 March 1751, p.3.

21   BL, Add. 70432, misc 14e, unfol., 31 July 1751.

22   Walpole, *Correspondence*, Vol. 9, p.107, 23 June 1750.

23 Lady Jane Coke, *Letters*, p.94, 28 January 1752.

24 BL, Add. 70432, misc 14e, unfol., 22 April 1752.

25 Lady Jane Coke, *Letters*, p.104, 12 June 1752.

26 Ibid., pp.110–111, 13 August 1752.

27 LMA, DL/C/277, ff.91, 101, Consistory Court of London: Register of Depositions; DL/C/555/050/3: Consistory Court of London, Cause Papers, Chudley v. Hervey, December 1768, Exhibit C.

28 Walpole, *Correspondence*, Vol. 37, p.364, 24 May 1753.

29 Lady Jane Coke, *Letters*, p.103, 9 October 1753.

30 *The Daily Advertiser*, 29 April 1754.

31 Walpole, *Correspondence*, Vol. 35, p.80, 30 April 1754.

32 Lady Jane Coke, *Letters*, p.150, 26 November 1754.

33 Oberkirch, *Memoirs*, Vol. 3, p.218, Paris 21 March 1786.

34 Lady Jane Coke, *Letters*, p.154, 7 January 1755.

35 HMC Hastings, Vol III, p.99, 3 July 1755.

36 Whitehead, *Original Anecdotes*, p.52.

37 Ibid., pp.52–53.

38 *The Daily Advertiser*, 21 January 1756, p.xxx.

39 PRO, RG 4/4330, 21 January 1756.

40 Walpole, *Correspondence*, Vol. 37, p.447, 4 March 1756.

41 HMC Hastings, Vol III, pp.117–118, 25 May 1756.

42 LMA, DL/C/555/050/4, Consistory Court of London, Cause Papers, Chudley v. Hervey, December 1768, Exhibit D.

43 LMA, DL/C/277, f.95, Consistory Court of London: Register of Depositions.

44 Ibid., f.85. The rate books for Hill Street show 'Mrs Chudleigh' as ratepayer for 11 April 1758, but by 19 December 'Meynell Esq' has moved in; the Duke's valet says the house had been finished by summer.

45 Sadly, Flitcroft's drawings have not survived. There is a fuller description in the *Survey of London: Volume XLV, Knightsbridge*, p.159.

46 Kielmansegge, *Diary of a Journey to England*, p.280, 15 March 1762.

47 Walpole, *Correspondence*, Vol. 9, p.276, 27 March 1760.

48 HMC Various, Vol. VIII. (MSS of the Hon Fred[k] Lindley Wood), p.187, 5 December [1758–1769].

49 *The Times; or Universal Daily Register*, 22 September 1788, p.3.

50 Whitehead, *Original Anecdotes*, p.53.

51   Ibid., pp.53–56.
52   *Some Letters and Records of the Noel Family*, p.58, Scarborough 4 August, Friday [1758]. The date suggested for the letter is 1760, but that year 4 August was a Monday. The next Friday 4 August was 1769, by which time Miss Chudleigh was the Duchess of Kingston.
53   Nottinghamshire Archives: Foljambe of Osberton, DD/FJ/ 11/1/2/235–236, 26 August 1758.

CHAPTER 6

1   Melville, *Trial of the Duchess*, p.260.
2   LMA, DL/C/280, f.355, Consistory Court of London, Deposition Books 1776–1780, Vol. 93.
3   Hampshire Record Office, Knollis Family, Earls of Banbury, IM44/66, f.24, [23] April 1776.
4   LMA, DL/C/280, f.355, Consistory Court of London, Deposition Books 1776–1780, Vol. 93.
5   Melville, *Trial of the Duchess*, p.260.
6   LMA, DL/C/280, f.356, Consistory Court of London, Deposition Books 1776–1780, Vol. 93.
7   Melville, *Trial of the Duchess*, p.261.
8   LMA, DL/C/280, f.356, Consistory Court of London, Deposition Books 1776–1780, Vol. 93.
9   Westminster Archives, Acc. 943, Box 3, Bundle 3, 28 March 1760.
10   Whitehead, *Original Anecdotes*, p.86.
11   *The Gentleman's Magazine*, Vol. XXIX (1759), pp.438–439, 14 September 1759.
12   Walpole, *Correspondence*, Vol. 9, p.276, 27 March 1760.
13   Ibid., Vol. 35, pp.299–301, 7 June 1760.
14   Northumberland, *Diaries of a Duchess*, pp.17–18, Sunday 22 May 1760.
15   Surrey History Centre, Manorial Records of Frensham Beale: surrenders, 1294/2/22, 10 September 1760; court rolls 1688–1761, 1294/1/3, ff.158–161, 10 September 1760; surrenders, 1294/2/23, 15 September 1760.
16   'Particulars of and Conditions of Sale for, a Valuable Estate called Pierrepont Lodge, Within three Miles of Farnham, in the

County of Surry. Which will be sold by Auction, By Mess. Langford, at their House in the Great Piazza', Covent Garden, on Tuesday the 24th Day of August 1779, p.2.

17   Whitehead, *Original Anecdotes*, p.82.

18   *The Gentleman's Magazine*, Vol. XXX (1760), p.486.

19   *Annual Register*, Vol. 3, 1760, p.139.

20   Ibid., p.178.

21   Ibid., p.146.

22   Ibid., p.147.

23   Walpole, *Correspondence*, Vol. 9, p.338, 7 February 1761.

24   Thrale, *Diary*, p.32.

25   Walpole, *Correspondence*, Vol. 9, p.338, 7 February 1761.

26   Quoted in Rimbault, *Soho and Its Associations*, p.167.

27   *Annual Register*, Vol. 4, 1761, p.206.

28   Ibid., p.210.

29   Ibid., p.213.

30   Ibid., p.214.

31   *The Gentleman's Magazine*, Vol. XXXI (1761), p.418.

32   Ibid., p.428.

33   *The London Evening-Post*, Thursday 24–Saturday 26 September 1761.

34   Walpole, *Correspondence*, Vol. 38, p.123, 25 September 1761.

35   Whitehead, *Original Anecdotes*, p.86. In October and November 1759, *The Beggar's Opera* ran (almost) every night, with Charlotte Brent singing the lead female role of Polly.

36   HMC Various, Vol. VIII. (MSS of the Hon Frederick Lindley Wood), p.179, 8 December 1761.

37   *The Gentleman's Magazine*, Vol. XXXII (1762), p.44.

38   Kielmansegge, *Diary of a Journey to England*, 15 March 1762.

39   *Public Advertiser*, Friday 2 July 1762, p.4.

40   LMA, DL/C/555/050/5, Consistory Court of London, Cause Papers, Chudley v. Hervey, December 1768, Exhibit E, 14 July 1762.

41   Ibid., DL/C/555/050/6, Consistory Court of London, Exhibit F, 14 August 1762.

42   Derbyshire Record Office, D3155/C3015, Chudleigh House 18 September 1762.

43   'Particulars of and Conditions of Sale for, a Valuable Estate called Pierrepont Lodge', op. cit., p.1.

44 Whitehead, *Original Anecdotes*, p.82.

45 'Particulars of and Conditions of Sale for, a Valuable Estate called Pierrepont Lodge', op. cit., p.2.

46 Whitehead, *Original Anecdotes*, pp.82–83, 91–92.

47 Manuscripts of the Marquis of Bute, 30 January 1763.

48 Walpole, *Correspondence*, Vol. 38, pp.203–205, 21 May 1763.

49 Beinecke, Library of Frederick W Hilles, 21 May 1763.

50 BL, Add. 35400 (Hardwicke Papers), f.137, London 1 October 1763: 'Yesterday the committee had an application from another Lady for Leave of the use of that Room [the Reading Room] for study, which we readily granted: and your Lordship would scarce have guess'd, that this Lady is Miss Chudleigh'; British Museum Standing Committee, Index to the Trustees' Minutes, p.884, 30 September 1763.

51 BL, Add. 35400 (Hardwicke Papers), f.138, 4 October 1763.

52 Whitehead, *Original Anecdotes*, p.96.

53 *London Chronicle*, Vol. XV, p.435, Saturday 5–Tuesday 8 May 1764.

54 Sutton, *Date Book*, pp.66–67, 24 August 1764.

55 Melville, *Trial of the Duchess*, p.226.

CHAPTER 7

1 Whitehead, *Original Anecdotes*, pp.22–23.

2 Ibid., pp.23–26.

3 University of Nottingham, Pw F 8717/1–2, Longleat 3 December 1764; Walpole, *Correspondence*, Vol. 38, p.473, 3 December 1764; Lady Mary Coke, *Letters*, Vol. 1, p.18, 5 December 1764.

4 Lady Mary Coke, *Letters*, Vol. 1, p.18, 5 December 1764.

5 LMA, DL/C/277, Consistory Court of London: Register of Depositions, ff.83, 85.

6 Casanova, *History of My Life*, Vol. 10, p.49.

7 Frederick the Great, *Oeuvres*, Vol. 24, pp.89–90, Potsdam 22 July 1765.

8 *London Chronicle*, 23–25 July 1765, p.87.

9 University of Nottingham, Ma 2 x 2 (iii) (g), Calais 21 June 1776.

10 Frederick the Great, *Oeuvres*, Vol. 24, pp.90–91, Pillnitz 3 August 1765.

11   Dresden, Nachlass Maria Antonia, Nr. 62, Bl. 155–194, f.155, Carlsbad 15 August 1765.

12   Chesterfield, *Letters*, p.2665, 1765.

13   Whitehead, *Original Anecdotes*, pp.26–27.

14   Chesterfield, *Letters*, p.2673, 25 October 1765.

15   University of Nottingham, Pw F 2799, Chudleigh House 13 April 1766.

16   Whitehead, *Original Anecdotes*, pp.32–33.

17   Dresden (Nachlass Maria Antonia, Nr. 62, Bl. 155–194), f.170, Calais 20 August 1774.

18   Whitehead, *Original Anecdotes*, p.40.

19   *London Chronicle*, 5–7 August 1766, p.134.

20   Chesterfield, *Letters*, p.2753, 1 August 1766.

21   NLW, Peniarth 418, f.80.

22   Lady Mary Coke, *Letters*, Vol. I, p.87, 30 October 1766.

23   *The Beauties of England and Wales*, Vol. XII, Part I, p.368.

24   Lady Mary Coke, *Letters*, Vol. II, p.200, 25 February 1768.

25   Ibid.

26   *The Experienced English Housekeeper*, by Elizabeth Raffald (London 1769).

27   Lady Mary Coke, *Letters*, Vol. II, p.261, 12 May 1768.

28   LMA, DL/C/277, f.85, Consistory Court of London: Register of Depositions.

29   Dresden (Nachlass Maria Antonia, Nr. 62, Bl. 155–194), ff.191–192, London n.d. [May/pre-10 June 1768].

30   Ibid., ff.157–158, London 10 June 1768.

31   Manuscripts of the Marquis of Bute, Chudleigh House 1 August 1768.

32   *Grenville Papers*, Vol. IV, pp.343–344, 13 August 1768.

33   Melville, *Trial of the Duchess*, p.283.

34   Lady Mary Coke, *Letters*, Vol. II, pp.330–331, 7 August 1768.

35   Ibid.

36   Melville, *Trial of the Duchess*, p.247: 'she did not acknowledge him for her legal husband'.

37   Dresden (Nachlass Maria Antonia, Nr. 62, Bl. 155–194), ff.159–160, 13 August 1768.

38   Melville, *Trial of the Duchess*, p.246.

39   NLW, Peniarth 418, ff.83–83a, 20 August 1768.

40   Melville, *Trial of the Duchess*, p.247.

41   Lady Mary Coke, *Letters*, Vol. II, pp.365–366, 370–371, 374.

42   Ibid., p.385

43   Montagu, *Letters*, Vol. 1, p.179.

44   *Grenville Papers*, Vol. IV, p.394, 31 October 1768.

45   Quoted in Melville, *Trial of the Duchess*, p.67.

46   Dresden (Nachlass Maria Antonia, Nr. 62, Bl. 155–194), ff.161–162, 18 November 1768.

47   LMA, DL/C/555/050/1–14, Consistory Court of London, Cause Papers, Chudley v Hervey.

48   LMA, DL/C/277, ff.75–76, Consistory Court of London: Register of Depositions.

49   NLW, Peniarth 418, f.113.

50   Melville, *Trial of the Duchess*, p.228.

51   LMA, DL/C/280, f.354, Consistory Court of London, Deposition Books 1776–1780.

52   Melville, *Trial of the Duchess*, p.250.

53   Dresden (Nachlass Maria Antonia, Nr. 62, Bl. 155–194), f.163, 14 February 1769.

CHAPTER 8

1   Lady Mary Coke, *Letters*, Vol. III, p.35, 3 March 1769.

2   Ibid., p.36, 5 March 1769.

3   Melville, *Trial of the Duchess*, p.289.

4   Whitehead, *Original Anecdotes*, p.11.

5   *London Chronicle*, 7–9 March 1769, p.230.

6   BL, Add. 35509 (Hardwicke Papers), ff.305–306.

7   Whitehead, *Original Anecdotes*, p.11.

8   Ibid., pp.58–59.

9   Dresden (Nachlass Maria Antonia, Nr. 62, Bl. 155–194), f.164, Friday 10 March 1769.

10   *London Chronicle*, 11–14 March 1769, p.242.

11   Ibid., 14–16 March 1769, p.250.

12   *Grenville Papers*, Vol. IV, p.414, 21 March 1769.

13   Oulton, *Queen Charlotte*, pp.106–107.

14   Lady Mary Coke, *Letters*, Vol. III, p.46, 19 March 1769.

15   Whitehead, *Original Anecdotes*, p.60.

16   Ibid., p.59.

17   Lady Mary Coke, *Letters*, Vol. III, pp.83–85.

18   Dresden (Nachlass Maria Antonia, Nr. 62, Bl. 155–194), f.167, 2 May 1769.
19   Norfolk Record Office, Walsingham (Merton) Collection, WLS/XLVIII/1/425 x 9, Bristol 19 August 1769.
20   Whitehead, *Original Anecdotes*, pp.67–72.
21   NLW, Peniarth 418, f.84, n.d., 'Thursday morn'.
22   See, for instance, Hodson, ed., 'The building and alteration of the second Thoresby House, 1767–1804'.
23   *Vitruvius Britannicus*, Vol. 5 (London 1771), p.3.
24   Christie's Catalogue, Thoresby sale, 10 June 1789.
25   BL, Add. 42232, f.28v., Diary of a trip into Derbyshire, n.d.
26   Kurakin, *Arkhiv*, Vol. V, pp.386–388, Thoresby November 1771.
27   BL, Add. 42232, f.28v, Diary of a trip into Derbyshire, n.d.
28   Whitehead, *Original Anecdotes*, pp.97, 100–101.
29   BL, Eg. 3539, f.182.
30   Whitehead, *Original Anecdotes*, p.118.
31   Ibid., p.48.
32   Ibid., p.118.
33   Ibid., pp.116–117.
34   Ibid., p.119.
35   Ibid., pp.122–123.
36   University of Nottingham, Ne C 3927, Thoresby 1 February 1770.
37   HMC Underwood, pp.423–424 (now BL, Add. 57928), 5 May 1770.
38   Whitehead, *Original Anecdotes*, p.143.
39   Surrey History Centre, Manorial Records of Frensham Beale, surrenders, 1294/2/29, 21 May 1771; 1294/2/30, 1 June 1771.
40   University of Nottingham, Ne C 3363, 7 June 1771.
41   Kurakin, *Arkhiv*, Vol. V, pp.386–388, Thoresby November 1771.
42   University of Nottingham, Ne C 3270, Thoresby December 1771.
43   Watzlawick, *Bio-Bibliographie*, p.7.
44   University of Nottingham, Ne C 2948/1–2, Thoresby 22 [January] 1772.
45   *Annual Register*, Vol. 15, 1772, p.72.
46   BL, Eg. 3516, f.148, 19 April 1772.
47   Plymouth and West Devon Record Office, Acc. 733, Box 3358, unfol., Plymouth 4 July 1772.
48   Sutton, *Date Book*, p.96, 13 October 1772.

49 University of Nottingham, Ne C 3271/1–2, Thoresby 6 [January] 1773.

50 University of Nottingham, Ne C 3269, Thoresby n.d., probably January/February 1773.

CHAPTER 9

1 University of Nottingham, Ne C 3273, 3 August 1773.
2 Ibid., Ne C 3257, 14 August 1773.
3 Ibid., Ne C 3246, Bath 18 September 1773.
4 Ibid., Ne C 3268, Bath 19 September 1773.
5 *The Gentleman's Magazine*, Vol. XLIV (1774), p.338.
6 Lady Mary Coke, *Letters*, Vol. IV, pp.231–232, 30 August 1773.
7 University of Nottingham, M 4150.
8 Walpole, *Correspondence*, Vol. 32, pp.145–147, 1 October 1773.
9 Delany, *Life and Correspondence*, 2nd Series, Vol. 1, p.554, circa 2 October 1773.
10 Walpole, *Correspondence*, Vol. 32, pp.145–147, 1 October 1773.
11 University of Nottingham, Ne C 3274, Kingston House n.d. [29 September 1773].
12 Delany, *Life and Correspondence*, 2nd Series, Vol. 1, pp.573–574, "Monday" 1773.
13 Whitehead, *Original Anecdotes*, p.171.
14 Surrey History Centre, 183/47/15.
15 BL, Add. 35509 (Hardwicke Papers), ff.305–306, 1775 [dated by recipient]
16 Walpole, *Correspondence*, Vol. 24, p.31, 23 August 1774.
17 *Public Ledger*, 25 October 1773.
18 Delany, *Life and Correspondence*, 2nd Series, Vol.1, pp.562–563, 20 October 1773.

CHAPTER 10

1 Whitehead, *Original Anecdotes*, p.181.
2 *The Noels and the Millbanks*, p.37, 24 February 1774.
3 *Notizie del Mondo*, Num. 16 (22 February 1774): 'Roma 16 Fevrario 1774, E giunta in questa Dominante proveniente da altre principali città dell'Italia la Dama Inglese Vedova Kingstor [sic]'; WSRO, Arundell MSS (letters of Father John Thorpe),

2667/20/22/2, f.29, Rome 19 February 1774: '. . . the Dutchess of Kingston arrived some days ago'.

4   WSRO, Arundell MSS (letters of Father John Thorpe), 2667/20/22/2, f.31, Rome 26 February 1774.

5   Walpole, *Correspondence*, Vol. 23, p.564, 29 March 1774.

6   WSRO, Arundell MSS (letters of Father John Thorpe), 2667/20/22/2, f.35, Rome 9 March 1774.

7   Ibid., f.40, Rome 19 March 1774.

8   Ibid., f.35, Rome 9 March 1774.

9   Ibid., f.50, Rome 2 April 1774.

10 Ibid., f.58, Rome 13 April 1774.

11 Hoare & Co Archives, Ledger F 1774–1775, ff.96–98.

12 Walpole, *Correspondence*, Vol. 23, p.566, 23 April 1774.

13 Grancourt, *Voyage d'Italie*, pp.100–101.

14 Walpole, *Correspondence*, Vol. 23, p.559, 12 March 1774.

15 WSRO, Arundell MSS (letters of Father John Thorpe), 2667/20/22/2, f.55v., Rome 9 April 1774.

16 Clifford of Chudleigh MSS, Ugbrooke Park (letters of Father John Thorpe): photocopies in WSRO, 2667/20/22/8, unfol., Rome 23 April 1774.

17 Ibid.

18 Ibid.

19 PRO, SP 93/29, ff.97–98, 26 April 1774.

20 Clifford of Chudleigh MSS, Ugbrooke Park (letters of Father John Thorpe): photocopies in WSRO, 2667/20/22/8, unfol., Rome 23 April 1774.

21 University of Nottingham, Pw F 2800, Rome 27 April 1774.

22 PRO, SP 98/79, f.68, 10 May 1774.

23 Clifford of Chudleigh MSS, Ugbrooke Park (letters of Father John Thorpe): photocopies in WSRO, 2667/20/22/8, unfol., Rome 23 April 1774: 'The Dutchess of Kingston is so charmed with Rome, that she is about purchasing Villa Negroni for £20,000 Stg; PRO, SP 93/29, ff.97–98, 26 April 1774: By Sir William Hamilton . . . 'Her Grace has offer'd Sixteen Thousand Pounds for the Villa Negroni at Rome.'

24 PRO, SP 98/79, f.68, 10 May 1774.

25 WSRO, Arundell MSS (letters of Father John Thorpe), 2667/20/22/2, f.63, Rome 30 April 1774.

26 Walpole, *Correspondence*, Vol. 24, pp.6–7, 17 May 1774.

27 *Notizie del Mondo*, No. 43, Saturday 28 May 1774, p.341: 'Genova 21 Maggio. Nell' istesso giorno [Wednesday 18 May] arrivò da Lerici, servita da 3 felughe la Duchessa Kingston.'

28 Walpole, *Correspondence*, Vol. 24, pp.6–7, 17 May 1774.

29 WSRO, Arundell MSS (letters of Father John Thorpe), 2667/20/22/2, f.77v. Rome 4 June 1774.

30 Dresden (Nachlass Maria Antonia, Nr. 62, Bl. 155–194), f.169, Genoa 28 May 1774.

31 University of Nottingham, Pw F 2801, Paris 28 June 1774.

32 HMC Rutland, Vol. IV, p.237, Lille 30 June 1774.

33 Quoted in Cross, 'Vasilii Petrov', p.243, 17 May 1774.

34 Whitehead, *Original Anecdotes*, p.178.

35 Ibid., pp.187–188.

36 Melville, *Trial of the Duchess*, p.238.

37 Ibid., p.241.

38 PRO, C 12/1051/2, ff.1–3.

39 PRO, C 24/2450, unfol.

40 Quoted in Mavor, *The Virgin Mistress*, p.167.

41 University of Nottingham, Pw F 2802, Calais 11 July 1774.

42 Lady Mary Coke, *Letters*, Vol. IV, p.378, 18 July 1774.

43 HMC Carlisle, p.271, 26 July 1774.

44 Delany, *Life and Correspondence*, 2nd Series, Vol. 2, pp.19–20, 27 July 1774.

45 Quoted in Mavor, *The Virgin Mistress*, p.167.

46 Lady Mary Coke, *Letters*, Vol. IV, pp.410–411, 8 October 1774.

47 University of Nottingham, Pw F 2803, Calais 28 [July] 1774.

48 Dresden (Nachlass Maria Antonia, Nr. 62, Bl. 155–194), f.170, Calais 20 August 1774.

49 Ibid.

50 Clifford of Chudleigh MSS, Ugbrooke Park (letters of Father John Thorpe): photocopies in WSRO, 2667/20/22/8, unfol., [Rome] 10 September 1774.

51 University of Nottingham, Pw F 2804, Calais 20 September 1774.

52 WSRO, Arundell MSS (letters of Father John Thorpe), 2667/20/22/2, f.77v., Rome 4 June 1774.

53 Clifford of Chudleigh MSS, Ugbrooke Park (letters of Father John Thorpe): photocopies in WSRO, 2667/20/22/8, unfol., [Rome] 10 September 1774.

54 WSRO, Arundell MSS (letters of Father John Thorpe),

2667/20/22/2, f.52v., Rome 6 April 1774: 'The Pope has lately been much out of order, & one night was twice let blood; he has also suffered by a stoppage of urine.'

55 Dresden (Nachlass Maria Antonia, Nr. 62, Bl. 155–194), ff.171–172, Dijon 8 October 1774.

56 Ibid.

57 Walpole, *Correspondence*, Vol. 24, p.59, 24 November 1774.

58 *Notizie del Mondo*, No. 92, Wednesday 15 November 1774, p.736; No. 93, Saturday 19 November 1774, p.744; Clifford of Chudleigh MSS, Ugbrooke Park (letters of Father John Thorpe): photocopies in WSRO, 2667/20/22/8, unfol., Rome 12 November 1774.

59 Clifford of Chudleigh MSS, Ugbrooke Park (letters of Father John Thorpe): photocopies in WSRO, 2667/20/22/8, unfol., Rome 2 December 1774.

60 Ibid., Rome 10 December 1774.

61 Ibid., Rome 7 December 1774.

62 *London Chronicle*, 8–10 December 1774, p.558.

63 BL, Eg. 3524, f.3, 12 December 1774.

64 Blackstone, *Commentaries*, Vol. IV, p.163.

65 Ibid., p.164.

66 PRO, C 33/444, f.48.

CHAPTER 11

1 Clifford of Chudleigh MSS, Ugbrooke Park (letters of Father John Thorpe): photocopies in WSRO, 2667/20/22/8, unfol., Rome 21 December 1774.

2 Dresden ((Nachlass Maria Antonia, Nr. 62, Bl. 155–194), f.173, Rome 2 January 1775.

3 BL, Eg. 3524, f.5, 17 January 1775.

4 Ibid.

5 WSRO, Arundell MSS (letters of Father John Thorpe), 2667/20/22/3, f.120, Rome 28 January 1775.

6 Dresden (Nachlass Maria Antonia, Nr. 62, Bl. 155–194), ff.176–177, Rome 4 February 1775.

7 Ibid., ff.181–182, Rome 11 [February] 1775.

8 PRO, C 33/442, f.160, 9 February 1775.

9 BL, Eg. 3524, ff.6–7, Rome 15 February 1775.

10   PRO, SP 98/80, ff.37–38, Florence 11 March 1775; Walpole, *Correspondence*, Vol. 24, pp.83–84, 11 March 1775.

11   BL, Eg. 3524, ff.6–7, Rome 15 February 1775.

12   Dresden (Nachlass Maria Antonia, Nr. 62, Bl. 155–194), f.183, Florence 8 March 1775.

13   Ibid., ff.185–186, Calais 9 April 1775.

14   Durham University Library, Archives and Special Collections, Palace Green Section: letters of Rev. Robert Wharton, No. 167, Letterbook I, f.4, Paris 24 March 1775.

15   Dresden (Nachlass Maria Antonia, Nr. 62, Bl. 155–194), f.184, Paris 22 March 1775.

16   Walpole, *Correspondence*, Vol. 24, pp.55–56, 11 November 1774.

17   Dresden (Nachlass Maria Antonia, Nr. 62, Bl. 155–194), ff.185–186, Calais 9 April 1775.

18   Frederick the Great, *Oeuvres*, Vol. 13, pp.91–92.

19   HMC Rutland, Vol. III, p.2, Calais 6 & 16 May 1775.

20   University of Nottingham, Pw F 2806, Kingston House 22 May 1775.

21   Ibid., Pw F 2805, Calais 14 May 1775.

22   Ibid., M 4147/4, 12 May 1775.

23   Dresden (Nachlass Maria Antonia, Nr. 62, Bl. 155–194), f.187, Calais n.d. [15/16 May 1775].

24   BL, Eg. 3524, f.8, Kingston House 20 May 1775.

25   *The Morning Post; and Daily Advertiser*, 24 May 1775, p.2.

26   Ibid., 25 May 1775, p.2.

27   *Annual Register*, 1775, p.123.

28   Dresden (Nachlass Maria Antonia, Nr. 62, Bl. 155–194), f.189, London 24 May 1775.

29   PRO, C 33/444, f.606v.-607v.; *Annual Register*, 1775, p.133.

30   Dresden (Nachlass Maria Antonia, Nr. 62, Bl. 155–194), f.193, [London] n.d. [circa 28 June 1775].

31   Colman, *Posthumous Letters*, p.316, n.d. [1775].

32   *The Morning Chronicle*, 4 August 1775, p.4.

33   Foote, *A Trip to Calais*, p.44.

34   *The Morning Post, and Daily Advertiser*, 7 August 1775, p.1.

35   Ibid., 14 August 1775, p.1.

36   *The Morning Chronicle*, 16 August 1775, p.4.

37   Bentham, *Collected Works*, Correspondence Vol. 1, 1752–1776, pp.244–246, 27 August OS/5 September NS 1775.

38 *The Morning Post, and Daily Advertiser*, 16 August 1775, p.4.
39 *The Morning Chronicle*, 19 August 1775, p.4.
40 Colman, *Posthumous Letters*, p.313, 29 August 1775.
41 Walpole, *Correspondence*, Vol. 24, pp.125–126, 7 September 1775.
42 Ibid., Vol. 28, p.224, 22 October 1775.

CHAPTER 12

1   University of Nottingham, Pw F 2808, Kingston House 3 November 1775.
2   Walpole, *Correspondence*, Vol. 24, p.143, 14 November 1775.
3   Almon, *Parliamentary Register*, Vol. 5, p.102, 20 November 1775.
4   University of Nottingham, Pw F 2809, Kingston House 18 November 1775.
5   *The Gentleman's Magazine*, Vol. XLV (1775), p.602, Sunday 3 December 1775.
6   *Town and Country Magazine*, 1775, p.656.
7   *Journals of the House of Lords*, Vol. XXXIV (1774–1776), p.527, Monday 11 December 1775.
8   *Calendar of Home Office Papers of the Reign of George III, 1773–1775*, p.498, Kingston House 11 December 1775.
9   *Journals of the House of Lords*, Vol. XXXIV (1774–1776), p.531, Tuesday 12 December 1775.
10 Almon, *Parliamentary Register*, Vol. 5, p.111, 12 December 1775.
11 Grosley, *A Tour to London*, Vol. 2, p.192.
12 University of Nottingham, Pw F 2810, [London] 14 December 1775.
13 HMC Carlisle, p.310, 12 December 1775.
14 *London Chronicle*, 21–23 December 1775, p.608
15 Walpole, *Correspondence*, Vol. 24, p.167, 9 January 1776.
16 *Journals of the House of Lords*, Vol. XXXIV (1774–1776), p.544, 25 January 1776.
17 *The Morning Chronicle; and London Advertiser*, 1 March 1776, p.2.
18 *London Chronicle*, 29 February–2 March 1776, p.212.
19 University of Nottingham, Pw F 2814, Kingston House 28 March 1776.
20 *Morning Post*, 3 April 1776, p.2.
21 *The Morning Chronicle; and London Advertiser*, 15 April 1776, p.2.

22 *Morning Post*, 8 April 1776, p.2.

23 *Public Advertiser*, 5 April 1776, p.3.

24 *London Chronicle*, Vol. 39, 19–21 March 1776, p.276.

25 A typical example is University of Nottingham, Ne C 2688: 'I fear your Grace will think me troublesome in asking the Favour of a Ticket for the approaching Trial . . .'

26 *Morning Post*, 15 April 1776.

27 *Daily Advertiser*, 12 April 1776.

28 BL, Add. 73563, ff.51–52, 6 April 1776.

29 Hampshire Record Office, Knollis Family, Earls of Banbury, IM44/66, f.23v., 4 April 1776.

30 Ibid., f.24, April 1776.

31 National Archives of Scotland, GD157/3324, Kingston House 12 April 1776.

32 *Morning Post*, 15 April 1776, p.2.

33 Ibid.

CHAPTER 13

1 Several different accounts of the trial were published at the time, including one by order of Lord Bathhurst. A more recent, and therefore more widely available, edited account is Melville, *Trial of the Duchess of Kingston*.

2 *Public Advertiser*, Tuesday 16 April 1776, p.2.

3 *Morning Post*, Tuesday 16 April 1776, p.2.

4 *Public Advertiser*, Tuesday 16 April 1776, p.2.

5 *The Morning Chronicle; and London Advertiser*, Monday 15 April 1776, p.3.

6 *Gazetteer and New Daily Advertiser*, Tuesday 16 April 1776.

7 Boswell, *Private Papers*, Vol. 11, Journal 1775–1776, pp.252–253.

8 *Annual Register*, Vol. 19, 1776, p.133, 15 April 1776.

9 *The Morning Chronicle; and London Advertiser*, Friday 19 April 1776, p.3.

10 Saussure, *A Foreign View of England*, p.57.

11 *Morning Post*, Tuesday 16 April 1776, p.2.

12 Bedford Archives, Wrest Park (Lucas) Papers, L30/14/315/13, 15 April 1776.

13 *Gazetteer and New Daily Advertiser*, Wednesday 17 April 1776, p.3.

14 More, *Letters*, p.43.

15 Ibid.

16 *Gazetteer and New Daily Advertiser*, Tuesday 16 April 1776, p.2.

17 *Morning Post*, Tuesday 16 April 1776, p.2.

18 *The London Evening-Post*, Saturday 13–Tuesday 16 April 1776, p.3.

19 University of Nottingham, Ne C 2800, 25 April 1776. From the content, it is clear the letter must have been misdated, however, and that it should have been dated 15 April.

20 More, *Letters*, p.41.

21 Ibid., p.42

22 Boswell, *Private Papers*, Vol. 11, pp.253–254, 16 April 1776.

23 More, *Letters*, p.42.

24 *Morning Post*, Wednesday 17 April 1776, p.2.

25 Ibid., Friday 19 April 1776, p.2.

26 Melville, *Trial of the Duchess*, p.222.

27 Ibid., p.231.

28 Ibid., p.282.

29 BL, Add. 73563, f.57, 19 April 1776.

30 BL, Add. 73563, f.59, 'Thursday morning' [18 April 1776].

31 *Public Advertiser*, Monday 22 April 1776, p.2.

32 George III, *Correspondence*, Vol. 3, p.352, [22] April 1776.

33 Melville, *Trial of the Duchess*, pp.271–280.

34 Ibid., p.286

35 *Daily Advertiser*, Wednesday 24 April 1776.

36 George III, *Correspondence*, Vol. 3, p.352, [22] April 1776.

37 Ibid.

38 *Annual Register*, Vol. 19, 1776, p.236.

39 Almon, *Parliamentary Register*, Vol. 5, p.102, 20 November 1775.

40 Bedford Archives, Wrest Park (Lucas) Papers, L30/14/315/30, 10 August 1776.

41 HMC Dartmouth, Vol. I, p.403, 25 March 1776.

42 More, *Letters*, pp.44–45, [22] April 1776.

43 Delany, *Life and Correspondence*, 2nd Series, Vol. 2, p.211, 27 April 1776.

44 More, *Letters*, pp.44–45, [22] April 1776.

CHAPTER 14

1 *Gazetteer and New Daily Advertiser/Morning Chronicle*, Thursday 25 April 1776.

2 Walpole, *Correspondence*, Vol. 32, pp.299–300.

3 *Morning Post*, Friday 26 April 1776, p.2.

4 *Public Advertiser*, Saturday 27 April 1776, p.3.

5 BL, Add. 42232, f.57, Calais 2 August 1777.

6 Blaikie, *Diary of a Scotch Gardener*, p.189.

7 *The St James's Chronicle; or, British Evening-Post*, 9–12 September 1775, p.1.

8 Quoted in Walpole, *Correspondence*, Vol. 32, pp.299–300.

9 *Lloyd's Evening Post and British Chronicle*, Friday 26–Monday 29 April 1776, p.422.

10 BL, Add. 73563, f.1, Calais 1 May 1776.

11 University of Nottingham, Ma 2 x 2 (iii) (g), Calais 21 June 1776.

12 Walpole, *Correspondence*, Vol. 6, p.311, 5 May 1776.

13 University of Nottingham, Ma 2 x 2 (iii) (g), Calais 21 June 1776.

14 Ibid., M 4147/7, Calais 7 May 1776.

15 From Calton, *Annals & Legends of Calais*.

16 LMA, DL/C/558/12, Consistory Court of London, Cause Papers, Chudleigh v. Hervey: Jactitation of Marriage July 1776, Exhibit A, 21 June 1776.

17 Ibid., 26 June 1776.

18 *Annual Register*, Vol. 19, 1776, p.159.

19 Walpole, *Correspondence*, Vol. 24, pp.226–227, 16 July 1776.

20 PRO, C 33/446, f.501, 26 July 1776; C 12/1051/2, ff.1–3.

21 Walpole, *Correspondence*, Vol. 24, pp.226–227, 16 July 1776.

22 Durham University Library, Archives and Special Collections, Palace Green Section: letters of Rev. Robert Wharton, 111, 26 February 1775.

23 Walpole, *Correspondence*, Vol. 24, p.242, 20 September 1776.

24 *The Morning Post, and Daily Advertiser*, 10 October 1776, p.2.

25 Ibid., 2 September 1776, p.2.

26 NHA Belarus, fond. 694, op.1, d.336, f.24, Munich 10 November 1776.

27 Prince de Ligne, *Memoir*, Vol. 1, p.311.

28 *The Morning Post, and Daily Advertiser*, 16 October 1776, p.2: 'Extract of a letter from Calais. On Saturday next, the Duchess of Kingston leaves this town on the way to Rome . . .'

29 NHA Belarus, fond. 694, op.1, d.336, f.24, Munich 10 November 1776: 'Je suis arrivee hiere a munich . . .'

Notes

271

30 Beckford, *Italy*, p.63, 23 July [1780].

31 PRO, SP 81/112, Munich 19 June 1777: 'The Elector a few days since took an opportunity of informing me that Lady Bristol had expressed a wish of having an establishment in this country, but having already made a vain attempt to be received at his Highnesses Court under the title of Dutchess of Kingston. . . His Highness repeated many expressions of respect and attachment to his Majesty, and added more than once that Lady Bristol should never be received at his Court as Dutchess of Kingston.'

32 NHA Belarus, fond. 694, op.1, d.336, f.24, Munich 10 November 1776: 'Je reste icy jusqu'a jeudi prochain [21 November].'

33 WSRO, Arundell MSS (letters of Father John Thorpe), 2667/20/22/4, f.268, Rome 2 November 1776.

34 PRO, SP 80/218, unfol., Vienna 30 November 1776.

35 Ibid.

36 *Annual Register*, 1777, p.164.

37 WSRO, Arundell MSS (letters of Father John Thorpe), 2667/20/22/5, f.290, 5 February 1777.

38 BL, Add. 73563, ff.23–24, Calais 19 March 1778.

39 NHA Belarus, fond. 694, op.1, d.336, f.19, 3 February 1777.

40 LMA, DL/C/558/54, Consistory Court of London, Cause Papers, Chudleigh v. Hervey: matrimonial cause appeal January–May 1777, 19 February 1777.

41 University of Nottingham, M 4147/10, 22 March 1777.

42 Ibid., M 4147/11, Kingston House 29 April 1777: 'I have the pleasure to let you know that Her Grace is Well and safe arrivd – at Callais.'

43 Ibid., M 4147/13, 19 May 1777.

44 NHA Belarus, fond. 694, op.1, d.336, f.20, 7 March 1777.

45 *The Gentleman's Magazine*, Vol. XLVIII (1777), pp.111–112.

46 Hannah More, *Letters*, p.43.

47 *Lloyd's Evening Post and British Chronicle*, Friday 26–Monday 29 April 1776, p.413.

48 *Public Advertiser*, Tuesday 30 April 1776.

49 University of Nottingham, M 4147/9, 3 March 1777.

50 Ibid., M 4148/17c, Calais 10 May 1777.

51 PRO, C 33/448, f.484v.

52 University of Nottingham, M 3305, 15 May 1777.

53 BL, Eg. 3525, ff.32–36, February/March 1789.

54 Archives Nationales de France, P-15, f.73; BL, Eg. 3525, ff.32–36, February/March 1789.

55 PRO, SP 81/112, Munich 19 June 1777.

56 Ibid., Munich 21 August 1777.

57 BL, Add. 73563, ff.11–12, Riga 25 November 1777.

58 PRO, SP 81/112, Munich 14 September 1777.

59 BL, Add. 42232 (A Journey to Paris by Theo Forrest), ff.57–57v., Calais 4 August 1777.

CHAPTER 15

1 Royal Bank of Scotland Archives, DR/427/73, f.1253.

2 *The Daily Universal Register* (*The Times*), 4 September 1786, p.2.

3 BL, Add. 73563, f.3, 'In Calais Road' 7 August 1777.

4 *The Gentleman's Magazine*, Vol. XLVIII (1778), pp.111–112.

5 BL, Add. 73563, ff.5–6, St Petersburg 19 September 1777.

6 Corberon, *Un Diplomate Français*, Vol. I, p.179, Sunday 28 September (NS) 1777.

7 PRO, SP 91/101, f.161, St Petersburg 11/22 August 1777; Russia had not yet adopted the Gregorian calendar, so its dates were eleven days behind the rest of Europe. Correspondents usually used both, as illustrated here. In the text, only the New Style date is given.

8 Coxe, *Travels into Poland, Russia, Sweden and Denmark*, Vol. 1, Book 4, pp.459–486 contains a good description of St Petersburg at around this time.

9 Centre for Kentish Studies, Norman MS U310/C3, 10 August 1784.

10 Wraxall, *A Tour*, p.258.

11 Tooke, *Life of Catharine II*, Vol. 2, p.269.

12 *The Gentleman's Magazine*, Vol. XLVIII (1778), pp.111–112.

13 PRO, SP 91/101, f.161, St Petersburg 11/22 August 1777.

14 University of Nottingham, M 4147/8, 1 December 1776.

15 Quoted in Melville, *Trial of the Duchess*, p.319.

16 PRO, SP 91/101, f.164, St Petersburg 18/29 August 1777.

17 *The Gentleman's Magazine*, Vol. XLVIII (1778), pp.111–112.

18 BL, Add. 73563, ff.5–6, St Petersburg 19 September 1777.

19 *SIRIO*, Vol. 23, p.63, Tsarko-Sélo 24 August (OS) 1777.

20 *The Gentleman's Magazine*, Vol. XLVIII (1778), pp.111–112.

21 Tooke, *Life of Catharine II*, Vol. 2, p.269.

22 NHA Belarus, fond. 694, op.1, d.336, ff.27–28, Calais 28 May 1778.

23 Tooke, *Life of Catharine II*, Vol. 2, p.278.

24 PRO, SP 91/101, f.164, St Petersburg 18/29 August 1777: '. . . She at present talks of staying here only a Fortnight . . . Richard Oakes.'

25 BL, Add. 73563, ff.5–6, St Petersburg 19 September 1777.

26 PRO, SP 91/101, f.182, St Petersburg 12/23 September 1777.

27 Ibid.; Corberon, *Un Diplomate Français*, I, p.179, Monday 22 September (NS) 1777; Tooke, *Life of Catharine II*, Vol. 2, p.196.

28 BL, Add. 73563, ff.11–12, Riga 25 November 1777.

29 Corberon, *Un Diplomate Français*, I, p.179, Sunday 28 September (NS) 1777.

30 BL, Add. 73563, ff.7–8, St Petersburg 23 September 1777.

31 Ibid., ff.13–14, Dresden 17 October 1777.

32 PRO, SP 91/101, f.182, St Petersburg 12/23 September 1777.

33 Ibid., f.190, St Petersburg 22 September/3 October 1777.

34 Tooke, *Life of Catharine II*, Vol 2, p.269.

35 NHA Belarus, fond. 694, op.1, d.336, ff.5–6, 3 March 1778, quoted in full in Felkersam, p.12.

36 Ibid., ff.27–28, Calais 28 May 1778, quoted in full in Felkersam, pp.12–14.

37 PRO, SP 91/101, f.190, St Petersburg 22 September/3 October 1777.

38 Ibid.

39 Ibid., f.201, St Petersburg 10/21 October 1777.

40 University of Nottingham, M 4147/15, 8 November 1777.

41 BL, Add. 73563, ff.7–8, St Petersburg 23 September 1777.

42 Ibid., ff.75–77, 24 October 1777.

43 Beinecke, Osborn MSS 17935, St Petersburg 7 November 1777.

44 University of Nottingham, M 4147/15, 8 November 1777.

45 BL, Add. 73563, f.9, St Petersburg 13 November 1777.

CHAPTER 16

1 BL, Add. 73563, ff.11–12, Riga 25 November 1777.

2   Ibid., ff.17–18, Konigsberg December 1777.

3   NHA Belarus, fond. 694, op.1, d.336, f.30v., [Konigsberg 15 December 1777].

4   BL, Add. 73563, f.15, nr Marienburg 25 December 1777.

5   Ibid., ff.19–20, Dresden 16 January 1778.

6   Ibid., ff.11–12, Riga 25 November 1777.

7   Frederick the Great, *Oeuvres*, Vol. 26, pp.37–38, n.d. The editor of Frederick's letters suggests a date of July 1765, presumably because Elizabeth was then travelling in Germany. This is highly unlikely, for in 1765 the world in general had no reason to assume she had more than one name, that of Miss Chudleigh; it was only after the trial that the question of names and titles became an issue.

8   Carlyle, *History of Friedrich II*, Vol. 6, Book XXI, pp.552–553, 8 October 1777.

9   NLS, Minto MSS 12980, f.95, Berlin 8 January 1778.

10 Ibid., f.96, Berlin 10 January 1778.

11 BL, Add. 73563, ff.11–12, Riga 25 November 1777.

12 NLS, Minto MSS 12980, f.96, Berlin 10 January 1778.

13 Ibid., Minto MSS 12994, f.207, 10 January 1778.

14 PRO, SP 88/115, unfol., 18 January 1778.

15 Ibid., unfol., 3 January 1778.

16 Ibid., unfol., 11 January 1778.

17 Ibid., unfol., 18 January 1778.

18 NHA Belarus, fond. 694, op.1, d.336, f.7, 16 January 1778, quoted in full in Felkersam, p.12.

19 BL, Add. 73563, ff.19–20, Dresden 16 January 1778.

20 PRO, SP 88/115, unfol., 18 January 1778: 'The Empress of Russia gave her a Gentleman a man of great confidence to accompany her to this place, & from hence he is to return.'

21 BL, Add. 73563, f.43, 'between Eisenach and Bercka', n.d. [between 16 January and 10 March 1778].

22 *Annual Register*, Vol. 21, 1778, p.168, 20 February 1778.

23 BL, Add. 73563, ff.21–22, Calais 10 March 1778.

24 NHA Belarus, fond. 694, op.1, d.336, ff.5–6, 3 March 1778, quoted in full in Felkersam, pp.12–14.

25 BL, Add. 73563, ff.29–30, Calais 15 April 1778.

26 Ibid., ff.23–24, Calais 19 March 1778.

27 Ibid., f.38, Calais 26 or 28 June 1778: 'Mr Dunning expresses

that Lord Bristol is vastly shockd that any person should doubt his word of honor . . .'

28 Ibid., ff.27–28, Calais 8 April 1778.
29 Ibid., ff.25–26, Calais 20 March 1778.
30 Ibid., ff.31–32, Calais [late April] 1778.
31 Ibid., f.86, 21 March 1778.
32 Ibid., ff.25–26, Calais 20 March 1778.
33 Ibid., ff.27–28, Calais 8 April 1778.
34 Ibid., f.33, Calais 2 May 1778.
35 University of Nottingham, M 4147/17, 14 April 1778.
36 BL, Add. MS 73563, ff.27–28, Calais 8 April 1778: 'I have bid a long farewell to my own country . . .'
37 *The Noels and the Millbanks*, p.102, 8 May 1778.
38 NHA Belarus, fond. 694, op.1, d.336, ff.27–28, Calais 28 May 1778, quoted in full in Felkersam, pp.14–15.
39 BL, Add. 73563, f.36, Calais 11 June 1778.
40 Ibid., ff.23–24, Calais 19 March 1778.
41 NHA Belarus, fond. 694, op.1, d.336, ff.17–18, Calais 4 June 1778, quoted in full in Felkersam, pp.15–16.
42 BL, Add. 73563, f.91, 25 June 1778.
43 Ibid., f.38, Calais 28 June 1778.
44 Ibid., f.91, 25 June 1778.
45 Ibid., f.38, Calais 28 June 1778.

CHAPTER 17

1 University of Nottingham, M 4147/18, 31 July 1778.
2 Walpole, *Correspondence*, Vol. 24, p.398, 1 August 1778.
3 NHA Belarus, fond. 694, op.1, d.336, ff.17–18, Calais 4 June 1778, quoted in full in Felkersam, pp.15–16.
4 University of Nottingham, M 4147/18, 31 July 1778.
5 *The Two Duchesses*, p.61, 15 August 1778.
6 *Gazetta Universale*, No. 66, Martedi 18 Agosto 1778: 'Roma 12 August, Domenica sera [16] arrivò a questa Dominante la Duchessa di Kingston.'
7 Walpole, *Correspondence*, Vol. 24, pp.404–405, 22 August 1778.
8 Ibid., p.398, 1 August 1778.
9 Beinecke, Osborn MSS 17935, Calais 13 November 1778.
10 Walpole, *Correspondence*, Vol. 24, pp.404–405, 22 August 1778.

11 Ibid., pp.409–410, 15 September 1778.

12 Bedford Archives, Wrest Park (Lucas) papers, L30/14/370/13 Rome 27 August 1778.

13 Knight, *Letters*, pp.70–71, 29 October 1778 .

14 Bedford Archives, Wrest Park (Lucas) papers, L30/14/370/13 Rome 27 August 1778.

15 Ibid.

16 BL, Eg. 3525, ff.11–16, 31 January 1789.

17 Ibid., ff.25–27, 13 February 1789.

18 Quoted in Mavor, *The Virgin Mistress*, p.166: present whereabouts of original unknown.

19 University of Nottingham, Ne C 2427, Calais 6 November 1778.

20 Ibid.

21 Quoted in Mavor, *The Virgin Mistress*, p.166.

22 Beinecke, Osborn MSS 17935, Calais 13 November 1778.

23 Quoted in Mavor, *The Virgin Mistress*, p.167.

24 Beinecke, Osborn MSS 17935, Calais 13 November 1778 .

25 Bentham, *Collected Works*, Correspondence Vol. 2, 1777–1780, p.207, 12/23 October 1778.

26 University of Nottingham, M 4147/20, 30 January 1779.

27 Beinecke, Osborn MSS 17935, Calais 6 February 1779.

28 Ibid., n.d.

29 Ibid., Calais 6 February 1779.

30 Quoted in Mavor, *The Virgin Mistress*, p.166: 'Self preservation is the first law in Nature.'

31 Beinecke, Osborn MSS 17935, Calais 3 March 1779.

32 BL, Add. 73563, f.41, Calais 10 April 1779.

33 Beinecke, Osborn MSS 17935, Calais 29 April 1779.

34 NHA Belarus, fond. 694, op.1, d.336, f.26, 12 May 1779, quoted in full in Felkersam, pp.17–18.

35 *SIRIO*, Vol. 23, p.141, St Petersburg 18 May 1779.

36 PRO, PRO 30/43/11, Gertrude Harris's travel journal, f.84, [Cronstadt] Monday 3/14 June 1779: 'After breakfast went on board the Czikiel a 75 gun man of war from whence on board the Empress yatch, & the Duchess of Kingstons . . .'

37 NHA Belarus, fond. 694, op.1, d.336, ff.27–28, Calais 28 May 1778, quoted in full in Felkersam, pp.14–15.

38 Beinecke, Osborn MSS (letters of Sir James Harris to Batt), f.3, St Petersburg, 25 January /4 February 1780.

39   PRO, PRO 30/43/11, Gertrude Harris's travel journal, f.84v., St Petersburg 6/17 June 1779.
40   Wraxall, *A Tour*, p.207.
41   PRO, PRO 30/43/11, Gertrude Harris's travel journal, f.85, St Petersburg Sunday 9/20 June 1779.
42   Ibid., f.93, Cronstadt Saturday 10/21 August 1779.
43   Radziwill, *Korespondencya*, pp.133–134, 7 July 1779.
44   Beinecke, Osborn MSS 3211, St Petersburg 18 October 1779.
45   William Richardson, *Anecdotes of the Russian Empire*, p.55.
46   Ibid., p.148
47   Beinecke, Osborn MSS 3211, St Petersburg 29 February 1770 [1780].
48   Ibid., 24 March /3 April 1780.
49   University of Nottingham, M 4147/21, April 1780.
50   Felkersam, p.18; Vorontsov, Vol. 32, p.195.
51   Beinecke, Osborn MSS 3211, 24 March/3 April 1780.
52   NHA Belarus, fond. 694, op.1, d.336, ff.24–25, St Petersburg 11 April 1780, quoted in full in Felkersam, p.18.
53   BL, Add. 33555, f.62v., St Petersburg 8 April NS 1780.
54   Beinecke, Osborn MSS (letters of Sir James Harris to Batt), f.3, St Petersburg, 15/26 April 1780.
55   *The Annual Register*, 1780, p.208, 14 April 1780.
56   *The Morning Chronicle, and London Advertiser*, 17 April 1780, p.2.

CHAPTER 18

1   PRO, SP 88/115, unfol., 19 December 1779.
2   PRO, FO 68/1, unfol., Dresden 19 March 1780.
3   Ibid., Dresden 26 April 1780.
4   PRO, SP 88/112, 2 September 1776; SP 88/115, unfol., 11 January 1778; FO 68/1, unfol., Dresden 3 May 1780; 31 May 1780 passim.
5   BL, Add. 33556 (Bentham Papers), f.127v., St Petersburg 17/28 May 1780.
6   Ibid., f.119v., St Petersburg 8/19 April 1780.
7   Ibid., f.124, St Petersburg 24 April/5 May 1780.
8   Ibid., f.127, St Petersburg 17/28 May 1780.
9   Radziwill, *Korespondencya*, p.135, 17 June 1780.

10   NHA Belarus, fond. 694, op.1, d.336, ff.10–11, Reval 25 June 1780, quoted in full in Felkersam, pp.18–19.

11   Ibid., f.9, Reval 27 [June] 1780.

12   Radziwill, *Korespondencya*, pp.37–38, Kiejdany 30 July 1780.

13   Ibid., p.163, 2 August 1780.

14   NHA Belarus, fond 694, op.1, d.336, f.12, September 1780, quoted in full in Felkersam, p.22.

15   Kearsley, *An Authentic Detail*, pp.107–111.

16   University of Nottingham, Pw F 2467, Brussels 2 October 1780.

17   Radziwill, *Korespondencya*, p.163, 2 August 1780.

18   Delany, *Life and Correspondence*, 2nd Series, Vol. 2, p.572, 3 November 1780.

19   NHA Belarus, fond. 694, op.1, d.336, ff.24v.-25, St Petersburg 11 April 1780, quoted in full in Felkersam, p.18.

20   University of Nottingham, Pw F 2467, Brussels 2 October 1780.

21   NHA Belarus, fond. 694, op.1, d.336, f.12, September 1780, quoted in full in Felkersam, p.22.

22   University of Nottingham, Pw F 2470, Brussels 10 November 1780.

23   Beinecke, Osborn MSS 3211, 21 November 1781.

24   Swinburne, *The Courts of Europe*, Vol. 1, p.372, Bonn 29 November 1780.

25   BL, Eg. 3524, f.11, 24 March 1781.

26   Wistinghausen, *Quellen zur Geschichte du Rittergüter Estlands*, p.91.

27   Beinecke, Osborn MSS 3211, St Petersburg 10 April 1781.

28   Wraxall, *A Tour*, pp.253–254.

29   Justice, *Voyage to Russia*, pp.39–40.

30   University of Nottingham, M 4148/12, 20 April 1781.

31   Ibid., M 4148/9.

32   Ibid., M 4148/8, Hull 16 April 1781.

33   Ibid., M 4148/9.

34   Ibid., M 4148/5, 12 April 1781.

35   Ibid., M 4148/6, 16 April 1781.

36   Ibid., M 3307/4, 15 April 1781.

37   Beinecke, Osborn MSS 3211, St Petersburg 10 April 1781.

38   Dimsdale, *An English Lady*, p.37, Igafer 6 August 1781.

39   Ibid., pp.37–38, Igafer 6 August 1781.

40   Beinecke, Osborn MSS 17936, Calais 5 October 1781.

41   Ibid., Osborn MSS 17864, Paris 27 December 1781.

42   BL, Eg. 3524, ff.13–14, Paris 2 February 1782.

43   Archives Nationales de France, Z/1J/1104, 7 August 1783.

44   *Lettre a Madame L****, p.3.

45   Beinecke, Osborn MSS 17934, Calais 27 May 1782.

46   BL, Add. 73563, f.9, St Petersburg 13 November 1777.

47   BL, Eg. 3524, ff.50–52, Paris 8 February 1786.

48   Royal Bank of Scotland Archives, DR/427/94, f.1022, I-Q 1782.

49   Beinecke, Osborn MSS 17662, Chudleigh 19 September 1782.

50   University of Nottingham, M 3308/15, 21 December 1782.

51   Ibid., M 3308/13b, November 1782.

CHAPTER 19

1   Dimsdale, *An English Lady*, p.37, 6 August 1781.

2   *The Northern Hero*, p.7.

3   Ibid., p.11.

4   Hampshire Record Office, Malmesbury MSS (letters of the 1st Earl of Malmesbury), 9M73/158/155, Chudleigh 25 December 1782.

5   PRO, PRO 30/43/19, f.2, St Petersburg Saturday 31 December 1782/11 January 1783.

6   *The Northern Hero*, p.12.

7   The full story – Semple's version of it, at least – is in *The Life of Major JG Semple Lisle, written by Himself*.

8   University of Nottingham, M 4148/17b, 15 April 1783.

9   *SIRIO*, Vol. 27, pp.273–274, 1783.

10   Archives Nationales de France, Z/1J/1132, 16 March 1785: contains several copies of the plans.

11   *SIRIO*, Vol. 27, p.273, St Petersburg 3 August 1783.

12   BL, Eg. 3524, ff.50–52, Paris 8 February 1786.

13   Ibid., f.16, 9 September 1783.

14   Ibid., ff.21–23, St Petersburg 4 October 1783.

15   University of Nottingham, M 3309/14, 24 October 1783.

16   BL, Eg. 3524, ff.25–31, 14 November 1783.

17   BL, Add. 33564, S. Bentham's Diary, September 1783–January 1784, f.31, St Petersburg January 1784: 'Jan 1st Monday . . . Tuesday . . . Called at Landskoy, dined at the Dutchess of Kingston . . . Thursday Called on Sangey who told me of the

English ministry being changed . . . Sunday Breakfasted at Fitzherbert dined by invitation at Dutchess of Kingston's, then to P. Dashkoff's . . .'

18 Royal Bank of Scotland Archives, DR/427/102, f.1022 & f.1026.

19 University of Nottingham, M 4148/2, 7 May 1784; M 4148/22, 24 May 1784.

20 Centre for Kentish Studies, Norman MSS, U310/C3, 10 September 1784.

21 University of Nottingham, M 3310/15, 19 June 1784.

22 Ibid., M 3310/25, 10 August 1784.

23 PRO, FO 65/11.

24 Centre for Kentish Studies, Norman MSS, U310/C3, 10 August 1784.

25 BL, Eg. 3524, ff.37–38, St Petersburg 31 October 1784.

26 Ibid., ff.39–40, St Petersburg 25 March 1785.

27 University of Nottingham, M 3311/3, 25 March 1785.

28 Ibid., M 3311/5, 30 March 1785.

29 BL, Eg 3524, ff.39–40, St Petersburg 25 March 1785.

30 University of Nottingham, M 4148/29, 28 April 1785.

31 Ibid., M 4148/33, 10 May 1785.

32 Ibid., M 4148/35, 31 May 1785.

33 BL, Eg. 3524, ff.39–40, St Petersburg 25 March 1785.

34 University of Nottingham, M 3311/12, 9 August 1785.

35 Ibid., M 3311/19, 2 October 1785.

36 Ibid., M 3311/20, 5 October 1785.

37 Ibid., M 3311/16, 18 September 1785.

38 Gemeentearchief Amsterdam, Rechterlijk Archief 5061, 641d, (quoted in Watzlawick, *Bio-Bibliographie*), 8 December 1785.

39 Oberkirch, *Memoirs*, p.237.

40 Ibid., p.238.

41 I am indebted to Helmut Watzlawick's excellent *Bio-Bibliographie de Stefano Zannowich* for this information.

42 Chamberlaine, *The Life and Memoirs of Elizabeth Chudleigh*, p.157.

43 Gemeentearchief Amsterdam, Rechterlijk Archief 5061, 641d (quoted in Watzlawick, *Bio-Bibliographie*), 8 December 1785.

44 Melville, *Trial of the Duchess*, p.312.

CHAPTER 20

1   BL, Eg. 3524, f.41, Calais 21 December 1785.
2   Ibid., ff.43–46, 25 January 1786.
3   Ibid., f.47, 30 January 1786.
4   University of Nottingham, M 3312/1, 21 January 1786.
5   BL, Eg. 3524, ff.50–52, Paris 8 February 1786.
6   Oberkirch, *Memoirs*, Vol. 3, p.218, Paris 21 March 1786.
7   *The Daily Universal Register (The Times)*, Paris 7 April 1786, p.3.
8   Oberkirch, *Memoirs*, Vol. 3, p.245, Paris 24 March 1786.
9   Barnett, *Richard and Maria Cosway*, p.115.
10 Oberkirch, *Memoirs*, Vol. 3, p.244, Paris 24 March 1786.
11 Ibid., p.218, Paris 21 March 1786.
12 Whitehead, *Original Anecdotes*, pp.121–122.
13 *The Daily Universal Register (The Times)*, Paris 7 April 1786, p.3.
14 Gemeentearchief Amsterdam, Rechterlijke Archief 5061, 641d (quoted in Watzlawick, *Bio-Bibliographie*), Paris 18 April 1786.
15 Watzlawick, *Bio-Bibliographie*, p.17.
16 Oberkirch, *Memoirs*, p.238, April 1786.
17 University of Nottingham, M 3312/16, 4 August 1786.
18 Royal Bank of Scotland Archives, DR/427/110, f.1437.
19 *The Daily Universal Register (The Times)*, 4 September 1786, p.2.
20 Jefferson, *Papers*, Vol. 10, pp.393–394, Paris Wednesday evening [20 September 1786].
21 BL, Eg. 3524, ff.53–54, 25 October 1786.
22 Jefferson, *Papers*, Vol. 10, p.506, Calais [late (28/29)] October 1786.
23 Printed in Barnett, *Richard and Maria Cosway*.
24 *The Daily Universal Register (The Times)*, Wednesday 1 November 1786, p.3.
25 Fondazione Maria Cosway, Lodi, Italy, letters of Maria Cosway, Calais 16 November 1786.
26 University of Nottingham, M 3313/24, 11 March 1787.
27 *The Daily Universal Register (The Times)*, Friday 29 June 1787, p.3.
28 BL, Eg. 3524, f.102; f.130.
29 Kearsley, *An Authentic Detail*, p.100.
30 Archives Nationales de France, O/1/201, f.52: 29 June 1787: 'La Duchesse de Kingston demande que la terre de St Assise qu'Elle

vient d'acquerir porte le nom de Chudleigh, qui est celui de sa
famille. bon.'

31   Jefferson, *Papers*, Vol. 11, pp.567–569, 9 July 1787.
32   *The Daily Universal Register (The Times)*, Friday 10 August 1787,
     p.3.
33   BL, Eg. 3524, ff.61–62, 17 September 1787.
34   University of Nottingham, M 3313/36, Calais 11 August 1787.
35   BL, Eg. 3524, f.57, 1 September 1787.
36   University of Nottingham, M 4148/38, 24 May 1786.
37   Felkersam, p.27.
38   University of Nottingham, M 3313/36, Calais 11 August 1787.
39   BL, Eg. 3524, ff.61–62, 17 September 1787.
40   *The Daily Universal Register (The Times)*, Saturday 23 June 1787,
     p.3.
41   Walpole, *Correspondence*, Vol. 33, p.572, 6 September 1787.
42   Royal Bank of Scotland Archives, DR/427/114, f.1021.
43   BL, Eg. 3524, ff.61–62, 17 September 1787.
44   Felkersam, p.24, 24 October 1787.
45   *The Daily Universal Register (The Times)*, Tuesday 13 November
     1787, p.4.
46   Private collection, Paris 11 February 1788.
47   Beinecke, Osborn MSS 3211, 11 April 1788.
48   Whitehead, *Original Anecdotes*, pp.196–197.
49   Archives Nationales de France, Y13581, 1788: 'Scelles [Sealings]
     Kingston (la duchesse de): decedée le 26 Août 1788, rue Coq-
     Héron, a l'Hotel du Parlement d'Angleterre.'

CHAPTER 21

1   BL, Eg. 3524, f.68, 30 August 1788.
2   Whitehead, *Original Anecdotes*, p.197.
3   BL, Eg. 3524, f.176, 18 November 1788.
4   Lincolnshire Archives, FL Glover 4/2/5, 24 December 1788.
5   University of Nottingham, M 3316/14, f.1, 26 January 1790.
6   Walpole, *Correspondence*, Vol. 34, p.20, 24 September 1788.
7   Kearsley, *An Authentic Detail*, p.1.
8   BL, Eg 3524, ff.76–79, enclosed with letter of 2 October 1788.
9   Ibid., ff.116–127, 4 October 1788.
10   Ibid., f.130, 1788, Duchess of Kingston's Debts at Paris.

11 Ibid., ff.138–139, 3 November 1788.

12 Ibid., ff.86–89.

13 Ibid., ff.80–84, 7 October 1786.

14 Ibid., f.98, 10 October 1788.

15 *The Times; or Daily Universal Register*, 25 October 1788, p.3.

16 BL, Eg. 3524, ff.138–139, 3 November 1788: 'the Body should be deposited there in some Vault or Repository, from whence it might be removed to England at a more convenient Time . . .'

17 Ibid., f.191, 10 December 1788: 'I beg leave to inform you, that instead of loosing a Month at Paris, which you was pleased to impute to me at our last Meeting I arrived there on the Evening of the 12th Septr and left it on the morning of the 19th . . . George Payne.'

18 Ibid., f.98, 10 October 1788.

19 Ibid., ff.138–139, 3 November 1788.

20 BL, Eg. 3525, ff.5–8, 4 January 1789.

21 BL, Eg 3524, ff.179–180: 'I hear also . . . that a Prise du Corps has been issued against Mr Meadows . . .'

22 Lincolnshire Archives, FL Glover 4/2/2, 17 November 1788.

23 Ibid., FL Glover 4/2/5, 24 December 1788.

24 BL, Eg. 3525, ff.160–161, 30 January 1793: 'The Executors not choosing to implicate themselves in the Testatrix's Effects in France, Mr Glover purchased of the next of Kin, their Interest, for £4500 (of which Mrs Elizabeth Chudleigh had a considerable, but what part, I do not exactly know) and by their wilful default, in taking out administration, he obtained the Grant, the consequence of that bargain, is well known to have been a loss to himself of £18,000.'

25 Lincolnshire Archives, FL Glover 4/2/45, 6 September 1790.

26 Ibid., 4/2/7, 2 February 1789.

27 Ibid., 4/2/25, 11 February 1790.

28 WSRO, Arundell MSS (letters of Father John Thorpe), 2667/20/22/6, Rome 1 November 1788.

29 BL, Eg. 3525, ff.11–16, 31 January 1789.

30 University of Nottingham, M 3316/1, 25 January/5 February 1790.

31 Ibid., M 3316/3, 20 May 1790.

32 Ibid., M 3316/12, n.d. [1790].

33 'A Catalogue of All the Rich Household Furniture, Pier Glasses of distinguished magnitude, Collection of Pictures, Sideboard of Plate, China, Linen, Fire Arms, Damask Hangings, and other Valuable Effects . . . which will be sold by auction by Mr Christie . . . On Wednesday May 20th, 1789 and three following days.'

34 'A Catalogue of [etc.] . . . At her Grace's seat at Thorseby [*sic*] Park . . . which will be sold by auction by Mr Christie, On the premises, on Wednesday, June 10, 1789, And Eleven Following Days, Sundays excepted.'

35 'A Catalogue of the Superb Jewels, Pearls, &c. of the Dutchess of Kingston, dec . . . Which will be Sold by Auction By Mr Christie, At his Great Room in Pall Mall, On Wednesday the 2d of February, 1791.'

36 BL, Eg. 3524, ff.86–89.

37 *The Gentleman's Magazine*, Vol. LVIII (1788), p.838.

Select Bibliography

PRINTED PRIMARY SOURCES
Printed diaries, letters, travel journals and memoirs

Almon, J — *The Parliamentary Register; or History of the Proceedings and Debates of the House of Lords*, Vol. 5, printed for J. Almon

Argyll, Duke of — *Intimate Society Letters of the Eighteenth Century*, ed. John D S Campbell, Duke of Argyll (London 1910)

Beckford, William — *Italy, with Sketches of Spain and Portugal* (London 1834)

Bentham, Jeremy — *The Collected Works of Jeremy Bentham*, ed. Timothy L S Sprigge (London 1968)

Blaikie, Thomas — *Diary of a Scotch Gardener at the French Court at the End of the Eighteenth Century*, ed. Francis Birrell (London 1931)

Boscawen, Hon Mrs — *Admiral's Wife: Being the Life and Letters of The Hon Mrs Edward Boscawen 1719–1761*, ed. C Aspinall-Oglander (London 1940)

Boswell, James — *Private Papers of James Boswell*, ed. Geoffrey Scott and Frederick A Pottle (18 vols, New York 1928–1934)

Burney, Charles — *Memoirs of Dr Charles Burney 1726–1769*, ed. S Klima, G Bowers, K S Grant (Nebraska 1988)

Casanova di Seingalt, Giacomo	*History of My Life*, trans. Willard R Trask (6 vols, London 1967–72)
Chesterfield, Lord	*Letters of Philip Dormer Stanhope, 4th Earl of Chesterfield*, ed. Bonamy Dobrée (London 1932)
Chudleigh, Lady Mary	*The Poems and Prose of Mary, Lady Chudleigh*, ed. Margaret J M Ezell (Oxford/New York 1993)
Coke, Lady Jane	*Letters from Lady Jane Coke to Her Friend Mrs Eyre at Derby 1747–1758*, ed. Mrs Ambrose Rathbone (London 1899)
Coke, Lady Mary	*The Letters and Journals of Lady Mary Coke*, ed. the Hon. James Archibald Home (Edinburgh 1889–96, facsimile Bath 1970)
Colman, George	*Posthumous Letters, from Celebrated Men; Addressed to Francis Colman, and George Colman, the Elder, with Annotations, and Occasional Remarks, By George Colman, the Younger* (London 1820)
Corberon, Marie Daniel Bourbé, baron de	*Un Diplomate Français à la Cour de Catherine II*, ed. Léon Honoré Labande (Paris 1901)
Coxe, William	*Travels into Poland, Russia, Sweden and Denmark* (London 1784)
Defoe, Daniel	*A Tour Through the Whole Island of Great Britain* (London 1724)
Dimsdale, Elizabeth	*An English Lady at the Court of Catherine the Great: The Journal of Baroness Elizabeth Dimsdale*, ed. Anthony G Cross (Cambridge 1989)
Foster, Vere, ed.	*The Two Duchesses, 1777–1859*, ed. Vere Foster (London 1898)
Frederick the Great	*Oeuvres de Frédéric le Grand*, ed.

	Johann D E Preuss (31 vols, Berlin 1846–57)
George III	*The Letters of King George the Third*, ed. Bonamy Dobrée (London 1935)
	The Correspondence of King George the Third, ed. the Hon. Sir George Fortescue (London 1928)
Grancourt, Pierre-Jacques Bergeret de	*Voyage d'Italie 1773–1774*, ed. Jacques Wilhelm (Paris 1948)
Granville, A B	*St Petersburgh: A Journal of Travels to and from that Capital* (London 1828)
Grenville Papers	*The Grenville Papers: being the Correspondence of Richard Grenville, Earl Temple and the Right Hon. George Grenville their Friends and Contemporaries*, ed. William J Smith (4 vols, London 1852–53)
Gwinnett, Richard	*Pylades and Corinna* (2 vols, London 1731)
Hervey, Augustus	*Augustus Hervey's Journal*, ed. David Erskine (London 1953)
Hervey, Lord John	*Memoirs of the Reign of George II*, ed. J Croker (London 1848)
	Lord Hervey and His Friends 1726–1738, ed. Giles Strangways, Earl of Ilchester (London 1950)
Hervey, John, Earl of Bristol	*Letter Books of John Hervey, 1st Earl of Bristol*, ed. Sydenham H A Hervey (Wells 1894)
HMC Carlisle	*Manuscripts of the Earl of Carlisle* (London 1897)
HMC Dartmouth	*Manuscripts of the Earl of Dartmouth* (3 vols, London 1887–99)
HMC Egmont	*Manuscripts of the Earl of Egmont:*

	Diary of the first Earl of Egmont (3 vols, London 1920–23)
HMC Hastings	*Manuscripts of the late Reginald Rawdon Hastings, Esq.* (3 vols, London 1928–34)
HMC Rutland	*Manuscripts of the Duke of Rutland* (4 vols, London 1888–1905)
HMC Townshend	*Manuscripts of the Marquess Townshend* (London 1887)
HMC Underwood	*Tenth Report on Historical Manuscripts, Appendix 1: Manuscripts of Charles Fleetwood Weston Underwood, Esq.* (London 1885)
HMC Various	*Report on Manuscripts in Various Collections* (8 vols, London 1901–13)
Home Office Papers	*Calendar of Home Office Papers of the Reign of George III, 1773–1775,* ed. Richard Arthur Roberts (London 1881)
Jefferson, Thomas	*The Papers of Thomas Jefferson,* ed. Julian P Boyd (Princeton 1950–) *The Jefferson Papers of the University of Virginia,* ed. Constance E Thurlow and F L Berkeley (Charlottesville 1950)
Justice, Elizabeth	*A Voyage to Russia,* 2nd edition (London 1746)
Kalm, Pehr	*Kalm's Account of his Visit to England on His Way to America in 1748,* trans. Joseph Lucas (London 1892)
Kielmansegge, Count Frederick	*Diary of a Journey to England in the Years 1761–1762,* trans. Philippa Kielmansegg (London 1902)
Knight, Lady	*Lady Knight's Letters from France*

	and Italy 1776–1795, ed. Lady Eliott-Drake (London 1905)
Kurakin, Prince Alexander	*Arkhiv kniazia FA Kurakina* (Saratov 1894)
Ligne, Prince de	*The Prince de Ligne: his memoirs, letters and miscellaneous papers*, ed. & trans. Katharine Wormeley (London 1899)
Malmesbury, Earl of	*Diaries and Correspondence of James Harris, 1st Earl of Malmesbury*, ed. his grandson the 3rd Earl (4 vols, London 1844)
Montagu, Elizabeth	*Mrs Montagu, Queen of the Blues, Her Letters and Friendships from 1762 to 1800*, ed. Reginald Blunt (London 1923)
More, Hannah	*The Letters of Hannah More*, ed. R Brimley Johnson (London 1925)
Morrison Papers	*The Collection of Autograph Letters & Historical Documents formed by Alfred Morrison* (2nd series, 1882–93): 'The Hamilton & Nelson Papers', Vol. 1, 1756–97
Murray of Broughton	*Murray of Broughton Memorials 1740–1747*, Scottish History Society Publications, Vol. 27 (Edinburgh 1898)
Noel Letters	*Some Letters and Records of the Noel Family*, ed Emilia F Noel (London 1910) *The Noels and the Milbankes, Their Letters for Twenty-Five Years, 1767–1792*, ed. Malcolm Elwin (London 1967)
Northumberland, Duchess of	*The Diaries of a Duchess: Extracts from the Diaries of the First Duchess of Northumberland*

	(1716–1776), ed. James Greig (London 1926)
Oberkirch, Baroness d'	*Memoirs of Baroness d'Oberkirch, Countess de Montbrison*, ed. Count de Montbrison (London 1852)
Oulton, Walley Chamberlain	*The Memoirs of Her Late Majesty Queen Charlotte* (London 1819)
Penrose, Rev. John	*Letters from Bath 1766–1767 by the Rev. John Penrose*, ed. Brigitte Mitchell & Hubert Penrose (Gloucester 1983)
Pembroke, Henry, Earl of	*Letters and Diaries of Henry, 10th Earl of Pembroke and His Circle 1734–1780*, ed. Lord Herbert (London 1939–42)
Radziwill, Karol Stanislaw	*Korespondencya Ks. Karola Stanislawa Radziwilla 1762–1790*, ed. Kazimierz Waliszewski (Krakow 1888)
Reynolds	*Sir Joshua's Nephew, Being Letters Written, 1769–1778, by a Young Man to His Sisters*, ed. Susan M Radcliffe (London 1930)
Richardson, Samuel	*Correspondence of Samuel Richardson*, ed. A L Barbauld (London 1804)
Richardson, William	*Anecdotes of the Russian Empire in a Series of Letters Written, a Few Years Ago, from St Petersburg* (London 1784, reprinted 1968)
Saussure, César de	*A Foreign View of England in the Reigns of George I and George II: The Letters of Monsieur César de Saussureto His Family*, trans. & ed. Mme van Muyden (London 1902)
Selwyn, George	*George Selwyn and His Contemporaries*, ed. John Heneage Jesse (London 1843)

	George Selwyn: His Letters and His Life, ed. E S Roskoe & Helen Clergue (London 1899)
Semple, James	*The Life of Major J G Semple Lisle, written by himself* (London 1799)
Sherlock, Martin	*Letters from an English Traveller* (London 1780)
SIRIO	*Sbornik Imperatorskogo Russkogo Istoricheskogo Obshchestva*, general ed. V.I. Saitov (148 vols, St Petersburg 1867–1916).
Swinburne, Henry	*The Courts of Europe at the Close of the Last Century*, ed. Charles White (2 vols, London 1841)
Thrale, Hester Lynch	*Thraliana: The Diary of Mrs Hester Lynch Thrale*, ed. K Balderston (Oxford 1942, 2nd ed. 1951)
Verney Letters	*The Verney Letters of the Eighteenth Century from the MSS at Claydon House*, ed. Margaret Maria Lady Verney (London 1930)
Vorontsov Papers	*Arkhiv kniazia Vorontsova* (40 vols, Moscow 1870–1895)
Walpole, Horace	*Correspondence* (48 vols, New Haven 1965–)
Wharton, Philip Duke of	*The Poetical Works of Philip Late Duke of Wharton* (London 1731)
Whitehead, Thomas	*Original Anecdotes of the late Duke of Kingston and Miss Chudleigh* (London 1792)
Wortley Montagu, Lady Mary	*The Complete Letters of Lady Mary Wortley Montagu*, ed. R Halsband (Oxford 1965–)
Wraxall, Nathaniel	*A Tour Through Some of the Northern Parts of Europe, Particularly Copenhagen, Stockholm*

and Petersburgh in a Series of
Letters, 3rd edition (London
1776)

SECONDARY SOURCES

Anon.   *The Northern Hero: Being a*
                            Faithful Narrative of the Life,
                            Adventures, and Deceptions, of
                            James George Semple, commonly
                            called Major Semple printed for
                            G. Kearsley (London 1786)

Anon.   *An Authentic Detail of Particulars*
                            Relative to the Late Duchess of
                            Kingston, printed for G Kearsley
                            (London 1788)

Anon.   *Histoire de la Vie et les Aventures*
                            de la Duchesse de Kingston
                            (London 1789)

Anon.   *Lettre a Mme L*** sur ce qui a*
                            precedé et suivi la mort d'Elisabeth
                            Chudleigh (London 1789)

Anon.   *The Life and Memoirs of Elizabeth*
                            Chudleigh, afterwards Mrs Hervey
                            and Countess of Bristol, commonly
                            called Duchess of Kingston
                            (Chamberlaine, London 1789)

Anon.   *The Life and Memoirs of Elizabeth*
                            Chudleigh (Randall, London
                            1788)

Anon.   *A plain state of the case of Her*
                            Grace the Duchess of Kingston:
                            with considerations, calling upon the
                            interference of the high powers, to
                            stop a prosecution illegally
                            commenced (London 1776)

Anderson, M S   *Britain's Discovery of Russia*
                            (London 1958)

Andrew, Donna T &   *The Perreaus and Mrs Rudd:*

McGowen, Randall	*Forgery and Betrayal in Eighteenth-Century London* (Berkeley/Los Angeles/ London 2001)
Andrieux, Maurice	*Daily Life in Papal Rome in the Eighteenth Century*, trans. Mary Fitton (London 1968)
Ashelford, Jane	*The Art of Dress: Clothes and Society 1500–1914* (London 1996)
Barnett, Gerald	*Richard and Maria Cosway* (Tiverton 1995)
Black, Jeremy	*Culloden and the '45* (Stroud 1990)
	The English Press in the Eighteenth Century (London 1987)
Blackstone, William	*Commentaries on the Laws of England*, 4th edn (Oxford 1770)
Blanning, T C W	*The Eighteenth Century* (Oxford 2000)
Bleackley, Horace	*The Story of A Beautiful Duchess: being an account of the life & times of Elizabeth Gunning Duchess of Hamilton & Argyll* (London 1907)
	Casanova in England (London 1923)
	Ladies Fair and Frail, Sketches of the Demi-monde during the Eighteenth Century (London/New York 1909)
Booker, John	*Travellers' Money* (Stroud/Dover 1994)
Britton, John and Brayley, Edward Wedlake	*The Beauties of England and Wales* (18 vols, London 1801–15)
Calton, Robert Bell	*Annals and Legends of Calais* (London 1852)
Cannon, J A	*Aristocratic Century: The Peerage of Eighteenth-Century England* (Cambridge 1984)

Carlyle, Thomas   *History of Friedrich II of Prussia, Called Frederick The Great* (6 vols, London 1865)

Carswell, John   *The South Sea Bubble* (London 1960)

Chagniot, Jean   *Nouvelle Histoire de Paris, Paris au XVIIIe Siècle* (Paris 1988)

Chancellor, E Beresford   *Knightsbridge and Belgravia: Their History, Topography and Famous Inhabitants* (London 1909)

Childe-Pemberton, William S   *The Earl-Bishop: The Life of Frederick Hervey, Bishop of Derry, Earl of Bristol* (London 1925)

Christie, Ian R   *The Benthams in Russia, 1780–1791* (Oxford 1993)

Cross, Anthony G   *By the Banks of the Neva: Chapters from the Lives and Careers of the British in Eighteenth-Century Russia* (Cambridge 1997)
By the Banks of the Thames: Russians in Eighteenth Century Britain (Newtonville MA 1980)
'The Duchess of Kingston in Russia', *History Today* XXVII (June 1977)
'Vasilii Petrov v Anglii (1772–1774)', *XVIII vek*, XI (Leningrad 1976), pp.243–245

Curtis Brown, Beatrice   *Elizabeth Chudleigh, Duchess of Kingston* (London 1927)

Davison, Dennis, ed.   *Eighteenth-Century English Verse* (London 1973, reprinted 1988)

Dean, C G T   *The Royal Hospital Chelsea* (London 1950)

Edwards, Averyl   *Frederick Louis, Prince of Wales, 1707–1751* (London 1947)

Farr, Evelyn   *Before the Deluge: Parisian Society in the Reign of Louis XVI* (London 1994)

Felkersam, A   'Gertsoginya Kingston i eyo prebyvanie v Rossii', *Starye Gody*, June 1913, pp.3–35

Foote, Samuel   *A Trip to Calais* (London 1778)

George, M Dorothy   *London Life in the Eighteenth Century* (London 1925)

Girouard, Mark   *Life in the English Country House* (London 1978)

Greenacombe, John, ed.   *Survey of London: Volume XLV Knightsbridge*, general ed. John Greenacombe (London 2000)

Hodson, J H, ed.   'The building and alteration of the second Thoresby House, 1767–1804', *A Nottinghamshire Miscellany:Thoroton Society Record Series 21* (Nottingham 1962)

Holmes, M R J   *Augustus Hervey: A Naval Casanova* (Durham 1996)

Jacks, Leonard   *The Great Houses of Nottinghamshire, and the County Families* (Nottingham 1881)

Johnson, C P C   'Phillips Glover and the Duchess of Kingston's French Estates', *Lincolnshire History and Archae ology*, Vol 11, 1976, pp.29–34

Knowles, Cecilia   *A History of Sparsholt and Lainston* (London 1981)

Leslie-Melville, R   *The Life & Work of Sir John Fielding* (London 1934)

Lewis, Wilmarth Sheldon   *Three Tours Through London in the Years 1748, 1776 and 1797* (New Haven 1941)

MacDonagh, Giles   *Frederick the Great* (London 1999)

Marples, Morris   *Poor Fred and The Butcher: Sons of George II* (London, 1970)

Mavor, Elizabeth   *The Virgin Mistress, A Study in Survival: The Life of the Duchess of Kingston* (London 1964)

Meara, Patricia   *Chelsea in the Eighteenth Century:*
                                Not Entirely a 'Village of Palaces'
                                (unpublished thesis, presented
                                1972)

Melville, Lewis   *Trial of the Duchess of Kingston*
                                (London 1927)
                                The Society at Royal Tunbridge
                                Wells in the Eighteenth Century –
                                and After (London 1912)

Mingay, G E   *English Landed Society in the*
                                Eighteenth Century (London 1963)
                                Land and Society in England,
                                1750–1980 (London 1994)

Osborn, J Lee   *Lainston and Elizabeth Chudleigh:*
                                The Amazing Duchess (Winchester
                                1914)

Pearce, Charles E   *The Amazing Duchess: being the*
                                romantic history of Elizabeth
                                Chudleigh, maid of honour, the
                                Hon. Mrs. Hervey, Duchess of
                                Kingston, and Countess of Bristol
                                (London 1911)

Pickard, Liza   *Dr Johnson's London* (London
                                2000)

Plescheef, Sergey   *Survey of the Russian Empire*, trans.
                                James Smirnove (London 1792)

Porter, Roy   *English Society in the Eighteenth*
                                Century (London 1982)

Reed, Christopher   'The Damn'd South Sea: Britain's
                                greatest financial speculation and
                                its unhappy ending, documented
                                in a rich Harvard collection',
                                Harvard Magazine, May–June
                                1999, pp.36–41

Ribeiro, Aileen   *The Dress Worn at Masquerades in*
                                England 1730–1790 (New York
                                1984)

Rimbault, E F   *Soho and its Associations* (London
                                1895)

Sebag Montefiore, Simon   *Prince of Princes: The Life of Potemkin* (London 2000)

Sherson, Erroll   *The Lively Lady Townshend and Her Friends* (London 1926)

Stainton, L   'Hayward's List: British Visitors to Rome 1753–1775', *Walpole Society*, 49 (1983)

Sutton, John Frost   *The Date Book of Remarkable and Memorable Events Connected with Nottingham and its Neighbourhood 1750–1850* (London 1852)

Sykes, Christopher Simon   *Private Palaces: Life in the Great London Houses* (London 1985)

Tooke, William   *Life of Catharine II, Empress of Russia*, 5th edn (Dublin 1800)

Treasure, Geoffrey   *The Making of Modern Europe 1648–1780* (London/New York 1985)

Troyat, Henri   *Catherine the Great*, trans. Emily Read (Henley on Thames 1979)

Turberville, A S   *The House of Lords in the XVIII Century* (Oxford 1927)

Turner, E S   *Amazing Grace: The Great Days of Dukes* (London 1975)

Walters, John   *The Royal Griffin: Frederick Prince of Wales 1707–51* (London 1972)

Vickery, Amanda   *The Gentleman's Daughter: Women's Lives in Georgian England* (London 1998)

Watzlawick, Helmut   *Bio-Bibliographie de Stefano Zannowich* (Geneva 1999)

Whiteley, W T   *Artists and Their Friends in England 1700–1799* (London 1928)

Wilton, Andrew and Bignamini, Ilaria, eds.   *Grand Tour: The Lure of Italy in the Eighteenth Century* (London 1996)

Wistinghausen, H von   *Quellen zur Geschichte der*

	Rittergüter Estlands im 18. und 19. Jahrhundert (1772–1889) (Hannover-Döhren 1975)
Wright, T	*England Under the House of Hanover* (2 vols, London 1848)
Wroth, Warwick William and Wroth, Arthur Edgar	*The London Pleasure Gardens of the Eighteenth Century* (London 1896)
Yorke-Long, Alan	*Music at Court: Four Eighteenth Century Studies* (London 1954), pp.74–93
Young, Sir George	*Poor Fred: the People's Prince* (Oxford 1937)

Index

Poniatowski, Stanislaw Augustus, King of Poland, 161, 184
Portland, Duke of, 79, 111, 116, 118–19, 120, 121, 130, 136, 137, 139, 157, 158
Portsmouth, 25
Posgate, Captain William (*Happy Meeting*), 209
possessions, disposition of, 240–4
Potemkin, Prince of Russia, 186, 188, 194, 197, 198, 217, 234
pregnancy and confinement, 35–6
'Princesse de Radzivil,' 207
Protestant Burial Ground, Paris, 241
Public Advertiser, 75, 151, 165
Public Ledger, 111
Pulteney, William, Earl of Bath, 17–18, 196
Purse-Bearer (Lords' Official), 146

Q

Quebec, General Wolfe's victory at, 68
Queensbury, Catherine, Duchess of, 22

R

Radziwill, Prince Karol Stanislaw, 161, 162, 164, 184, 186, 188, 197, 201, 204, 205–8
Raffald, Elizabeth, 81
Ranelagh Gardens, 22–3, 38, 41–2, 44
Raphael (Raffaello Sanzio), 172, 242
Rastrelli, Bartolomeo, 172
Raynes, Dr Thomas, 105, 111
Recques-sur-Hem, 188
remains, disposition of, 240–1, 244
Revalsche Woechenliche Nachrichten (Tallinn), 208
Reynolds, Sir Joshua, 17
Rice, Joseph (footpad), 11
Richard III (Shakespeare, W.), 65
Richardson, Samuel, 38
Richmond, Duke of, 45
Rickmansworth, fishing water at, 57, 59–60
Riga, 180, 205
Rochford, Lord, 85
Rogers, Sir John, 103
Rohan, Cardinal, 242
Rome, 113–16, 120–1, 122, 125–8, 190–1, 215, 242
Rosen, Baron Johann von, 208
Royal Hospital, Chelsea, 7–8, 10–12, 36, 58
Royal Opera House, Covent Garden, 23, 68
Rudd, Mrs. Margaret Caroline, 1, 137, 165
rumour and innuendo, 32, 41, 65–6, 83–4, 94, 107–8, 110, 141, 160
Russia, 165, 171–9, 197–202, 204–5, 207–11, 216–18, 219–24, 242–3

Rutland, Duke of, 130

S

St Assise, estate of, 232–3, 240, 241
St James's Palace, 21, 43, 49, 67, 68, 92
St Martin-in-the-Fields, 7, 8, 10
St Peter's, Rome, 115
St Petersburg, 171, 175–9, 194, 197, 198–201, 204–5, 209–10, 217–18, 219–24, 243
Salisbury, Bishop of, 100
Sanday, William, 210, 223
Saxony, 77–8, 80
scandalous allegations against, 117–18
Scarborough, 60
Scrope, Thomas, 39
Séchand, Abbé, 169, 231
second marriage, 91–2
Selwyn, George, 2, 58, 119, 139
Semple, Major James, 216–18
Seymour, Anthony, 243
Sher(r)ing, Samuel, 107, 111, 119, 166
Shuckburgh, Richard, 70
Shuckburgh, Sir George, 240
Simpson, Mr (Thoresby architect), 98
Sixtus V, Pope, 116
social success and wealth, 69–74
society
    dinners, typical menu for, 81–2
    discretion in, 2
    divorce, 27, 40
    earthquakes (and reaction to), 46–8
    education of ladies, 13–14
    fashion trends, 18–19
    footpads, 11
    marriage, 27, 29
    masquerades, sinful entertainments, 42–5
    matchmaking, 27
    optimism for George III's reign, 65–6
    poor rates, 14
    winter (1763-4), severity of, 70–1
    see also London
South Sea Company (and Bubble), 8–9, 11
Speake, Mrs (cousin), 199
Spearing, Mayor James, 62, 142, 143
Stockholm, 218
story-telling, gift for, 22
Strafford, Lord, 68
Stuart, Prince Charles Edward, 30
Syon House, 86

T

Talbot, Lord, 148